Tales From *Out There*

The Barkley Marathons,
The World's Toughest Trail Race

Frozen Ed Furtaw

Tales From *Out There*
The Barkley Marathons,
The World's Toughest Trail Race

Available for purchase at:
https://www.createspace.com/3427508

The front-cover and front-page artwork was created by Holly Proctor and Gary Cantrell and is used with permission. The back-cover photograph was taken by Rich Limacher and is used with his permission. Other photographs in the book were taken either by the author or by others who are acknowledged near the respective photographs.

To contact the author, write to:
Ed Furtaw, PO Box 5085, Pagosa Springs, CO 81147
or e-mail to: efurtaw@skywerx.com

EAN13: 9781450547017

Tales From *Out There*
The Barkley Marathons, The World's Toughest Trail Race

Table of Contents

Gary Cantrell, at left, prepares to signal the start of the 2009 Barkley Marathons. The author, Frozen Ed Furtaw, stands just in front of the gate, ready to start his stop watch and begin the race. This photo was taken by Peter Jolles.

Preface and Acknowledgements

I have always enjoyed telling stories about the Barkley Marathons. After all, it has been one of the most interesting and adventurous aspects of my life for over 20 years. For several years I said casually that "some day, when I am retired and have time, I am going to write a book about the Barkley." Well, that day finally arrived, and that book is now in your hands.

This book is the history of the first 24 years (1986-2009) of the Barkley Marathons. In writing this book, I have attempted to be as factually accurate as possible. However, there are inevitably some errors or omissions, due to the ease with which information becomes obscured or lost with the passage of years. I asked Gary Cantrell, the main creator and perpetrator of the Barkley Marathons, to review a draft of this book and give me his comments and corrections. I am grateful for his comments, but Gary declined to offer corrections in areas where he saw errors. He said that, this being the Barkley, it was appropriate for some misstatements to remain. To him, legends about the Barkley do not need to be true to be of value. Thus some factual errors remain in this book, but this is due to my ignorance of the true facts, not to my desire to tell untrue or exaggerated stories. In my opinion, the true story of the Barkley Marathons is extreme and interesting enough that it does not need to be exaggerated to be compelling and amazing.

Since the Barkley Marathons is an ongoing annual event, its story is not finished. Hopefully, there will continue to be many more runnings of the Barkley race, and more tales to be told about it. Therefore, a later edition of this book or its successor may be written at some future date. This would provide the opportunity to correct errors or omissions that others may find in this book. I would especially like to fill the gaps in the yearly lists of runners and their results. I encourage anyone to contact me with information for corrections, or suggestions of additional information that they would like to see included in a possible later version of this book.

I acknowledge and am grateful to several people for assisting me in various ways in the creation of this book: to Gary for his comments on the earlier draft; to Barkley runner Stu Gleman for his encouragement to keep working on this book when it seemed at times that no one else really cared about it; to my sister Susie O'Brien for her helpful suggestions and edits; to Barkley runners Rich Limacher, Carl Asker, and Mike Dobies for their comments on the earlier draft; to my wife Gail for lovingly helping with editing and for tolerating me throughout my work on this book; and mostly, to Gary Cantrell and Karl Henn for creating the wonderful monster known as the Barkley Marathons. It has made my life more interesting.

Enjoy the tales from *out there*!

Frozen Ed

Ed Furtaw
PO Box 5085
Pagosa Springs, CO 81147
E-mail: efurtaw@skywerx.com

Chapter 1
Introduction to the Barkley Marathons

It was about 3 o'clock in the morning Sunday when I fell into Phillips Creek. The immersion in cold water up to my waist caused my already fatigued brain to become even more numb. This contributed to my wandering aimlessly in the dark for the next two hours while never getting more than a hundred meters from the creek. It was another Barkley Marathons, and I was *out there* in deep woods trying to find a faint trail in the dark. But that is a tale from 1992, and I'm getting ahead of the story. Before beginning the detailed tales of the Barkley Marathons, the reader should be aware of a few general facts: what ultrarunning is, what the Barkley is, and what my relationship to the Barkley Marathons is that enables me to write this story.

The Barkley Marathons is an ultramarathon foot race that takes place in and around the Frozen Head State Park and Natural Area in the Cumberland Mountains of eastern Tennessee. The Barkley Marathons have been held annually (except 2002) since 1986. Nominal race distances in various years have been between 50 and 100 miles.

Based on its 23-year history of starters and finishers, the Barkley is arguably the toughest trail race, and the most difficult endurance foot-race to finish, in the United States and possibly in the world.

The official name of the event, *Barkley Marathons*, is nearly always pluralized, even when referring to a single running of the race or to the event as a singular noun. Hence I frequently use the singular form of a verb when referring to the Barkley Marathons, even though the word *Marathons* appears to be plural. When referring to the various Barkley events that have been held over the years, *Barkley Marathons* is a plural noun. Thus *Barkley Marathons* can be either singular or plural. When I asked Gary Cantrell, the event's creator, why he used the plural form *Marathons* in the event name, he said it was simply because the Barkley was more than one marathon. Among the people who participate in the Barkley Marathons, the phrase *the Barkley*, or the single word *Barkley*, are commonly used to refer to this event.

Races longer than the standard 26.2-mile marathon distance are usually referred to as *ultramarathons*, or simply *ultras*. The term *ultrarunners* is commonly applied to the runners who run ultras. In recent years, approximately 300 ultramarathon races have been held annually in the United States. An estimated 10,000 different U.S. runners run in these events each year, and the average ultrarunner runs about two or three such races per year. Most of these races are run on trails, with several percent of the races held on roads and tracks. Typical race distances include 50K (50 Kilometers, about 31.1 miles), 50 miles, 100K, 100 miles, 24 hours, and 2, 3, and 6 days.

The claim that the Barkley Marathons is the "toughest" trail race, and the most difficult foot race to finish, is based on the fact that it has one of the lowest percentages of finishers, and one of the longest course-record finishing times, among the regularly held ultras. Just over 1% of the starters have finished the Barkley 100-mile race. This low finishing rate is otherwise nearly unheard of in the sport of ultramarathon running. Most of the other races at the extreme-endurance end of the spectrum of ultramarathons typically have 50% or higher finishing rates within their respective time limits. More information on the comparison of the "toughest" ultramarathons appears in Chapter 29.

The Barkley is unusual among ultramarathon races in that the course is purposely designed and adjusted to keep it at the outer limit of human endurance. As will be described in this book, the history of the Barkley is one of escalation in difficulty over the years to make it ever more difficult. This ratcheting-up of its difficulty is the fundamental reason why so few runners are capable of finishing within the time limits and other rules. The Barkley is designed for most of them to *not* finish, while still being attainable by a small percentage of runners. Adding to the mystique of the Barkley is the fact that there has been controversy on several occasions as to whether an individual was or was not an official finisher. Many runners disdain the Barkley and the very concepts that it represents; this also has added to controversy about the Barkley.

In recent years, another form of controversy has affected the Barkley Marathons: an attempt by the Tennessee Department of Environment and Conservation (TDEC) to shut down the race after it had been held for 18 years. However, due to political intervention and negotiations between Barkley creator/director Gary Cantrell and TDEC officials, the race is being allowed to continue with course alterations to protect the environment.

In this book I will make the case that the Barkley Marathons is simultaneously both the world's most difficult foot race, and an often-humorous parody of the sport of ultramarathon running. The fact that it can be both is a tribute to the creativity and sense of humor of Gary Cantrell. Gary is intentionally probing, in a very challenging and fun way, the limits of the human spirit and running endurance. The athletes who gather at Frozen Head every spring to attempt the Barkley are a colorful bunch. The result is a rich history and a lot of sometimes hilarious, sometimes poignant stories of athletes running and playing at the limit of human endurance. Some of the more humorous and fascinating stories about the Barkley include the following, all of which are described in more detail in the appropriate chapters:

• The Barkley Chickens
• The connection to James Earl Ray, the convicted assassin of Dr. Martin Luther King, Jr.
• The Soviet invasion and tornado warning in the year of "Hell and High Water"
• Various runners lost overnight on loop one
• The runners who got too close to the prison and were questioned at gunpoint by prison guards
• The record for futility set in 2006: one checkpoint in over 31 hours
• What it means to be "tapped out."

In addition to these colorful stories, I think that the history of the Barkley Marathons is also rich in inspiring lessons about human nature and life itself. The most important of these lessons lie in both the failures and successes of the Barkley runners in pushing the limit of endurance. Numerous Barkley runners in recent years have far exceeded the achievements of those in the earlier years of the Barkley. This is why Gary has had to frequently increase the difficulty of the Barkley: the runners keep finding ways to do better on the Barkley course. Thus the history of the Barkley is a story of the evolution of human capability.

In Barkley's early years, I was one of its top competitors, as the reader will discover in due course. When I first entered the Barkley in 1988, I had been running ultramarathons for about five years, and had completed about 18 such races. Back then, I was a good ultrarunner, typically finishing in about the top quarter of the field. Since then, I have remained a frequent ultrarunner and a Barkley aficionado who has followed closely the history, evolution, and amusing stories surrounding the Barkley. I have participated in 13 of the 23 runnings of the Barkley Marathons to date (through 2009). Thus, aside from the two gentlemen who have created and annually organize the Barkley, I am probably in as good a position as anyone to write a book about the Barkley.

This book is not predominantly about me; it is about the Barkley as an historic and annual event. However, I will be telling many of the stories from the first-person perspective of a frequent participant. Hence this book is part history and part memoir. It has been suggested to me that this should be two different books: the objective history of the Barkley, and my own personal story at the Barkley. However, other commenters have expressed the preference that the two aspects remain together. I have chosen this latter direction. To me, the historical story of the Barkley Marathons and my personal role in it are inseparable.

I suspect that many readers of this book will be other ultrarunners who have heard of the Barkley and have an interest in learning more about it, and possibly entering it. I believe they will find that the story of the Barkley Marathons is a fascinating one. However, I also think that this story will be of interest even to those who do not run ultramarathons, because it provides observations and lessons about human nature and performance at the limit of endurance.

The chapters of this book tell the story of the Barkley in a logical sequence. First is an overview of the event, the course, its creators, and its venue. This is followed by a more detailed chronological history of the event in a series of chapters, each describing one year's results and highlights. Some very interesting and colorful things happened *out there*. I hope you enjoy reading about them.

Chapter 2
Overview: Why the Barkley Is So Difficult

Disbelief.   My first reaction to seeing information about the Barkley Marathons was disbelief: I thought that there must be an error in the race listing in the late-1985 *UltraRunning* event calendar.   It said that the 50-mile Barkley Marathons had 24,850 feet of elevation climb.   I was familiar with the mountains of eastern Tennessee, and I did not think that there was a 50-mile trail there that had anywhere near that much elevation change.   I actually thought that there must be a decimal-point misprint in *UltraRunning*—the Barkley Marathons probably had 2,485 feet of climb, not 24,850 feet.   However, when I read later in 1986 that no one had finished the inaugural running of that 50-mile race, I realized that race director Gary Cantrell had devised a tough course that maybe did have that much climb.

[Note: Throughout this book I will frequently refer to *UltraRunning* magazine.   Various issues of that periodical have been some of my major sources of information about each year's running of the Barkley Marathons.   Because the word *ultrarunning* is also sometimes used to refer to the sport rather than to the magazine, I will refer to the magazine as *UltraRunning*.]

In February 1987, I saw Gary at the Birmingham Track Club's 50-mile race.   I remember talking to Gary in the hallway of the motel where we both happened to be staying that weekend.   Gary had a topographic map of the Frozen Head State Park and Natural Area in Tennessee, where the Barkley race was held.   The date for the second annual Barkley Marathons was approaching, and Gary was trying to generate interest among the runners to come and try the Barkley.   I was amazed to see the elevation contour lines on the map—there were way too many of them, and they were packed very closely together, indicating some very steep terrain.   Gary clearly was trying to impress me with the difficulty of the Barkley.   However, I already had other race plans for that spring: I was attempting to run all eight ultras in the Southern Ultra Grand Prix Series.   So I had to forego Barkley for 1987.   A couple months later I read the *UltraRunning* article about the second running of the Barkley.   To my amazement, no one had finished it again, despite its 24-hour time limit for 50 miles.   As a point of comparison, I had finished the Birmingham Track Club 50-mile that year in 7 hours and 12 minutes.   I also knew that even the most difficult ultramarathon trail races, such as the mountainous 100-milers in the western United States, usually had well over 50% of their starters finish the race within the time limits.   The fact that no one had finished the Barkley in two years was difficult to understand and accept.   That was all the incentive I needed.   I was determined to attempt the Barkley in 1988.

Why is the Barkley Marathons so different, and so much more difficult to finish, than other foot races?   These are the questions that will be addressed in this chapter.

The first thing that the reader must understand about the Barkley Marathons is that it truly is an ultramarathon trail race.   Many runners in the ultrarunning community have claimed that it is not a real race, not a trail race, etc.   These claims are generally made by good ultrarunners who are not personally familiar with the Barkley course, and who can run 50 miles on other difficult trail courses in under 12 hours. When they deny the reality of the Barkley Marathons, they are exhibiting the same sense of disbelief that I did initially—they cannot comprehend just how difficult the Barkley really is. To understand that, the runner must experience it first-hand. One trip around the Barkley course will reveal the grim reality about just how difficult it really is. For me, it did not take even a full loop around the course to realize its difficulty; it took only about the first three or four miles.

In early 1988, I made my first trip to Frozen Head State Park to explore and train on the Barkley course. My girlfriend, Gail (now my wife of more than 20 years), went with me from Raleigh, North Carolina, where we lived at the time. We were both pretty strong hikers. We set out to hike as much of a loop as we could. After several hours, we had only gotten a few miles, and we had had considerable difficulty following the trail in many places. After about five hours and as many miles, we studied the map of Frozen Head and found a way to bushwhack, off-trail, across a ridge to a jeep road, which we then took back to the campground. This eye-opening introduction to the Barkley course was rather startling. I had never before been on such a difficult trail. I knew that this would indeed be a race different from those I had run before.

The following is a description of each of the many factors about the Barkley event that make it so difficult. In general, I have tried to list the factors in order of significance. The first factors listed are those that (in my opinion) contribute the most to why Barkley is different and more difficult than other races.

Event design philosophy. The Barkley course and race event are intentionally designed, and frequently changed, to keep it at the outer limit of human possibility. The design of the Barkley is intended to minimize the number of finishers. This is in contrast to most ultramarathon events, which have aid, course markings, generous time limits, allowing of pacers, and other design factors chosen so that most runners finish the event. At the Barkley, there is an exaggerated atmosphere of runners struggling against the course and their own limits rather than racing against each other. This underlying philosophy to create an event at the edge of possibility is why the various physical factors, listed below, are intentionally included in the event design to make it difficult.

Distance. The basic race course consists of multiple loops that start and end in the Big Cove Campground at the Frozen Head State Park and Natural Area near Wartburg, Tennessee. Although the specific route prescribed for each year has varied, the loop in general has always approximately followed the perimeter of the Natural Area. Each loop is about 20 miles, although the actual distances have not been (and probably cannot be) accurately measured. The issue of "actual distances" of the Barkley Marathons is controversial; much more will be said later about this subject. In most years, the nominal race distances have been a five-loop, 100-mile race, and a three-loop, 60-mile "Fun Run."

A topographic map of the Frozen Head State Park and Natural Area is on page 7. The darkened lines show the various routes that have been used for the Barkley Marathons over the years.

On page 8, a Schematic Map shows the various routes as a network of trail segments. Each segment is numbered, and the Table on page 9 gives estimated distances and elevation changes for each trail segment. Segments are numbered in the chronological order in which they were first used in the course. This Schematic Map will be referred to throughout this book, in the chapters describing each year's race. Each different course variation will be described, and defined as a sequence of trail segment numbers from the Schematic Map. This will enable the reader to trace the course for each year on the Schematic Map and on the topographic map. The Schematic Map and accompanying data will also be used to estimate the distance and climb for each different course configuration. This method allows a comparison of the relative difficulty of the courses that were used over the history of the event.

Most participants believe that the course length is actually longer than stated by Gary. For example, one runner who carried a Global Positioning System (GPS) device around the loop (before Gary prohibited GPS use during the race) estimated that a nominal 20-mile loop was actually about 27-28 miles. Based on painstaking measurements in 2007 with a scale on the topographic map of Frozen Head, I estimated the distance to be about 22.48 miles. This was based on the most recent ("Hell for the Highway") course. However, based on later field measurement data from 2008, reported in Chapter 27, I now think that the best estimate of the true distance of each loop on the Hell for the Highway course is about 26 miles.

A loop of twenty-some miles is not long by normal standards of ultramarathon distances. However, the difficult terrain and conditions (described below) make a Barkley mile similar in time and difficulty to two miles on other courses. Many runners, including myself, have noted that their times to complete one loop at Barkley are similar to their times to run 50 miles elsewhere. One major result of this fact is that each loop at Barkley takes many hours. In recent years, typical times to complete one loop are in the range of 8 to 14 hours. This, along with the lack of aid on the course, means that runners must carry a day's (or night's) worth of food, clothes, and supplies on each loop. Only water is available on the course; beyond this, runners must be self-sufficient on each loop.

Another difficulty that is incurred by the large-loop nature of the course is the psychological hurdle of leaving the campground on later loops. The runners knows that it will be many hours before they will be back at the campground for aid. Therefore it is mentally tough to leave the comforts of the campground and hcad back *out there*. It is especially daunting to go *out there* when it is dark, and raining, and cold, and you are alone in the woods.

Time Limits. In conjunction with the distance, the time limits within which each loop must be completed make the race more difficult than most runners can complete. The time limits for the current races are 40 hours for 60 miles (three loops; 13 hours and 20 minutes per loop), and 60 hours for 100 miles (five loops; 12 hours per loop). These are very liberal time allowances *per mile* compared to most other ultras. Most other 100-mile trail

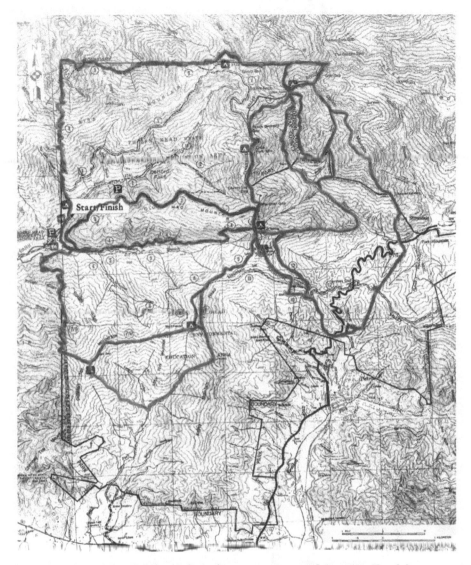

**Frozen Head Map showing routes used by the Barkley
Marathons in various years.**

races have time limits between 30 and 38 hours. The Hardrock Hundred,
held in the high-elevation mountains of Colorado, has the longest time limit
of the other 100-mile trail races, at 48 hours. Despite the apparently liberal
time limits at the Barkley, many good ultrarunners over the years have been
unable to complete even one loop within the time limit. For virtually any
race, the time limits are an inherent part of the difficulty. If the time limit
were to be significantly increased, the percentage of runners who would
finish it within the longer time limit would likely increase. For example, if
the Barkley 100-mile time limit were increased to, say, 120 hours—five full

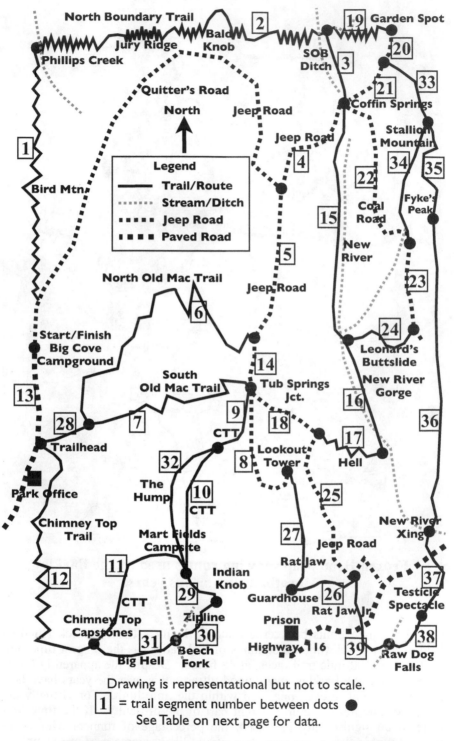

Drawing is representational but not to scale.

1 = trail segment number between dots ●

See Table on next page for data.

Barkley Marathons Course Schematic Map

Table of trail segment distances and elevation changes.

Trail Segment Number	Name	Estimated distance, miles*	Estimated Elevation Gain, ft**	Estimated Elevation Loss, ft**
1	Bird Mountain Trail	4.1	1,520	1,580
2	North Boundary Trail	5.1	2,680	1,640
3	Old Coal Road	0.5	490	0
4	Jeep Road	0.7	120	20
5	Jeep Road	1.3	170	240
6	North Old Mac Trail	3.2	0	1,550
7	South Old Mac Trail	2.7	1,640	0
8	Lookout Tower Road	0.4	270	0
9	Chimney Top Trail Northeast	1.1	130	220
10	Chimney Top Trail Southeast	0.7	140	120
11	Chimney Top Trail South	1.6	660	540
12	Chimney Top Trail West	4.0	360	2,080
13	Paved Park Road	0.6	80	0
14	Jeep Road	0.3	110	20
15	New River Trail	1.4	40	960
16	New River Gorge	0.7	10	350
17	Hell	1.0	1,370	40
18	Jeep Road	0.4	80	30
19	North Boundary Trail	1.0	680	0
20	Jeep Road	0.3	70	70
21	Jeep Road	0.3	0	190
22	Coal Road	1.3	20	350
23	Coal Road	0.4	0	0
24	Leonard's Buttslide	0.3	0	590
25	Jeep Road	1.1	0	660
26	Old Prison Mine Trail	0.4	0	40
27	Rat Jaw	0.8	1,020	0
28	South Old Mac Trail	0.2	0	30
29	Indian Knob Trail	0.2	120	0
30	Zipline	1.1	0	1,600
31	Big Hell	1.1	1,600	0
32	The Hump Trail	0.8	380	360
33	Stallion Mtn. ridge-line	0.3	210	0
34	Barley Mouth Branch	0.6	0	730
35	Stallion Mtn.-to-Fyke's Peak ridge-line	1.0	160	270
36	Fyke's Folly	1.4	10	1,650
37	Testicle Spectacle	0.8	860	0
38	Meth Lab Hill	0.7	0	920
39	Rat Jaw Jr.	0.8	860	40

* Distances estimated by map scaling, hypotenuse calculation, adjustment for switchbacks as discussed in Chapter 27, and rounding to nearest 0.1 mile.
** Elevation changes estimated from elevation contours on *Frozen Head State Park Trail Map*. Changes are given for the clockwise direction around the loop.

days and nights—I suspect that there would be many runners capable of finishing it by doing one loop per day in daylight for five consecutive days. The point is that time limits are an integral part of the difficulty or "toughness" to complete a race. In the case of the Barkley Marathons, the time limits are certainly a major factor in why it has one of the lowest finishing percentages in the world.

Sleep Deprivation. Because of the distance, difficulty, and time limits, finishing the Barkley means that the runner must run around the clock at least once for the three-loop race, and at least twice for the 100-mile. Thus the runner must deal with sleep deprivation, or at least with very little sleep for one or two nights during the event. In the stories of some of the years' races, mention will be made of how runners dealt with sleep management. This factor had a major impact in some results, and there have been some dramatic tales of hallucinations and loss of normal contact with reality as a result of lack of sleep during the Barkley.

Elevation Change. The Barkley course really does have over 10,000 feet of elevation climb per loop, with an equal amount of descent. Many of the steepest climbs are at slopes of about 1,600 feet per mile. And many of those slopes contain briers and blown-down trees. The steepness of much of the terrain is so severe that it is impossible to "run" in the normal sense of the word. A slow walking pace is the best that can be maintained on most climbs. For example, the hill known as Big Hell climbs 1,600 feet in approximately one mile; this climb usually takes me about 45 minutes, whereas my normal running pace on relatively flat trails is usually around 10 to 12 minutes per mile. The unusual steepness, in the uphill, downhill, and side-hill slopes, causes severe stress to the joints and muscles. The steep slopes also contribute to blisters on the feet for many runners. The overall amount of elevation gain, about 54,000 feet for the five-loop 100-mile race in recent years, is more than in any other ultra race that I am aware of. The steepness and amount of elevation change contribute significantly to the course slowness and difficulty, as well as to the pain and injuries that runners experience.

Trail conditions. Various parts of the loop are on different types of trail, including some well-maintained hiking trails, some old non-maintained trails, some old 4-wheel drive roads, a short section near the campground on paved road, and some sections that are cross-country with no trail to follow. While some of these surfaces are good for relatively fast running, many of the non-maintained and off-trail sections are very difficult and slow to traverse. This is especially true of those sections of the course that are extremely steep, rocky, and/or overgrown with briers.

Unmarked Course. The Barkley course is not marked for the race. Good navigation and orientation skills are required of the runners. This is one major difference from most trail ultramarathons, and one major factor why Barkley is so much more difficult and slow-paced compared to other races. The fact that the course is unmarked makes it slower to traverse, because the runner must frequently consult map, course description, compass, and surrounding environment in order to stay on course. Beyond this, most runners do actually deviate from the optimum line through the woods, thus adding distance and time. The use of GPS is prohibited during the race.

In many cases, runners get lost and spend significant time, energy, and distance getting back onto the course in a known location. The course being unmarked is a major difficulty of running Barkley in the dark. All Barkley race completions have taken in excess of 23 hours; thus running in the dark, on an unmarked course through dense woods, is an inescapable requirement for a Barkley finish.

Although the course itself is not marked for the race, Gary provides a detailed written description of the course that runners are required to follow. This makes the Barkley different from an orienteering or ROGAINE race. In these latter types of races, runners are free to choose and follow any route they want between checkpoints. At the Barkley, runners must follow a prescribed route. Some runners have been disqualified for not following the required route, even though they collected pages from all the checkpoint books (described below). These controversial episodes occurred in 1988 and 2001. These events are described in their respective chapters.

Gary's course descriptions are themselves of interest and perhaps some controversy and ridicule. Some of the descriptions of the route to be followed can be confusing, especially to runners who are not thoroughly familiar with the course. For example, in the 2006 course description, the route to follow from Book 7 (Indian Knob) reads as follows: "Look down. See that brier choked, steep hillside? That is the Zip Line Trail. Go down, and bear only a little to the left." The runners are not following an actual "trail" there. They are picking their ways down a steep, boulder-strewn and brier-infested mountainside. Each time I have gone down that hillside I have followed a different route, with much zig-zagging around boulders and cliffs. The nature of the course makes it difficult if not impossible to prescribe accurately the exact route to be followed. As a result, each runner may take a slightly different line through the forest on the non-trail sections of the course such as the Zip Line Trail.

The descriptions are usually colorfully written, and sometimes sarcastic and humorous. For example, Gary refers to the regular, maintained, hiking trails at Frozen Head State Park as "candy ass trails." Additional comments on some of the course descriptions will be included in later chapters about the specific years.

No Aid. There are no aid stations on the Barkley course, except that (usually) bottled water is provided at two locations on the loop. Other than water from these locations, or water from streams along the course, runners are allowed to take aid only at the campground at the start and finish of each loop. This factor is again unlike other ultra races, which typically have aid for the runners every few miles. This lack of aid is another major factor that makes the Barkley both physically and psychologically more difficult than other races. Runners must plan for and carry everything they will need (except water) for many hours of running at a stretch. This requires not only careful preparation, but also physically carrying a several-pound load.

No Pacers. Pacers are not allowed at the Barkley as they are at most 100-mile trail races. Pacers at other races can provide on-course motivation, companionship, navigational help, and even load-carrying assistance ("muling") to runners; hence the prohibition of pacers is a factor that makes the Barkley more difficult than other races.

Weather. Weather at the Barkley is frequently rainy, since it occurs in a rainy season in that part of the country. Running in the rain or on a wet course adds significantly to the difficulty and slowness at the Barkley. This is exacerbated by the unmaintained nature of most of the course, which results in non-level running surfaces. When wet and muddy, these sloped surfaces are very slippery. This causes feet, legs, and back to work harder to maintain balance and forward progress. Wet course conditions also contribute to foot blistering. Sometimes parts of the course have been more like small streams rather than trails. There have been several years when snow fell during the Barkley, especially in the higher elevations. Temperatures can also be a significant factor in adding to the difficulty of the Barkley. In various years it has been very cold—into the 20-degree range at night in the mountains, and relatively hot—into the 80s in daytime. Temperatures near either of these extremes have proven to contribute to high drop-out rates at the Barkley. In the chapters about each year, comments will be made about weather conditions and their impact on the race.

Out There. This phrase has long been used by Gary and Barkley runners to refer to the backcountry, isolated nature of the route. When a runner is *out there* on the course, we know that they could be miles and hours from being seen by another person. The course takes runners to places that are rarely visited by anyone other than Barkley runners. To me, this isolated aspect is one of the things I enjoy most about Barkley. In my 2006 single-loop run at Barkley, I ran the majority of the loop—about eight hours—without seeing another runner. To run for so long, even while near the middle of the pack of contestants, gave me a great sense of joy of being *out there* in the woods, slowly working my way around the toughest Barkley loop yet. Throughout the stories of Barkley, the phrase *out there* occurs frequently. This is why I have incorporated that phrase into the title of this book. I think the phrase is also metaphorical for the extreme nature of the Barkley compared to other runs. The Barkley is *out there* in a psychological sense as well as in the physical sense of being away from civilization in the back woods.

Checkpoint Books. Even though the Barkley course is not marked, the runners must go to each of about ten different checkpoint locations on each loop, where books have been placed in advance. Each runner must remove a page from each book. These pages are turned in and checked at the end of each loop, as proof that the runner actually went to all the checkpoints. As you will read in the 1997 Barkley story, one top runner lost one of the pages that he had collected, and was technically disqualified. Retrieving and storing book pages adds a little time to each loop, even when the runner goes directly to the books. A bigger factor is the additional time that it sometimes takes to actually find the books. There have been many times when runners have been unable to find one or more books, and those runners have been disqualified for not completing the loop.

Most of the books used over the years have been old paperback books. Some of the titles have been sources of amusement in themselves. Gary tries to select books that have appropriate or humorously relevant titles. For example, some of the book titles from the 2006 race were: *South of Sanity, Too Deep for Tears, Great Expectations,* and *The Endless Game.*

Each year in the weeks prior to the Barkley event, Gary and some of his friends spend a considerable amount of time and effort hiking around the course to place the books. They usually put each book in a place where no one other than a Barkley runner would be likely to see it. For example, the book at the bottom of the Zip Line Trail is placed into the hollow trunk of a tree in a location that can be seen only from directly in front of the hole in the tree.

The idea of using books as unmanned checkpoints on the course was developed with some input from me, back in 1988. That story will be told in its respective chapter.

Briers. Many of the cross-country and poorly maintained trail sections are thickly overgrown with sharp briers. Gary and others call them *sawbriers*, probably because as you run through them, they saw into your clothing and skin. I originally thought that Gary made up that name, but I eventually learned that *sawbriers* is a common name for a genus of thorny vines known as *Smilax*. There are reportedly 14 different species of *Smilax* in the southeastern United States. I do not know which species are prevalent at Frozen Head, but I know that they are a thorn in the side of the runners, so to speak. They offer scratches and pain rather than the refuge from Brer Fox that Brer Rabbit sought when he wanted to be thrown into the brier patch. Sawbriers are only one of several kinds of thorns that the runner will encounter at the Barkley. There are also blackberry briers, and thorns on locust trees.

Many runners wear protective clothing for defense against these briers. The runners' clothes usually get snagged and ripped by the briers, so many Barkley runners wear clothing that they are willing to sacrifice. One successful Barkley runner wore long-legged light pants with big denim patches sewn onto the fronts of the legs to protect him from briers. Another runner made himself a pair of pants from rip-stop nylon. In my early years of running the Barkley, I wore orienteering knickers, a type of nylon shorts that went down to my knees, with gaiters that came up to my knees. I would put these knickers and gaiters on when I got to bad brier patches, and take them off for the open areas. Although this protected me well from the briers, I eventually realized that it was slowing me down to have to repeatedly put the knickers and gaiters on and take them off. Now I just wear old tights that I am willing to get torn up. I also use leather-palm gloves for protection from the briers.

I have come to realize, as Gary has written, that the briers at Barkley are a relatively minor nuisance compared to many of the other obstacles at the Barkley. Gary has opined that the briers have never stopped a determined runner the way other factors such as weather and exhaustion have. He also once wrote that the briers would give you "fewer scratches than you would get baptizing a cat." But the briers can be a big psychological fear factor. The important thing is to protect yourself adequately so that when you throw yourself into the brier patches, like Brer Rabbit, you do not fear the briers.

On the next page is a photo of Gary, e-mailed by him in 2009, demonstrating how to shave with sawbriers.

Blowdowns. Many of the cross-country and poorly maintained trail sections have large blown-down trees (blowdowns) lying across them. These obstacles prevent actual running in many areas, including on some of the downhill sections. Some blowdowns can be climbed over. Others can be crawled under, and still others can be traversed around. It can take several seconds or more to get past each blowdown, so they can significantly slow down the runner's progress and increase energy expenditure.

Reversal of direction. In most years, the Barkley loops have been run in the clockwise direction (when viewed from above). Beginning in 1996, runners were required to run the loop in the reverse (counterclockwise) direction on the third and fourth loops. Runners embarking on a fifth loop were allowed to choose the direction in which to circumnavigate that fifth loop. The seemingly simple change of direction reversal adds to the time and difficulty of the run. It is more difficult to run in the reverse direction because the loop looks and feels different than what the runner is used to from running clockwise. For example, some climbs go up the side of a mountain on no trail. When ascending a mountain, there is no doubt about the way to the top. However, when descending the same mountain, the runner could end up anywhere at the bottom. Thus reversing the direction of running the loop adds navigational complication to the route. There have been several instances of runners losing time—up to a couple of hours—or even losing their way completely and dropping out, while trying to follow the course in the less-familiar reverse direction.

No teams on fifth loop. Most runners recognize that running with someone else helps pass the time and makes a given distance seem easier. Beginning in the first year of the Barkley Marathons, it became obvious to runners that running the Barkley course was significantly easier with a partner or in a small team of several runners. Running the Barkley with a partner helps with navigation as well as coping with the long durations for which the runners are on the loop. In 2001, two top runners ran the Barkley together, after each had spent several years running mostly alone on later loops, and neither had been able to finish five loops alone. Running as partners, they finished the 100-mile Barkley together, becoming just the second and third 100-mile finishers. Following this, Gary instituted a new rule that, if there should be more than one runner on the fifth loop, they would be required to run that loop in directions opposite from each other, thus effectively breaking up possible teams for the final loop. This led to a dramatic finish in the 2004 race. (See Chapter 23.)

Season. The Barkley is held in the early spring, usually near the first of April, on what Gary refers to as The Fool's Weekend. This time of year contributes to the difficulty of the Barkley in at least two ways. As mentioned above, this season brings highly variable and frequently wet weather. In addition, the season tends to increase the difficulty of training for the Barkley, because the training period for most of us ultrarunners in preparing for an ultra is typically a few months preceding the event. This places the Barkley training period in the winter. For most of us, training is more difficult in the winter because of short daylight, cold, snow, and wet winter conditions. Training for Barkley thus imposes more hardship on runners than does training for ultras in other seasons. Very few among the other extreme endurance-running events in the U.S. occur in this early spring season.

Taunting and humiliation. As if the Barkley race itself were not tough enough, runners must endure constant joking and taunting by Gary. However, in my opinion, Gary's joking approach to the Barkley and its runners (including himself) is part of the fun. Furthermore, I think this aspect of the Barkley is consistent with one of my beliefs about the Barkley: that it is a lesson and an exercise in humility. Gary likes to announce in advance that "no one will finish." One of his frequently repeated lines, in articles and entry-form information, is the statement to runners that "the Barkley will squash you like a bug." I have more to say about Gary and some of the strange requirements that he imposes in the later chapters.

Camping. Another factor that contributes to the difficulty of the event in a rather obscure way is the near-requirement to camp at the campground where the loop starts and ends. Camping is not literally required, but one of Gary's customs is to not announce the starting time in advance. In recent years he has blown a conch shell in the campground on the morning of the race as a signal that the race will start in one hour. This puts the burden on runners to spend the night at the campground, or else to risk missing the start of the race. The story of Milan Milanovich's demise in the 2006 race shows the importance of not missing the start as a result of spending the night before the race off-site.

Event size. The Barkley is not among the larger ultra races, some of which have several hundred runners each year. Because of limitations of the size of the camping area and related facilities at Frozen Head State Park, the number of runners in most years has been limited to about 35. This entry limit has been filled in most recent years as the race's reputation has spread throughout the American and international endurance-running communities. The relatively small number of runners means that many runners are alone on the course for much of the time. This adds to the difficulty of route finding. As will be described in the chapters on each year's event, Barkley runners have included world-class, middle-of-the-pack, and back-of-the pack ultra-runners from across the U.S. and around the world. All but a very small fraction of them have ended their attempts in failure. The race could probably attract a much bigger number of runners if it were feasible and allowed. As it is, getting into the race is itself somewhat of a secret process that helps prevent race management from being overloaded with applicants.

Entry Requirements.   Because of the limited number of runners allowed each year, in most years more runners apply for entry than can be allowed in. Therefore, Gary, as Race Director, must select those who will be allowed entry. Other applicants go onto a waiting list. Gary gives preference to former Barkley runners, especially those who have had some success there.   Gary also enjoys seeing how the top ultrarunners fare against the Barkley, so elite runners with significant accomplishments and reputations are also given some preference in the selection of the entrants each year. Each year, he usually allows several "Virgins," i.e., first-time Barkley entrants, into the race. Of course, he doses out extra kidding to those Virgins. He has even joked about some year requiring Virgins to start the run by going the opposite direction on the loop from the veterans who have run previous Barkleys.

The Barkley entry application form is usually a joke in itself. One of my favorites was in 2005 when the entry form had the large bold headline "Start thinking of excuses...." The form usually has a few insults, such as "no women, they are too soft," but in reality I think Gary enjoys seeing women ultrarunners attempt Barkley. Indeed, there have been several noteworthy Barkley runs by women. These stories will be discussed in their respective years' chapters. Gary has also accommodated numerous entrants from foreign countries, mostly European. Some very colorful stories surround the international runners; these will also appear in their respective chapters.

One of the entry requirements is to write an essay entitled "Why I Should Be Allowed to Enter The Barkley." I have had a lot of fun over the years writing those essays and reading the essays of other runners. For each year for which I wrote an essay, my essay is included in this book, at the end of the corresponding chapter. These essays will give the reader a glimpse into the evolution of my personal thoughts and feelings about the Barkley Marathons over the years.

In recent years, the entry form has required entrants to give their ages in non-Earth planetary years. One year, it was Jupiter years, another year Neptunian years. A couple of years ago it was Plutonian years—just after Pluto was demoted from planetary status. Typically several runners either cannot correctly figure out their planetary age, or ignore the question. Gary then uses that failure to poke fun at those who cannot figure out the math.

Another entry requirement is a fee of $1.60. This fee corresponds to a rate of one cent per mile, counting the 60-mile and 100-mile runs separately.

This tradition of a 1-cent-per-mile fee was established in the early years of the Barkley. This was done as a spoof—and sort of rebellion on Gary's part, I think—of the then-popular entry fee of one dollar per mile that many ultra-marathons charged. (Now, in 2009, most U.S. ultramarathon entry fees are typically closer to $2 per mile.) In addition to the monetary fee, each runner is asked to bring Gary a designated item that changes from year to year, such as a white long-sleeved dress shirt, a pair of socks, or a pack of cigarettes. Virgin entrants are asked to bring a license plate from their state of residence. Over the years, Gary has accumulated an impressive collection of license plates from around the country and world. Each year, he hangs these license plates on display at his campsite beside the gate at which the loops start and finish. Below is a picture, taken by me in 2008, of Gary sitting at his camp-site with his Willys truck in the foreground and the license plates hanging around the campsite.

Chapter 3
The People behind the Barkley

Gary Cantrell. The story of the Barkley Marathons largely reflects the personality of the individual who is primarily responsible for the creation, evolution, and annual directing of the Barkley Marathons: Gary Cantrell.

Gary was a very good ultrarunner in the early 1980s. He has run over 105 miles in a 24-hour track race, and over 150 miles in a 48-hour run. He has also run many thousands of miles on the back roads of Tennessee. In his basement a large map of the state of Tennessee hangs on the wall. All the back roads of each county are shown. Gary has highlighted the roads where he has run, and most of the roads in central Tennessee are highlighted. To this day, Gary does long road runs. However, it appears that his competitive running days are over. He has had severe back problems and other health conditions that prevent him from running ultras as he once could.

Gary began organizing ultras near his home in the early 1980s. He used to hold a long-distance road race called the Idiot's Run. *Idiot* was his own self-applied nickname. However, he is certainly far from being an idiot. He has attended several colleges and universities, and has a Bachelors Degree in Accounting from Middle Tennessee State University. He is employed as the City Treasurer for Shelbyville, Tennessee. He is an accomplished dry-stone mason, building walls and landscapes with stone while using no mortar. He also is or has been a coach of middle-school and high-school basketball, baseball, and softball. He has largely coached his own children in sports, and his oldest son attended the Illinois Institute of Technology on a baseball scholarship.

In addition to the Barkley Marathons and the Idiot's Run, Gary also organized a 24-hour track run in 1984. He also created and directed for many years the Strolling Jim, a 42-mile road race held each year in the town of Wartrace, Tennessee, near where Gary lives. This race has now been held for over 25 consecutive years, making it one of the oldest ultramarathons in the U.S. In the mid-1980s, Gary was also a co-organizer of the Southern Ultra Grand Prix Series, a schedule of numerous ultramarathons across the southeastern U.S., in which event finishers received points based on their finishing place, and the Series winners were given awards at the end of the Series. I consider Gary to be a benefactor to the ultrarunning community by organizing and directing many events over the past quarter-century.

I have known Gary for over 20 years, and I consider him a friend. I admire him greatly for his many skills and accomplishments. I especially think that his creation and nurturing of the Barkley Marathons over the past 20+ years is a gift to me and to the ultrarunning community.

One of Gary's best features, and one that is essential to his ability to create an event such as the Barkley, is his sense of humor. Gary is irreverent about nearly everyone and everything. I think that is a necessary quality for someone to even conceive of an event that has the characteristics of the Barkley Marathons. However, I also know that Gary has a deep respect for the runners who are willing to risk ridicule and failure by attempting the

Barkley Marathons, and especially for those who have overcome the obstacles that he has created, by succeeding at the Barkley.

Many ultrarunners are familiar with Gary as a regular writer in *UltraRunning*. In my opinion, Gary is one of the best writers covering the sport of ultramarathon running. His columns are usually subtly humorous, as well as insightful. Gary knows a lot about the sport, and he is very good at describing it in all its dimensions. His writings reveal a unique and studied perspective on human athletic performance. I always enjoy his columns and articles in *UltraRunning*.

I especially enjoy reading what Gary writes about the Barkley. After each running of the Barkley (except 1987), Gary has written an article in *UltraRunning* about the event. (In 1987, the Barkley article in *UltraRunning* was written by Fred Pilon, who was then a co-editor of that magazine and a multiple-year Barkley runner.) These articles have been one of the main sources of the information that I have collected into this book. Other sources include Gary's other writings about the Barkley, including e-mails, entry forms, and course descriptions. I have also collected many comments from others who have written about Barkley in various e-mails, Internet websites, and articles. These sources of information will be acknowledged throughout this book.

In about the year 2000, Gary found a nickname that he now frequently applies to himself in his e-mail writings about ultramarathons. That nickname is Lazarus Lake, which he commonly shortens to *laz*. Gary told me that on one of his cross-state highway runs across Tennessee, which he calls the Vol State Road Race, he was spending a night in a motel in a small town in western Tennessee. He looked into the local phone book that was in the motel room. For some reason, the name Lazarus Lake in that phone book struck him. He decided to adopt it as his ultrarunning pen name. Gary has written that he had health problems early in his life that make him feel fortunate to be alive. Perhaps his choice of laz as a nickname reflects that sentiment. In recent years he has used that name for himself in most of his Barkley-related writings. However, because I had known him for so many years before he became laz, I will normally refer to him as Gary in this book. Many Barkley runners know him better as laz, and there are probably some people who read his e-mail writings who do not even know that his actual name is Gary Cantrell. I would have preferred that he stick with *Idiot* as his nickname.

Karl Henn. Karl is a long-time friend of Gary. Gary's nickname for Karl is *Raw Dog*. One of their common pursuits has always been hiking. Together they explored the Frozen Head area on many occasions in the 1970s and 80s. It was on these trips together to Frozen Head that Gary conceived of a foot race there. So Karl was with Gary when the Barkley was developed into an ultramarathon event. Karl was also a runner and has run a few ultramarathons including a couple of loops of the Barkley in the early years, but he was not a regular ultrarunner as Gary was. Karl is a much more reserved person than Gary. Although Karl was involved from the beginning in creating and designing the Barkley Marathons, he has played a secondary role to Gary in the development of the Barkley. Karl has been more of a behind-the-scenes instigator, while Gary has been the overt director and spokesman of the event. It is my opinion that the Barkley reflects Gary's personality far more so than Karl's. However, Raw Dog's influence is significant enough that, in all likelihood, the Barkley would not exist if it were not for him.

One area where Karl has had an influential role in shaping the Barkley is related to Karl's profession. He is a mine inspector for a government agency. Much of the area in and around the Frozen Head State Park and Natural Area contains and has been mined for coal. Because of his job, Karl is familiar with these mining areas, and with the companies that still conduct nearby coal mining. Karl has provided information to Gary about former mining roads that have been included in some of the Barkley routes over the years. Karl also has provided contact with some of the coal-mining companies to obtain permission for the Barkley to cross private land that was formerly mined.

Although Raw Dog is not a frequent ultrarunner, he is a strong hiker. He has helped Gary over the years in exploring the area and laying out the Barkley course. He hikes in with Gary to place the checkpoint books prior to each year's event. And Karl is usually there at the Barkley, camping out and observing the goings-on.

In recent years, Karl's son, Davy Henn, has entered the Barkley as a runner. Davy is the youngest person to ever complete a loop during a Barkley race. Beginning in 1997, Davy also became the Barkley's official bugler. As a Boy Scout, Davy was his Scout troop's bugler. In 1997, Gary had the idea to salute each Barkley runner who dropped out or was disqualified, with their personal rendition of *Taps* played on a bugle. The *Taps* tune, of course, is the familiar military tune that is played to signal bedtime... or death. Most Barkley runners get "tapped out" when their Barkley attempt ends in failure, as nearly 99% of the attempts do.

Barry Barkley. The Barkley Marathons was named to honor Mr. Barry Barkley. Barry is a long-time friend of Gary. Barry has long been a farmer whose home and farm are near Wartrace, Tennessee, where Gary lives. Barry has a long history of supporting Gary in the ultra races that Gary has directed. On one of the early Barkley entry forms, Gary says that the reason for the Barkley is "to honor Hoghead Barkley for his ten years of service to the ultra community." So apparently Barry's nickname, at least for Gary, is *Hoghead*.

For the Barkley event, Barry has always donated chickens from his farm to serve the runners and race personnel. Special mention should be made here of Gary's preparation of the Barkley Chickens. Gary brings several cases of these donated, frozen chicken quarters to the race. At the campground the day before and during the Barkley race, Gary cooks Barkley Chickens for anyone who wants some. His method of preparation is legendary, and it even has a special name: *digitally prepared chicken*. This is appropriate because he manually places the frozen chicken quarters on the fire pit, and then digitally applies barbeque sauce by directly applying it to the cooking chicken with his fingers. The chicken then cooks over an open log and/or charcoal fire. Thus, after a few minutes, the Barkley Chickens are burnt on the outside while still partially frozen on the inside. Diners must assume their own responsibility for ensuring that their Barkley Chicken is properly cooked.   Below is a picture of Gary digitally preparing some Barkley Chickens.   This photograph was taken by Alan Geraldi at the 2009 Barkley.

I have met Barry Barkley only once, at Gary's house many years ago. He seems to be a very nice and friendly person. To the best of my knowledge, Barry has never attended a Barkley Marathons. So to most entrants in the Barkley Marathons, Barry Barkley is only a name; the person behind that name remains unknown. However, for Gary to have named the event after him implies that Gary holds Barry in deep respect. And since the runners at the Barkley love and respect Gary and the Barkley event, Hoghead Barkley's name will forever be held in esteem by those associated with the event.

Chapter 4
Frozen Head

According to information from the Tennessee Department of Environment and Conservation, the area now known as Frozen Head State Park and Natural Area was previously known as Morgan County State Forest. The area had been logged in the early 1900s. Some of the trails there were built in the 1930s by the Civilian Conservation Corps. A huge forest fire burned much of the area in 1952. The area was transferred to the Tennessee Division of State Parks in December 1970, and subsequently called Frozen Head State Park. In 1988, the park's 11,876 acres, with the exception of the interior developed area of 330 acres, was classified by the state as Natural Area. This designation has legal significance, with restrictions on development and activities.

The nature of the geographical area within and around the Frozen Head State Park and Natural Area is an essential feature of the Barkley Marathons. This area is characterized by steep mountainsides that are heavily wooded with mostly hardwood trees and heavy underbrush. This latter characteristic of the forest has led this area to be referred to as the Brushy Mountains.

Elevations range from about 1,300 feet above sea level in the valleys to about 3,300 feet at many of the mountaintops. Frequently, this amount of elevation change takes place over distances of only a fraction of a mile, resulting in steep mountainside gradients of up to about 50%, with even steeper cliffs. Frozen Head Mountain, from which the State Park and Natural Area get their name, is the highest peak in the Natural Area at 3,324 feet elevation. A lookout tower is located atop Frozen Head. From this tower, one can overlook much of the area. The view reveals the steep terrain and heavily wooded nature of the area.

The sedimentary nature of the land in this area tells us that in a past geological era, this area was under water. Much of the land in and around the Frozen Head Natural Area contained coal deposits, and much of it has been mined over the past century. Remnants of past mining activity are scattered around the area and some of these are seen around the Barkley course. Much of the mining here was done by inmates from the state prison.

In part because of this rugged terrain, there are multiple prisons located adjacent to the Frozen Head Natural Area. The Morgan County Prison is located along the paved road that leads into the park headquarters. This is a lower-security-level facility. However, a more infamous maximum-security prison, the Brushy Mountain State Penitentiary, is located along the eastern edge of the Natural Area. This penitentiary gained national attention when, on June 10, 1977, James Earl Ray escaped from it, and headed into the Brushy Mountains. Ray was the convicted assassin of the Reverend Dr. Martin Luther King, Jr. James was serving a life sentence at Brushy Mountain. He escaped along with six other prisoners, crossing what the guards called the "fifth wall" of the Penitentiary, the mountain slope into the Frozen Head area. Ray was captured 54 hours later. His escape and the ensuing chase through the Frozen Head area became part of the historical inspiration for the Barkley Marathons.

Gary claims that when he heard about Ray's escape through Frozen Head, he was surprised to read that in 54 hours *out there* on the lam, Ray had managed to get only about five miles from the prison. He was scratched, hungry, and exhausted when the bloodhounds finally found him, hunkering under leaves on the forest floor.

Gary and Karl have spent a lot of time hiking and exploring the Frozen Head area since the 1970s. So they knew how rugged the terrain was. But when they learned about James Earl Ray's run in the woods there, Gary figured that *anybody* should be able to get much farther than that in over two days. With this seed planted in the Idiot's brain, the idea grew, and soon Gary was pondering the absurd notion of a long-distance race through this incredibly rugged terrain at Frozen Head.

With continued years of exploring the Frozen Head area, Gary and Karl eventually knew enough about the area to conceive of a loop route that generally follows the perimeter of the Natural Area. This led to Gary announcing, in mid-1985, that the first Barkley Marathons would be held at Frozen Head in March, 1986. Thus was born the Barkley Marathons.

Chapter 5
1986: In a Class by Itself

The first Barkley Marathons was held on March 1, 1986. An amazing thing happened: *no one finished.*   The headline of the May 1986 *UltraRunning* article about the event, written by Gary Cantrell, declared that "The 'Trail' Wins the Barkley Marathons." This result was nearly unprecedented, but it set a significant precedent.

I have reviewed many old issues of *UltraRunning* from the years just prior to the first Barkley. The only evidence I found about any previous ultramarathon race which had no finishers was a small and obscure track race called the Lilac City 150 Km, held in Rochester, NY on June 9, 1984. This race had seven starters, who all quit before reaching the 150 Km distance. The cause for this was attributed to extreme heat and humidity (*UltraRunning* November 1984, page 25). It is difficult to consider a track race of less than 100 mile as tougher than any of the many 100-mile trail races. Clearly the unusual weather at this one event, rather than the inherent toughness of the course, was the reason for no finishers. Other than this one event, there is no evidence that in the several years before the first Barkley, there had been any other reported ultramarathon races in which there were no finishers. However, later years' results of subsequent Barkley events will show that the no-finisher precedent was followed by several other years with no finishers.

To understand just how unusual this no-finisher result was in 1986, I have reviewed a couple of articles in older issues of *UltraRunning* that listed the "toughest" ultramarathons. In the January-February 1985 edition of *UltraRunning*, the editors (at that time, Peter Gagarin, Fred Pilon, and Stan Wagon) ran several articles and lists summarizing the ultras run in calendar year 1984. One of these was a short article titled "The Toughest Ultras??" The editors stated that they based their "toughest" ratings on the races with the lowest finishing percentages, and a minimum starting field of 30 runners. This lower limit of 30 runners is probably why the Lilac City track race was not listed among the toughest. The toughest race on this list was the New York 100-mile, which had the lowest finishing percentage of any ultra reported in 1984. This race had 67 starters and 21 finishers, for a finishing rate of 31.3%. Of the seven toughest races listed, four were 100-milers, one was a 50-mile (with a 38.8% finishing rate in thunderstorms), one was a 70-mile, and one was an Alaskan race of 150 miles with no aid. This latter race had 17 finishers of 35 starters, for a 48.6% finishing rate, an astonishing fact that reveals the incredible toughness of ultramarathon runners in general. Each of those seven toughest races had at least 13 finishers. The article also stated that many of the listed races were repeats from the previous year. However, I could not review the earlier list because I do not have the January-February 1984 or any earlier issues of *UltraRunning*. I started subscribing to *UltraRunning* with the March 1984 issue.

In the January-February 1986 issue of *UltraRunning*, there is similarly a short article listing the toughest ultras of 1985. Again, the New York 100-mile was considered the toughest ultra of the year, with a 34.8% finisher rate.

Five ultras made the list, each with a finishing rate between 34.8% and 50%; all five races had at least 20 finishers. The article went on to list two additional races as "Honorable Mention," because these races had fewer than 30 starters: the Mister Rogers 165-mile Fun Run with 2 finishers of 16 starters, and the Alaska Mountain and Wilderness Classic (~200 miles) with 2 finishers of 14 starters.

Thus the pre-Barkley candidates for "toughest" ultra were mostly races at least twice as long as Barkley, and every candidate for the "toughest" title prior to Barkley had had at least two finishers. In view of these pre-Barkley considerations of the toughest ultra, it is not surprising that when the first Barkley had *no finishers,* it was a significant phenomenon in the world of sports.

Rightfully, the Barkley Marathons immediately became reputed as the toughest ultramarathon. In the January-February 1987 *UltraRunning* magazine article entitled "The Toughest Ultras," several 1986 races, each having from 2 to 45 finishers, were listed as in previous years. However, the Barkley was reported "In a Class by Itself." The article, presumably written by Fred Pilon, went on as follows: "1. The Barkley Marathons (0 out of 13 finished). In fact no one got more than 2/3 of the way. Organizer Gary Cantrell claims it is just 50 miles, but it may be 60 or 70 miles, with no trail in places. It's on again for 1987, but if you want to give it a try, make sure you're properly suited for it. Cantrell, after all, used to organize something called the Idiots Run."

Barkley's reputation as the toughest ultra continues to this day, with low completion percentages to justify the claim. This reputation eventually was a factor in some of the Barkley's most interesting races, such as the year in which a team of elite ultrarunners from the Soviet Union came to compete in the Barkley. That is part of the story of the 1991 Barkley, in Chapter 10.

Gary's *UltraRunning* report on the 1986 Barkley Marathons stated that there were 13 starters, but it did not list all 13. Several names are mentioned throughout the article. Those reported as having started the run were Gary Cantrell himself, Doyle Carpenter, Fred Pilon, Tom Green, Richard (Tom's nephew), Ken McMaster, Gary Buffington, and Damon Douglas. This list includes several well-known ultrarunners of those days. For example, Doyle Carpenter was a farmer from eastern Tennessee who in 1988 set a U.S. over-age-40 record for the 48-hour run, with over 219 miles. Fred Pilon, as noted earlier, was an editor of *UltraRunning* and a finisher of many ultras. Tom Green was also a veteran of many ultras, and he was the first runner to complete the "Grand Slam" of the four major 100-mile trail races in one year; in fact, he did this remarkable accomplishment later in 1986. Cantrell, Buffington, McMaster, Carpenter, and Pilon were all directors of ultra races. Hence this starting field, although rather small, had a considerable amount of ultramarathon experience.

In about 2006, while starting to compile information for this book, I asked Gary Cantrell if he still had records from the early years of Barkley. I was hoping to obtain complete lists of all the entrants and how each fared at Barkley. However, Gary told me that he had discarded all of his old Barkley records in a state of disgust after the controversy over the 2001 Barkley. That story will be told in Chapter 20.

In the 1986 *UltraRunning* article, the race distance is stated as 50 miles (+-), with 24,850' climb, and a 24-hour time limit. As I noted near the beginning of Chapter 2, this amount of elevation climb was difficult to believe, given that it is held in an area where it is only about 2,000 feet vertically from valley bottom to hilltop. The explanation for this conundrum is that the Barkley course goes up and down many steep, long hills, and it goes up and down them multiple times.

As all Barkley Marathons courses have been, the course of the first Barkley was basically a loop around the Frozen Head State Park and Natural Area, starting and ending at the Big Cove Campground. However, this first year's course had the unusual characteristic that the first loop was run in the counterclockwise direction. In all subsequent runnings of the Barkley, the course has started by going in the clockwise direction. The 1986 experiences of most runners being unable to follow the North Boundary Trail (NBT) in the counterclockwise direction on the first loop made Gary decide to start the run clockwise in subsequent years. The NBT seems to be easier to follow in that direction, although many runners (including myself) have gotten lost on the NBT while trying to go clockwise. Regarding the NBT, Gary once told me that his brother-in-law had worked on maintaining the NBT back in 1973. That was probably the last time the NBT was maintained prior to the 1986 Barkley.

Doyle Carpenter and Fred Pilon apparently ran much of the first loop together, and led it most of the way. The *UltraRunning* article says that they got off-trail after Jury Ridge, which is on the NBT, and would have been more than three-quarters of the way around the loop. They ended up on the jeep road that runs roughly parallel to and south of the NBT, and took this road back to the start/finish campground. A couple of noteworthy Barkley precedents were established by these front-runners: runners tended to stay in pairs or small groups, and runners tended to get lost, or at least off the intended course. These trends have remained prevalent throughout the history of the Barkley. As noted in Chapter 2, the reason for getting lost is the nature of the trail: it is unmarked, unmaintained, overgrown, brier-infested, eroded, strewn with deadfalls, and has many switchbacks. These characteristics are especially applicable in what Gary has called "the grim North Section." The fear of getting lost is a primary motive for runners to stay in teams. It was noted in the article that several other runners stayed in pairs. The article also stated that three of the starters had actually gotten off-course right near the start, by taking the wrong trail up toward the Frozen Head lookout tower. A reason for this early error was that they were late to the start of the race. This problem has occurred numerous times, especially by runners who do not camp at the park the night before the race.

Tom Green and his nephew, Richard, were the first runners to finish the prescribed loop, in a time that was stated as "breaking nine hours." However, they chose to not start another loop. Gary Cantrell and Gary Buffington also completed the intended route of the first loop, with no intention of going further. Only one runner, Damon Douglas, started a second loop, and he ran into the night. Although later statements from Gary suggest that Damon did not follow the prescribed route, Gary's description in the *UltraRunning* article of Damon's second loop is a classic example of Gary's colorful writing: "Now it was Douglas alone, out in the dark. What form of fun he had out there only Damon could tell. Whatever kind it was he had a lot of it, dragging it into 35 miles after 17:08:48. Considering he could win without finishing, and stood no chance of finishing within 24 hours… then there were none." Note that the phrase *out there* already appears in this, the first article about Barkley.

Below is a list of the known starters and their results from this first running of the Barkley Marathons. Other starters and loop-finishing times are unknown.

1. Damon Douglas   Finished two loops in 17:08:48; probably not all on the intended course.
2. Tom Green   Finished one loop under nine hours.
3. Richard Green   Finished one loop under nine hours.
4. Ken McMaster   Finished one loop in about 9:30.
5. Gary Cantrell   Finished one loop in 12:18.
6. Gary Buffington Finished one loop in 12:18.
7. Fred Pilon   Finished one loop; time unknown; not all on the intended course.
8. Doyle Carpenter Finished one loop; time unknown; not all on the intended course.

13 Starters

Damon Douglas had written an article that appeared in the July-August 1985 issue of *UltraRunning*. It was entitled "Tough Trail Running in New Zealand." Ironically, he described a section of trail in a New Zealand race as "the roughest in the world" that took him over 17 minutes per mile. Note that in comparison, his average pace at the Barkley was over 29 minutes per mile. From Damon's article, and the fact that he was listed as a finisher in several trail races in the years preceding the 1986 Barkley, it appears that he was a very experienced long-distance runner. His picture was even on the cover of an issue of *UltraRunning* in 1983. From other event finisher listings, we can see that Damon was a good but not elite runner. It appears that he was either 51 or 52 years old at the time of the 1986 Barkley. Following his relative victory at Barkley in 1986, he did not enter subsequent Barkley Marathons, and his name appears in *UltraRunning* in only a couple of other 30 Km and marathon trail race reports. Maybe his experience at the 1986 Barkley cured him of his proclivity for running ultramarathons!

Gary stated in the *UltraRunning* article that the first loop was 20 miles, and that Damon ran two loops for 35 miles; so Damon's second loop must have been about 15 miles. A course elevation profile graph accompanies the *UltraRunning* article. From this elevation profile, and discussion about the 1986 route with Gary many years later, it appears that the intended route was as described below.

From the campground, the first loop was run counterclockwise. The route went south on the main paved park road to the main trailhead a little north of the Ranger Residence. The route then took the Chimney Top Trail all the way to its end near Tub Springs, at the junction of several trails and the main jeep road that goes through the park. The course then went up the road to the base of the lookout tower at the top of Frozen Head peak. The course then went back down the road to Tub Springs Junction, then down the South Old Mac Trail to its junction with the North Old Mac Trail, near the main trailhead. From there the course went up the North Old Mac Trail, back up to the jeep road just a few tenths of a mile north of Tub Springs Junction. Then the course followed the jeep road northward a little over a mile, and then took the jeep road eastward to Coffin Springs. From there, the route went northward down an old coal-mining road about half a mile where it intercepted the North Boundary Trail. The route then went westward on the NBT to the northwestern corner of the State Natural Area, at Phillips Creek. From there, the course went south on the Bird Mountain Trail across Bird Mountain just west of its peak, and then down to the main jeep road. At that point, it was just a couple hundred meters down the jeep road to the campground where the loop started and ended. On the Schematic Map of the loop on page 8, the route of this first counterclockwise loop was the following sequence of trail segments: 13, 12, 11, 10, 9, 8 (up), 8 (down), 7, 6, 5, 4, 3, 2, 1.

Loop two was apparently intended to be run clockwise around the loop, beginning with the Bird Mountain Trail, the NBT, and the coal road to Coffin Springs, then south along the jeep roads to Tub Springs Junction, then on the Chimney Top Trail and park road back to camp. The sequence on the Schematic Map was 1, 2, 3, 4, 5, 14, 9, 10, 11, 12, 13. This second loop would be shorter than the first loop, because the South and North Old Mac Trails, plus the out-and-back on the dirt road to and from the fire tower, were not done on the second loop. Thus the second loop was about five or six miles shorter than the first. Apparently Gary considered it to be 15 miles, which is the distance of the Boundary Trail as given on the park map. Based on the elevation graph in *UltraRunning*, the third loop was intended to be the reverse of the second loop, run in the counterclockwise direction as the first loop had been, but again without the Old Mac Trails and fire-tower road included (the sequence 13, 12, 11, 10, 9, 14, 5, 4, 3, 2, 1 on the Schematic Map). However, the intended route for the third loop is a moot point, because no one attempted loop three.

Gary noted in his article that next year's Barkley would "Go with the Douglas route." Perhaps this referred to running the loop in the clockwise direction, because for the next several years, all loops were run in only the clockwise direction. This comment in Gary's article also suggests that Damon had not in fact followed the route that Gary had prescribed.

Another change in subsequent years' runnings of the Barkley was the date. Whereas the first Barkley was held on March 1, all other Barkley events have been held in late March or early April. The early date in 1986 brought cold weather and snow, so as he stated in his 1986 *UltraRunning* article, Gary decided to move the race to a slightly later date in hopes of warmer weather.

Another statement by Gary in the *UltraRunning* article reveals an important aspect of the Barkley and Gary's intentions. He called the fact that nobody finished the first Barkley "A rousing success all around." I think this statement reveals what has become the unique and defining aspect of Barkley: Gary does not want many runners to be able to finish Barkley. It is intended to be a contest between the course and the runners; a contest that the runners usually lose. In fact, I think this philosophy is subtly implicit in the title of his article: "The 'Trail' Wins the Barkley Marathons." We will continue to see evidence of this Barkley philosophy as the stories of later years at the Barkley unfold.

Although Gary called the first loop 20 miles, and the second and third loops 13 miles each, the true distances were undoubtedly longer than those estimates. As noted above, an *UltraRunning* article, presumably written by Fred Pilon, had speculated that the course length "may be 60 or 70 miles." Using the estimated distance and elevation-change data from the Table on page 9, I estimate that the distance of the first loop was about 26.4 miles. The estimated climb and descent are about 8,260 feet each. Likewise, I estimate the distance of the intended second and third loops to have been about 20.0 miles each, with about 6,460 feet each of ascent and descent. Adding these loop distances, I estimate the distance of the intended 1986 race to have been about 66.4 miles. Note that this is very near the middle of Fred Pilon's speculated range. My estimate of the total three-loop elevation change is 21,180 feet each of climb and drop, whereas Gary had stated that it was 24,850 feet. The true value probably lies somewhere between these estimates.

The apparent tendency of Gary to understate the distance of the Barkley appears to be part of his normal mode of operating. This tendency was noted in an article in the July-August 1986 issue of *UltraRunning* written by the well-know ultrarunner and ultramarathon historian, Nick Marshall. Nick wrote a multiple-part Ultra Quiz, and one of the questions was about the true lengths of several ultras that were each advertised as 40 miles in length. Gary's Strolling Jim 40 was one of those races. Nick noted that its true length was 41.2 miles. Nick then stated: "In relation to the SJ, it must be obvious that Gary Cantrell is a devious trickster." I think that the history of the Barkley Marathons, starting from this first year, proves that Nick understood Gary's personality pretty well, even way back in 1986.

Another peculiarity of the Barkley that originated in its first year was the entry fee. It was 25 cents for 1986. This amount was so low, at a time when most ultra entry fees were in the range of a few dollars to $75, that I think it was another manifestation of Gary's disdain of normalcy. However, the 1987 Barkley entry fee was doubled to 50 cents, with the offer of a "full refund if you stick it out and have a cubic inch of your body not in extreme pain." This started his tradition of charging one cent per mile. It is good to know that Gary is not into race directing for the money.

Gary ended the 1986 *UltraRunning* article about Barkley by stating: "Of course it is still impossible to run 50 miles on that trail in a day, but if anyone wants to try, we'll be doing it again next spring." We will see in the next few chapters how good this taunting prediction was, that the Barkley was "impossible."

Chapter 6
1987: Still No Finishers

If the first Barkley's result of no finishers was unusual in the sport of ultrarunning, the second annual Barkley Marathons proved to be even more unusual; again *no one finished.* This outcome is even more remarkable because the fact that no one had finished in the first year should have put the ultrarunning community on notice that this event was not to be taken lightly. Where the element of unexpected difficulty was certainly a factor in the first Barkley, this difficulty factor should not have been such a surprise in the second Barkley. Nevertheless, Gary's 1986 prediction that 50 miles in 24 hours at the Barkley was "impossible" was proven true, at least for another year.

The article in *UltraRunning* about the 1987 Barkley appeared in the June 1987 issue. It was written by Fred Pilon. This was to be the only time in the history of the Barkley, at least through the 2009 race, that Gary did not author a Barkley article in *UltraRunning*. Fred wrote a very interesting article about his own experiences during the run, but his article lacked some of the factual details that Gary usually provides about the entrants. In fact, Fred's 1987 article named only two other runners besides Fred himself. The article stated that there were "About a dozen starters." Later information from Gary put the number of 1987 starters at 16.

This was Fred's second attempt at Barkley, and his second DNF (Did Not Finish). The theme of his article was the issue of "closure." He implied that he was somehow psychologically avoiding finishing the Barkley course on purpose. This was not to be Fred's final run at Barkley, by a long shot. We will see in later chapters whether or not Fred achieved the closure that he referred to in 1987.

Besides Fred, the other two runners named in the article are Tom Possert and Mac Williamson. Fred notes that Tom was the winner of the previous year's 70-mile Laurel Highlands Trail race, and that Mac was the second-place finisher of that year's Pacific Crest Trail 50-miler in California. The article didn't mention it, but at that time, Tom had recently run 147+ miles in 24 hours at the Across The Years track race in late December 1986. At that time, that was the 5th-best all-time American performance at 24 hours. The 24-year-old Possert had also run the Wolfpack 50-Mile race in Ohio just the previous weekend, finishing second in 7:07:22. Mac Williamson, at 21 years old, had finished the Pacific Crest Trail 50-mile in 6:49:43. So these two named entrants were both accomplished ultrarunners with impressive credentials. Thus, as was also the case in the 1986 Barkley, the 1987 Barkley starting field was small but included some very experienced and accomplished runners. In fact, in the case of Tom Possert, we could say that he was at that time one of the best ultrarunners in the United States.

There are a couple of black-and-white photographs in the article. One shows Tom going down a steep, rocky, and leaf-covered section of trail. The location of that photo appears to be on the Chimney Top Trail near its high point. The other picture is of Fred leaning forward to get under some fallen trees across the trail. These photos do a good job of portraying the obstacle-course nature of the trail.

From Fred's description of the 1987 course, we know that the direction of running the loop was clockwise, starting with the North Boundary Trail. Fred and Tom ran together. It seems that they were teaming up in order to better stay on course. Together they attempted to navigate the first loop, but apparently they made a slight deviation from the intended course when they could not follow the badly overgrown trail from Coffin Springs down along the western side of the upper part of the New River. This was to have been a new section of the course compared to the 1986 route. Instead they went to the eastern side of the New River and ran southward, parallel to the river on an old mining road. They then went cross-country down the steep side of the New River gorge to re-join the intended route, the old trail along the New River. They then went up from the New River to Frozen Head Mountain on a steep slope that Gary would eventually name "Hell." This incredibly steep hill had an old, virtually indiscernible trail that passes through a former coal-mining area. Fred noted in his article that he and Tom passed by several coal seams, wells, and old pulleys and wheels left over from the mining activities. From the top of Hell, the runners probably went to the top of Frozen Head Mountain, and then on the Chimney Top Trail down to the park, and then the park road to the campground. However, this detail on the latter portion of the 1987 course is lacking in Fred's article.

Based on the above description, and using data from the Schematic Map and Table on pages 8 and 9, the intended route of the 1987 loop was presumably the following sequence of trail segments, to be run three times: 1, 2, 3, 15, 16, 17, 18, 8 (up), 8 (down), 9, 10, 11, 12, 13. This loop has an estimated distance of 22.0 miles. Thus the estimated three-loop total race distance was 66.0 miles, although Gary still referred to it as 50 miles. The estimated elevation gain per loop was 7,830 feet, for a three-loop total climb of 23,490 feet, with an equal amount of descent.

Fred states that he and Tom finished the first loop in about seven hours. However, on the 1988 Barkley entry form, Gary stated that the fastest time for one loop in previous races was 7:22. Since the fastest loop time in 1986 was stated as "breaking nine hours," this 7:22 must refer to Fred and Tom's first-loop time from this year (1987). Gary also stated on the 1988 entry form that the distance of that loop was 16.67 miles. After completing this first loop, Fred and Tom then went out on a second loop, hoping to complete it before dark.

Based on Fred's report in *UltraRunning*, it appears that no one other than Tom and Fred went beyond one loop. In his article, Fred stated that Possert pulled ahead of him early in the second loop. Pilon rested for a while on the trail, then resumed running. He stated that halfway through the loop, he caught back up to Tom, who had stopped to wait for Fred. Tom asked Fred whether he wanted to go through Hell again. In his article Fred wrote: "I decline. We both know that no one will do it twice. Not this year. With the decision to quit behind us, we finally get to run." So they apparently did not take the trail through Hell on their second loop, but took one of the better park trails back to camp. Fred reports that he and Tom finished their second loop in "14¼ hours." He also reported that the race had a 36-hour time limit that year.

Besides Tom and Fred, the only other runner named in Fred's article is Mac Williamson. Gary recalls that Mac had told him by telephone before the race that "I'm gonna do the 50 miles in nine hours or die." Fred reported that he eventually learned that Mac had showed up late (another occurrence that had happened to some of the runners in 1986), and was seen only at the end of his first and only loop. Mac apparently claimed to have run the loop in 5 hours, but Fred reported that he and Tom had not seen Mac out on the course, so Mac must not have run the same course as Fred and Tom. As best I could determine by reviewing race results in *UltraRunning*, Mac subsequently finished a different 50 mile race later in 1987, at age 22, in 6:09:45; this is listed in the January-February 1988 *UltraRunning* list of 1987 ultra finishers. However, after that, Mac virtually disappeared from the ultra scene. Perhaps his experience at Barkley helped him realize that he really didn't want to be an ultrarunner.

In later years, Gary told me some of his recollections of this 1987 running of the Barkley. Apparently he himself did one loop that year, as he had in 1986. He remembers doing at least part of the loop in 1987 with his friends Webb and Linda Sledge. A group of six Marines also had come to run Barkley that year, under the leadership of a Sergeant Stone. Sergeant Stone told Gary that he had led his men in several 50-mile hikes, including the JFK 50-miler in Maryland, the oldest regularly held ultramarathon in the United States. He told Gary before the Barkley race that "If we can finish the JFK, we can finish anything." He had told his men that they would have to do extra duty if they did not finish the 50 miles. During the Barkley, one of the Marines, realizing that he would not be finishing this 50 miles, was heard asking Sergeant Stone: "How much extra duty, Sir?" Gary also remembered that Linda found some deer antlers, and as they were going up Hell hill, Linda asked one of the Marines to carry the antlers for her. Being a gentleman, the Marine did as requested. On the entry form for the following year's Barkley (1988), Gary made fun of the Marines' failures by noting among the entry requirements: "NO marines, Linda Sledge likes to kick their tails."

The following list includes the known starters of the 1987 Barkley and their results. Numbers in parentheses are the runners' known numbers of Barkley starts, including 1987. Other starters and loop-finishing times are unknown.

1. Fred Pilon (2)   Finished one loop in 7:22; finished two loops in
                           about 14¼ hours, not all on the intended course.
2. Tom Possert (1)   Finished one loop in 7:22; finished two loops in
                           about 14¼ hours, not all on the intended course.
3. Gary Cantrell (2)   Finished one loop; time unknown.
4. Mac Williamson (1)   Results unknown.
5. Linda Sledge* (1)   Results unknown.
6. Webb Sledge (1)   Results unknown.
7. Marine Sgt. Stone (1)   Results unknown.
8. Marine #2 (1)   Results unknown.
9. Marine #3 (1)   Results unknown.
10. Marine #4 (1)   Results unknown.

11. Marine #5 (1)   Results unknown.
12. Marine #6 (1)   Results unknown.
16 Starters
* Female runners' names are underlined in this and other lists in this book.

Again this year, as in the first Barkley, runners were not able to, or chose not to, accurately follow the intended course that Gary had prescribed. This problem is a perennial characteristic of the Barkley. In the next chapter, we will see how Gary subsequently employed a method for verifying that runners actually reached each of several checkpoints on the designated course.

Chapter 7
1988: A Finisher at Last!

This third year of Barkley was when it became personally interesting to me, because this is when I first entered the Barkley. As I described at the beginning of Chapter 2, Gary had talked to me in early 1987, encouraging me to enter that year's Barkley. However, I had other race plans that year, and so it was not until early 1988 that I decided to give the Barkley a try. I knew from the first two years' race reports that Barkley was not your ordinary 50-miler, and that much of its difficulty was due to the inability of runners to follow the prescribed course. So I decided that I would familiarize myself with the course in advance.

In late 1987 or early 1988, Gary mailed me a map of the Barkley course. The map had the tentative route of the 1988 Barkley course marked with various colors of highlighters. Gary had hand-written on the map the following outline of the course:

North Section	0-7 [miles]	17-24	33-40
New River	7-10	24-27	40-43
South Section	10-17	27-33	43-50

It helps in understanding the Barkley course to break down the loop into these three sections. Throughout the years, although the course has been changed many times, this generalization of dividing the loop into the three sections—North, New River, and South—is always a valid way to analyze the loop. I could see from the mileages provided by Gary on the map that the race would consist of three clockwise loops. At that time, he still called the total distance 50 miles. However, this would change before the 1988 race was actually held.

Armed with this map, I went to Frozen Head several times and familiarized myself with the entire loop. From the records that I kept, it appears that I made three trips to Frozen Head prior to that year's race, and did a total of five training hikes/runs on the Barkley course.

The first trip was in late February with Gail, then my fiancee (now my wife of 20+ years). We started up the Bird Mountain Trail, past the sign that said "Trail Closed," and hiked the first few miles of the North Boundary Trail (NBT). It was eye-opening to find that trail so difficult to follow. It was badly overgrown and had many large trees fallen across it, making the trail nearly indiscernible in places. After several hours of slow hiking and bushwhacking while attempting to follow the NBT, we took the easy shortcut from the NBT to the jeep road near Bald Knob. Little did I know then that I would take that jeep road many times in subsequent years, as my retreat from the Barkley course back to camp to quit. In fact, that road back to camp has come to be known as Quitter's Road. From my early 1988 notes, it appears that Gail and I then ran on the jeep road from Bald Knob to Coffin Springs to check out that location, which was to be the first aid-drop station on the Barkley course. From there we ran down the jeep road back to the park campground. The following day, I hiked from the trailhead parking lot up to the Frozen Head Lookout Tower, the second aid location on the Barkley course, and then ran along the Chimney Top Trail (CTT) back to the parking lot. The CTT was to be the third, or South Section, of the Barkley loop.

My archives of Barkley-related papers include a couple of old envelopes in which Gary had mailed me information about the Barkley. On an envelope postmarked the 20-something (partially indiscernible) of December 1987, Gary addressed me as "Ed 'Frozen Head' Furtaw." On another envelope postmarked 15 Jan 1988, he addressed me as "Frozen Head Ed Furtaw," and then on a later update of course changes mailed in early March, 1988, he called me "Frozen Ed." This latter note was the first recorded instance when Gary called me by the "Frozen Ed" nickname. Over the years I have proudly used this nickname in conjunction with ultrarunning, and especially at Barkley. I feel that it was an honor from Gary for him to call me that. In that note, Gary wrote: "Myself and Mr. Henn are planning to recon. the course in Feb. or March. Very much would like to do it with you. Will be in touch on that subject." I eagerly accepted this invitation. Thus, my second reconnaissance trip to Frozen Head was in early March, when I met there with Gary and Karl.

Prior to this meeting, Gary had told me of the past years' problems of runners not following the prescribed course, and the need for him to have a method of ascertaining that the runners did indeed follow the intended course. I suggested the use of paperback books placed at checkpoints, with the idea that each runner could tear the next page out of each book and return those pages to Gary at the end of each loop. This would prove not only that the runner reached the required locations, but also establish the order of runners' arrival of each checkpoint. I took an old paperback book and drilled a hole through the upper left-hand corner of it. I then tied an old running shoe lace through the hole. I took that book to Gary and explained the concept to him. He liked the idea, and adopted it. Subsequently, this use of paperback books as confirmation of runners reaching the required checkpoints has become a regular feature of the Barkley Marathons. In later years, Gary improved on the concept by assigning each runner a different number on each loop. He keeps a record of each runner's number for each loop. Runners must retrieve that particular page number from the book at each of the various checkpoints, and turn those pages in at the end of each loop. This method allows race officials to ascertain whether a given runner reached a given checkpoint. As described in Chapter 25, this method helped us in 2006 when we sent search parties out onto the course to try to find a missing runner.

Gary, Karl, and I did a long hike on the Barkley course on March 5, 1988. We hiked from the Big Cove Campground up the jeep road and all the way to the northeastern corner of Frozen Head State Park, at the mountaintop called the Garden Spot. There we found numerous painted trees and rocks indicating the park property boundary. Gary referred to the rock formation at this location as the "Druid Shrine."

From the Garden Spot we followed the route that would be the continuation of the Barkley course. We went down to Coffin Springs and then cross-country to the southeast, down to an old railroad bed. Gary pointed out a few places where you could see the old rail bed dug into the ground. It was amazing to me to realize there there had actually been a railroad there in the past. Following this rail bed downhill, we came to a coal-mining road that approximately follows the 2,600-foot elevation contour along the western side of Stallion Mountain. That coal road is outside the eastern boundary of Frozen Head State Natural Area. We went south and eastward along this road, passing an old mining auger, a big machine with a large drilling tool for digging coal.

We then passed the Barley Mouth Branch (creek), and soon came to a large rock outcropping that Gary called Standing Rock, where we turned westward and dropped steeply down toward the New River. We then turned and paralleled the New River going southeasterly and downstream, along a bench that was again the old railroad bed, high above the eastern side of the river. This was one of the most spectacular parts of the course. The New River is at the bottom of this gorge, down a sheer cliff that drops off from the edge of the trail. The trail follows the old shelf that was carved into the canyon wall for the railroad. The river below cascades over a series of small waterfalls and rapids. We followed this overgrown trail until it eventually dropped down to the river and crossed to the west side of it. A little farther downstream we came to the bottom of the hill that Gary called Hell. Some old concrete pillars were visible in the ground at this point; Gary called these "stockades" and claimed that they were part of the foundation of old prison structures.

Hell is an incredibly steep ascent that goes westward straight up the side of Frozen Head Mountain. I was amazed at the steepness of the climb. We had to literally pull ourselves uphill from tree to tree in the steepest places. The overgrown condition made things even more difficult, but the brush and trees at least gave us something to hold on to, to keep us from falling or sliding backward down the hill. Hell hill goes up about 1,200 feet of climb, from about 1,700' elevation to 2,900', in the first 0.7 miles. I was astounded to see that there were paint blazes on some of the trees along this hill. This was actually an old trail! Gary explained that it was an old mining trail used by the prisoners from the nearby Brushy Mountain Penitentiary.

As we hiked slowly, almost torturously, up this hill, we passed through several sites with old mining ruins of various kinds, including metal parts, cables, remnants of coal piles, and holes in the ground. Fred Pilon had mentioned these old mining artifacts in his Barkley article last year. Somewhere several hundred feet up Hell, I dropped one of my gloves. Gary had wisely advised me to bring leather gloves for protection from the briers and branches. Gary and Karl stopped for a smoke break while I went back down for several minutes to retrieve my glove. When I rejoined Gary and Karl, we continued upward and passed through a heavily brier-infested area that Gary called Sawbrier Point, and continued trudging to the jeep road at about 3,000' elevation.

On this dirt road, just at the point where it makes a big switchback, we turned right and continued uphill for a few more tenths of a mile, to the junction at Tub Springs with the jeep road that runs from the Big Cove Campground to the Frozen Head Lookout Tower. From there, I don't recall the details of where we went that day, but I suspect that we took the South Old Mac Trail, the shortest trail route, back down to the campground. On race day, the course would go up to the lookout tower, and then back to Tub Springs Junction, and then on the Chimney Top Trail back to the park and campground.

The following day, I did about a 15 mile run/hike in about five and a half hours. I believe I did about two-thirds of the race loop, including the North Boundary Trail, the Garden Spot, Coffin Springs, the coal road, the New River, Hell, and the jeep road to Tub Springs Junction. I again took the South Old Mac Trail back to the parking area. My time from the start to the Garden Spot was 3:02, and 4:48 to the Tub Springs junction. My notes also show that I was lost for about 8 minutes at the bottom of Hell.

I also made a one-day trip to Frozen Head for more training later in March. My old running log book from 1988 shows the following incomplete entry on March 21: "Ran/hiked ~13.0 miles 5: " During this run I took pencil notes on a piece of paper that I can still decipher. I counted switchbacks along the North Boundary Trail, as well as noted my times at several locations. It took me 1 hour and 55 minutes to go from the parking area to the northwest corner of the State Natural Area. My time was 3:09 to the Garden Spot, where I wrote: "EXHAUSTED; THIRSTY; SOCKS SAGGING". I then took the jeep road back down to my car. Most of my normal runs in those years were at about 8 minutes per mile, so a 13-mile run that took me 5+ hours (about 24 minutes per mile) illustrates the extreme difficulty of running on this route at Frozen Head.

As I recall, in the three visits I made to Frozen Head in preparation for the race (in late February, early March, and March 21), I covered all portions of the course at least once. On one of these reconnaissance trips, I think the March 21 run, I found a pedometer along the NBT in the vicinity of Bald Knob. As I recall, the reading on the pedometer where I found it was 6.2 miles. I picked up the pedometer, thinking that it was probably registering the distance from the campground to where I found it. I suspected it was lost by someone else who was also training for the Barkley. Who else would be *out there* on that overgrown, abandoned, "closed" trail?

Another way that I prepared for the Barkley was to make an elevation profile graph of the loop. I carefully measured the trail length with a scale on the map that Gary had sent me. I read the elevations at each major peak and valley from the elevation contours on the map. I then plotted the elevation profile on graph paper, and added annotation of various landmarks along the course, including numbers of switchbacks on the major climbs. A copy of this graph is shown on the next page.

This graph and my distance/elevation data are dated March 20, 1988. So this graph was produced the day before my last training run at Frozen Head. Interestingly, Gary later generated a computerized spreadsheet of data describing the course, with location names, distances, and elevations. My

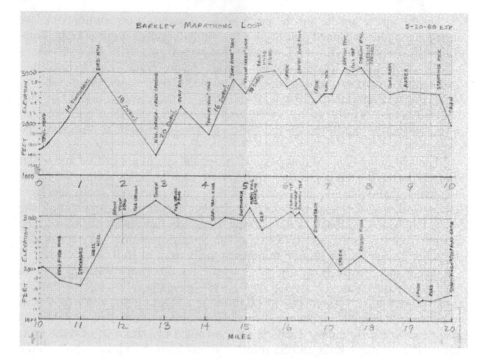

hand-measured data had estimated a loop length of 20.4 miles with 7,794 feet each of gain and drop per loop, whereas Gary's spreadsheet had the "actual miles" per loop at 18.33, with 8,680 feet each of gain and drop. I rounded the total distance to 20.0 miles for the graph. However, based on subsequent measurements, I now believe that the distance and climb were more than these earlier estimates. Referring to the Schematic Map and Table on pages 8 and 9, the sequence of trail segments for this year was 1, 2, 19, 20, 21, 22, 23, 24, 16, 17, 18, 8 (up), 8 (down), 9, 10, 11, 12, 13. The estimated distance of this loop adds up to 23.7 miles, so the three-loop race was actually about 71.1 miles long. Elevation gain and drop per loop were each about 8,070 feet, for a three-loop total of 24,210 feet.

In addition to preparing the elevation graph, I also wrote out a detailed list of things for my drops bags, a page of plans for what flashlights and batteries to have at each aid-drop location, and a "Game Plan" with a time schedule that I hoped to follow. I planned to finish the first loop in 7:30, take a 30-minute break to eat, drink, re-supply, and get a leg massage from Gail. I expected to get to Hell on loop two between 6 and 7 PM. I noted: "7 PM dark approaching. Get the hell out of Hell." It was my specific goal to get to the top of Hell hill on loop two before dark. I also estimated a 10 PM time for completion of loop two, for an elapsed time of 17 hours after the start of the race. I planned to then "Stop. Rest. Massage. Eat. Sleep. ? 2AM EST → 3AM EDT Get up. Start hiking in dark. Set watches ahead 1 hour." I noted the time limits to start and finish the third loop, and the approximate times of daylight and nightfall. I even planned to adjust my watch for the start of Daylight Saving Time. However, I did not predict a finishing time.

Besides training on and memorizing the Barkley course, another way that I prepared myself for the 1988 Barkley was to take up the sport of orienteering. I did this to train myself in backcountry navigation with map and compass, a skill that is surely helpful for running the Barkley. My training log shows that I ran a 6.75-kilometer orienteering race with 14 controls, in about 77:30 on February 27, in Umstead State Park near Raleigh, North Carolina, where I lived at the time. Interestingly, a 100-mile race was started in 1995, and has been held annually in Umstead State Park every year since then. This Umstead 100 Mile Endurance Run is frequently held on the same weekend as the Barkley. Prior to the 1988 Barkley, I also bought a pair of orienteering knickers and gaiters. These clothes were intended to protect the legs when running through brush. The gaiters came up almost to the knees and had thin pads to protect the shins. I wore these during Barkley as protection from the briers.

My three pre-race visits to Frozen Head to familiarize myself with the loop were extremely valuable training. They not only taught me the course, but also gave me a good feel for the difficulty of the race. I could see that this was nothing like the 50-mile races I had run. I knew that I had to approach it as similar in effort to a 100-mile race. In June 1987, I had finished the Old Dominion 100-mile trail race in Virginia, in 22:48. I could tell from my Frozen Head training runs that the Barkley, although eventually called only 55 miles that year, would be comparable to the effort it took me to run the Old Dominion. This training on the course also pretty much convinced me that I was capable of finishing the race within its time limit.

The entry form for 1988 was titled: "THE BARKLEY MARATHONS The Race That Eats Its Young." This slogan, "the race that eats its young," has subsequently been used many times on Barkley information and T-shirts. On the T-shirt that I got at the 1988 race, there was a drawing of some wolf-like animals chewing on a fallen runner at the bottom of a mountain. The caption on the T-shirt was "The Barkley Marathons Eats Its Young."

Gary mailed a course update to the entrants prior to the race. This update announced the rule requiring runners to retrieve book pages at each of three locations on the course. He described the three locations in detail on a separate sheet of paper. These locations were the Garden Spot, the coal mine road near Standing Rock, and the bottom of Hell hill. He also stated that the starting time would be 5 AM. He claimed that this early start was to help runners reach "Hell" twice before dark. He warned the runners that Daylight Saving Time would begin during the race. He imposed a 36-hour cutoff to be an official finisher. He further stated in that update that "we are going to call the dam thing 60 miles." But he said that "It probably falls just a little short of 60." His official breakdown was: "8 miles to Coffin Springs, 4 miles to the firetower, and 8 more miles in." He then rated the sections on "the Gary Grim Gradient:" North Section 7.8, New River (Hell) 9.7, and South Section 3.6. For comparison, he listed a few other races and gave their Gary Grim Gradient ratings as: Pine Mountain 3.7, Groundhog 50-mile 3.4, and Strolling Jim 1.9. Despite Gary's statement that he was going to call the Barkley distance 60 miles, in his post-race *UltraRunning* article he reverted to calling it 55 miles.

In that update, Gary stated that "Frozen Ed, the Raw Dog and myself took a leisurely hike through that segment [the New River section] just last weekend." This statement places the date of the update at about March 7-13, 1988. He went on to try to scare the entrants by noting: "It will bite you on the ass. Reaching the northeast boundary marker [the Garden Spot] was easy. Finding both Coffin Springs and the mine road were also easy. However, descent from Standing Rock, down the south side of Barley Mouth Branch (the first 1/4 mile planted in thorny locust trees) was incredibly draining and left very little time to recover before the 'sweetest half mile in ultra-marathoning' where we climb 1300 feet from the Stockades to the jeep road. During that short section Frozen Ed took a locust thorn thru the palm and got a sawbrier imbedded in his calf. The Raw Dog and myself got only minor cuts and puncture wounds. However, my hamstrings feel today as if they have hard knots tied in them. Believe me, there aren't four miles to compare to Hell anywhere else on this planet. There is no way you'll be finishing this race. See you on the Fools Day."

In a handwritten note to me on this update information, Gary wrote: "Frozen Ed, If you do run with the top dogs, then you lose your advantage! If you can avoid being a guide, I think you can not just finish, but WIN. Big. See you soon, Gary." This statement by Gary turned out to be prophetic, as you will see. He was correct in alluding to my course knowledge as being an advantage.

Gary was at his most eloquent as a writer when he wrote in the June 1988 *UltraRunning* article about the Barkley, regarding the importance of navigation to stay on course. He wrote: "The runner cannot afford to lapse into a semi-comatose state of pure running and suffering. Failing to stay alert for even a moment can lead to a wander off the trail, and finding it again can be quite difficult." I have often since then thought about that phrase, "semi-comatose state of pure running and suffering," as a poetic description of running. I agree with Gary that there is a significant difference between "pure running" without the need to navigate, when the runner can zone out and let the mind wander, compared to trail running *out there* in the forest where there is a risk of getting lost or off-course, and thus the runner must stay intently focussed on his surroundings and whereabouts. The Barkley, because it is run on an unmarked course, epitomizes the latter type of running.

The Barkley race started on Saturday, April 2 that year. Gail and I drove from Raleigh, North Carolina, to Oak Ridge, Tennessee, on Friday, and stayed in a motel. I didn't yet understand the importance of camping at the Big Cove Campground the night before the race. Interestingly, Tom Possert was also staying at that same motel that night. I had met Tom at one or two other ultras in recent years, so I recognized him when I saw him at the motel. Gail and I went to his room and talked to him for a while on Friday evening. He was methodically measuring out some drink-mix powder for the race. In our conversation with Tom, I mentioned the pedometer that I had found on the North Boundary Trail. Tom said that he had lost that pedometer while training on the Barkley course. I gave the pedometer back to him.

Staying in that motel turned out to be a bad mistake, because when Gail and I tried to sleep, we were kept awake by loud teenagers partying in the room next to ours. As I recall, we were able to get only a couple hours sleep after the party wound down. We had to get up early and drive to Frozen Head for the 5 AM start of the the the race. Before we left the motel Saturday morning, we tried to return the favor to the next-room revelers by turning our television on and turning the volume up really loud with the television facing the wall of the offending party.

In Gary's subsequent article in *UltraRunning* about the 1988 race, he mentioned the following eight names of those who were starters: Tom Possert, Eric Clifton, me, Fred Pilon, Richard Schick, Doyle Carpenter, Carl Barshinger, and Eileen Elliot. Others whom I am quite sure started that year were Bruce Ensign, John DeWalt, Jim Dill, and Gary himself. Gary had printed copies of essays from that year's entrants, and I have a copy of those essays. Based on these essays, the following other runners were also entrants that year (although this does not guarantee that these runners all actually started the race): Gary Buffington, Ken McMaster, Jim Estes, Bill Seiler, Karl Henn, and Dan Sullivan. Gary also named the following entrants who had failed to submit an essay, for which Gary called them "pimples" and said that "for the duration of the Barkley time limit they shall be referred to as: weasel eater, weenie noses, sleaze skiers, pond scum, pustules, and, worst of all, Vinnie Testaverdes." The names following this list of insults were: Fred Pilon, Linda Sledge, Webb Sledge, Wally Shiel, Doyle Carpenter, Jim Dill, Steve Warshawer, Tom Possert, Tom Carter, Bob Alexander, and David Cochran.

The above lists of entrants include 25 different runners. In the *UltraRunning* article, Gary states that there were 19 starters. The complete list of starters is unknown, One runner named above who I am sure did *not* run was Steve Warshawer. I wish Steve had been there. He was one of the top ultrarunners in the country at that time, and I would have liked to have seen how he could have done on the Barkley course. As it was, there were several national-class ultrarunners in the starting field, notably Possert, Clifton, and Carpenter. So as in the previous year, the 1988 Barkley had several top national ultrarunners among its competitors.

At Frozen Head on Saturday morning, the race got underway on a course that had been freshly watered by rains throughout the previous night. I remember getting to Coffin Springs on the first loop, and Gail was there. There was an aid-drop at that location. In those early years, Gary actually took runners' drop bags to both Coffin Springs and the Frozen Head fire tower as on-course aid for the runners. I had carefully prepared a box or bag for each aid station, with things including flashlight and batteries, drinks, food, and clean socks.

As recounted by Gary in his *UltraRunning* article about the 1988 race, Possert and Clifton led the race through two loops. Gary referred to them as "speedsters" running at a "suicidal pace," and stated that "the faster trail didn't prepare us for the monumental running of Possert and Clifton. Flying with reckless abandon, they completed the first 18 1/3-mile loop in an earth-shaking 5:50 for Clifton and 5:52 for Possert." I completed the first loop in third place, in 6:54, over half an hour ahead of my "Game Plan" schedule. Pilon was fourth in 8:00, with Schick and Carpenter next in 10:58.

It is remarkable to note that Clifton's time of 5:50 for the first loop in this 1988 race remains as the fastest time ever run on any loop in any Barkley race through 2009.

After I finished the first loop, Gary noted that I took a nearly half-hour break at the campground to re-supply and get a leg massage from Gail. I was employing a strategy of saving myself for the third loop.

On the second loop, I remember falling on a wet, mossy rock on the north side of Bird Mountain and hurting my knee. My running log notes show that this injury was still bothering me up to 13 days later. However, I continued onward in pain. At Coffin Springs on the second loop, I remember that Eric Clifton's wife, Shelby, was there. She asked me whether I planned to go up to the Frozen Head lookout tower on this loop. I replied that of course I was! That was part of the race. She then informed me that Possert and Clifton were not going to the lookout tower. They somehow had interpreted the rules as making the top of Frozen Head mountain optional, not mandatory. I was dumbfounded to hear this. I expressed my belief that it was mandatory, and that I was certainly going to go there.

In looking over the course description that I have from 1988, which Gary titled "The Barkley Marathons Course Deprecation," I see that the directions for the Frozen Head mountain section read as follows: "Take a right on the Jeep Road [at the top of the Hell hill-climb] and follow it to Tub Spring where you can get water again. Then continue up to the firetower atop Frozen Head itself where supply drop number two will be located. From this point go back down the Jeep Road to where the three way intersection is and follow the trail that goes to Mart Fields and Chimney Top." From this description I cannot see how Clifton and Possert could interpret the top of Frozen Head as optional. However, several years later I asked Eric Clifton about it, and he definitely remembered that he and Possert thought that it was optional, not required. One possible explanation for the confusion may be that, as best I can recall, Gary may have told us runners verbally, rather than in writing, to go up the stairs to the top of the lookout tower on the first loop, but there was no need for us to do so on the second or third loops. Perhaps Tom and Eric had misinterpreted this to mean they could skip the *road* to the lookout tower rather than the *stairs* up the lookout tower on loops two and three. Regardless of the explanation, I think the confusion illustrates a fundamental principle about human perception: different people will interpret what they hear differently, even though they all were told the same thing. Although I could not understand their interpretation, I do believe that Clifton and Possert had no intention to cheat. If so, they would not have been so open about skipping Frozen Head Mountain. If they were trying to cheat, they would have done this surreptitiously, not openly. But by skipping this out-and-back to the base of the lookout tower, they were shorting the loop by about 0.8 mile and about 270 feet each of climb and descent.

As the race progressed, Possert finished his second, slightly shortened, loop, in a total time of 12:46. He headed out on his third loop after taking a 15-minute break. Clifton finished his second loop about 90 minutes later, and then quit. I came in again in third position, in 15:09, nearly two hours ahead of my Game Plan. I then, as Gary wrote, "crawled off to sleep, planning to rise at 3 a.m. for loop three." I remember several things about my decision to get some sleep in my car between loops two and three. One factor was my desire to avoid the North Boundary Trail in the dark. This trail was difficult enough to follow in the daylight. I assumed that it would be nearly impossible in the darkness. So sleeping after the second loop was an explicit part of my pre-race Game Plan. I was also exhausted from the effort of running those first two loops. Add to this the fact that I had gotten very little sleep in the noisy motel the night before the race. I thought a few hours of sleep would help me on the third loop. However, as the night progressed, it began raining. So when my intended 3 AM wake-up time arrived, I decided to continue sleeping until near the time limit for starting the third loop, which was 24 hours after the start, or 6 AM Daylight Saving Time (rather than 5 AM, since we had lost an hour to the daylight saving time-switch at 2 AM).

When I finally got up to start my third loop, I witnessed the fateful moment when Possert finished his third loop, in 23:47. He came into camp wearing a large and bright headlamp with a battery pack worn on a belt around his waist. This was quite innovative in those days before LED headlights were commonplace—it is the first time I can recall having seen a runner wear a headlight. Tom's performance was truly impressive. However, by now Gary knew that Tom had skipped the top of Frozen Head on the latter two loops, so Gary, very painfully I am sure, informed Tom that he was technically disqualified. Gary described this moment in the *UltraRunning* article by stating: "For all the courage and conditioning Tom had shown during his magnificent run, it was at the moment of disappointment that he showed his true class. As he lay exhausted on his back in the cold rain, being deprived of what he had so painfully earned, he responded with a weak smile, 'You do what you have to do—I know what I did and I'm satisfied with my effort. That was the hardest 24 hours I've ever experienced.'" Gary then paid well-deserved high tribute to Possert, as he wrote: "Tom will not be recorded as the winner of the 1988 Barkley. An extrapolated finish time of 24:47 for the entire 55 miles cannot be counted as official. However, in the south they say that the true measure of a man is not how he wins, but how he faces losing. Tom was a man among boys on the trail. But his class in the face of bitter disappointment stands alone as the brightest moment that will ever be seen at the Barkley."

I was the only other runner besides Possert to run a third loop, which Gary described in the *UltraRunning* article as "a tribute to raw endurance." My preparation paid off. I successfully navigated the three loops without getting off course. After over eight hours of downtime and sleep between loops two and three, I did the third loop in 8:27, finishing in a total time of 32:14:50.

Thus, in its third year, the Barkley Marathons finally had an official finisher.

Below is a list of the known starters, their numbers of Barkley starts, and all known loop-finishing times for 1988. Other starters and loop-finishing times are unknown.

1. Frozen Ed Furtaw (1)   6:54   15:09   32:14:50
2. Tom Possert (2)   5:52   12:46* 23:47*
3. Eric Clifton (1)   5:50   14:16*
4. Carl Barshinger (1)   Probably finished two loops; times unknown.
5. Eileen Elliot (1)   Probably finished two loops; times unknown.
6. Fred Pilon (3)   8:00
7. Richard Schick (1)   10:58
8. Doyle Carpenter (2)   10:58
9. Gary Cantrell (3)   Finished one loop; time unknown.
10. Bruce Ensign (1)   Results unknown.
11. John DeWalt (1)   Results unknown.
12. Jim Dill (1)   Results unknown.
19 Starters
* Disqualified for short-cutting the loop.

As I approached the finish line, I was expecting a congratulatory crowd to greet me. However, when I arrived at the campground, only Karl's wife, Cathy Henn, and their two children were there. Gary, Karl, and Gail had driven up the jeep road in a pickup truck to retrieve the drop bags from the two aid stations. Apparently everybody else had gone home. So there wasn't much fanfare at the finish. I stopped my stopwatch and rested while awaiting the return of the others.

When Gary, Karl, and Gail returned, they congratulated me. Gary then presented me with the Barkley Cup. This was a pewter mug that was the trophy for winning the Barkley Marathons. The name "Barkley" was engraved near the top of the cup. Beneath this name was engraved:
1986   0
1987   0
Gary told me that I could get my name engraved on the cup, but that I could only keep it until next year's Barkley. Then I had to return it to him to be given to next year's winner. I got it engraved with "1988   Ed Furtaw" below the line for 1987. This engraving cost me $4.50. Gary later told me that this Cup had been Hoghead Barkley's drinking mug when Hoghead was a college student. On the next page is a photo of Gail's hand holding the Barkley Cup. More will be said about the Barkley Cup, including its disappearance, in later chapters.

Gary's pre-race statement that I could not only finish, but win the race, had proven correct. However, I did not have to worry about the "top dogs" learning the course from me. Possert already knew the course, apparently as well as I did (except for the part about skipping the top of Frozen Head on loops two and three). Clifton was too fast to hang back with me, and all the other runners were too slow to keep up with me. So my course knowledge and preparation paid off without me losing the advantage by serving as a guide to others.

I consider my victory at Barkley in 1988 to be one of the most significant accomplishments in my running career. Although Tom was clearly the best runner there that year, I became the first finisher in the history of the Barkley Marathons. This is something about which I have always been proud. Even if

Tom had finished the proper course and won, I would still have been happy to have finished second. My goal in running the Barkley was to finish it, and to prove to myself, Gary, and the world that it could be done. I would have accomplished that even if Tom or someone else had finished first.

I thought that my completion of the Barkley, and Tom's virtual domination of the course, would open the door for others to also succeed, now that it had been proven to be do-able despite Gary's taunts that no one could do it. However, I was not yet fully aware, way back then, of the true nature of the Barkley in Gary's mind. I didn't realize that he would make it even tougher, to push it further toward impossible. Gary informed us of his plans at the end of his *UltraRunning* article about the 1988 Barkley, when he wrote: "Naturally, the burning question among the remaining Barkley almost-veterans was: 'What will you do to the course now?' Well, the joke is on the runners once again. For the Barkley Marathons is like a Christmas package that opens only to reveal another package inside. Only in this case the inside package is larger than its container. Over the past three years the Barkley has been cleared, rerouted to faster stretches, marked, and measured accurately (sorry, but it really is only 55 miles). The triple-loop is just perfect. But next year there will be an additional option of completing 100 miles on these trails, getting in over 50,000 feet of wonderful climbing. The limit will still be 36 hours for the 55-mile, and 50 hours for 100 miles. Two miles an hour ain't much. I'm sure there are plenty of 'real runners' out there who believe they can do it. We'll see."

Thus Gary turned victory into a form of punishment. Because the Barkley had been finished, he was going to make it even more difficult. We will see in later chapters how Gary did this, and how, over the years, he has continually crafted the Barkley to keep it at the limit of possibility.

++++++++++

Below is a copy of my essay that was required for entry into the 1988 Barkley Marathons.

Why I Should Be Allowed To Enter The Barkley Marathons
(January 9, 1988)

There are several reasons why I should be allowed to enter the Barkley Marathons, and I will elucidate some of them in this essay. There are actually an infinite number of reasons why I should be allowed, but I don't have the time to write them all, so I will constrain myself to the more obvious ones.

First of all, I should be allowed in because I am still, despite all your rantings and all the historical evidence, unconvinced that I can't be the first to finish it. You owe it to the course to let it eat me... or try. I notice this race "eats its young." This brings us to the second reason why I should be allowed to enter: I will not be "young" any longer, as my 40th birthday occurs before Barkley this year (Feb. 28). I plan to run lots of races in my first Master year, and Barkley will probably be the first. Hopefully, it will teach me some humility, which of course is one of the main reasons why there should even be ultramarathons. A reasonable argument could probably be made that I should be required to run Barkley, but I won't go quite that far.

Another reason I should be allowed to run Barkley is that I am willing to openly admit it's folly and thus to claim my rightful place in it as a fool.

Actually, a manifestation of the Spirit has directed me to enter Barkley; therefore it would be contrary to the tao of the universe to attempt to deny me entrance.

There are also several more mundane, physical arguments for my running Barkley. I have done some orienteering (including successful competition) and I am very adept at using maps and finding my way in unknown territory. I plan to come well-equipped for a two-day ordeal. I also plan to bring my lovely crew to laugh at me. I should be allowed in, if for no other reason, just so all the others there can enjoy the pleasure of her company.

One final reason which I will mention is that I should be allowed to enter Barkley because I was actually crazy enough to sit down and write an essay on why I should be allowed to do something crazy. So that proves I should be allowed, right?

Ed "Frozen Head" Furtaw

Chapter 8
1989: The Course Bites Back

I noted near the end of the last chapter that I thought that Possert's and my results in the 1988 Barkley would show others that it was possible to complete the course within the time limit, thus opening the door for others to complete it. Gary also stated this belief in his article in *UltraRunning* about the 1989 Barkley, in which he wrote that Tom and I had "combined to destroy the Boundary Trail's illusion of invincibility." He also opined that "it seemed the natural order of things that more finishers would follow with the ground now broken." However, the results of the race of 1989 did not fulfill this optimistic projection.

In January 1989, Gail and I got married and moved from North Carolina to Las Vegas, Nevada. We started new jobs. Hence when the time for the 1989 Barkley approached, I sadly informed Gary that I would not be able to attend. With my new job, I did not have the vacation time available to travel across the country and run in that year's Barkley. I packaged the Barkley Cup and mailed it to Gary, ostensibly for him to present to the 1989 Barkley winner.

Because I was not there, I do not have much information about the 1989 Barkley beyond what is provided in the *UltraRunning* article that was written by Gary. I have an unused entry form that Gary had sent me, and a printout of Gary's spreadsheet with locations, distances, and elevation data. This spreadsheet was revised from the 1988 spreadsheet, to accommodate the course changes for 1989.

The addition of the 100-mile race was the major change on paper. The traditional three-loop run was retained, but it was now referred to on the entry form as the "short one." The 100-mile was referred to as "the long run." The short run was again three loops and was stated to be 55 miles, and had a 36-hour time limit. The long run was called 100 miles, and the time limit was 50 hours. It consisted of six loops. The loops were mostly the same as the loop from 1988, with the exception described below. The first two loops of both race distances were slightly longer than the loop of 1988. All subsequent loops in both races were shortened by taking the South Old Mac trail from the Tub Springs Junction back down to the park, rather than the Chimney Top Trail. On the entry form, Gary again taunted the runners by saying: "You gotta finish 55 in 27:30 or better to be 'allowed' to continue. You won't. And even if you did, you wouldn't go on. The Barkley will squash you like a bug."

Regardless of this rhetoric about the 100-miler, the major change in reality for 1989 was the addition to each loop of another extreme climb. The addition of the six-loop 100-miler was not a change in the reality of the runners because no one was even thinking of attempting six loops. At most, three loops remained the goal for all, at least for several more years to come.

The new major climb that was added was called the Rat Jaw. In 1988, when the course got to the top of Hell hill, it turned *right* on the jeep road and went up to Tub Springs Junction, then up the jeep road to the lookout tower at the top of Frozen Head mountain. For 1989, the course turned *left* on the jeep road at the top of Hell and went steeply downhill for about a mile, with about 600 feet of elevation drop. There it turned right on an old prison mine road, went for a fraction of a mile past some old mining ruins, and came to a powerline running steeply up and down the south face of Frozen Head mountain. Just past the powerline was an old guardhouse that had been part of the prison facilities. The guardhouse was a small cinder block structure completely surrounded by chain-link fence with barbed wire on top, with the barbed wires slanted outward. This suggests that the guards stayed inside the guardhouse; the barbed wire was to keep the prisoners out, not in. For several years beginning in 1989, this guardhouse was one of the book locations. In some years, runners actually had to crawl under the chain-link fence to get to the guardhouse to retrieve a book page. A photo of the guardhouse, that I took during the 1991 Barkley race, is shown below.

The route turned northward near this guardhouse and went steeply uphill in the partial clearing that had been cut into the forest beneath the powerline. This uphill section was heavily overgrown with blackberry briers, which are sometimes over head-height. This climb goes up about 1,020 feet in about 0.8 miles from where the runners start up, to the very top of Frozen Head mountain, at the base of the lookout tower.

The name *Rat Jaw* for this grueling climb could have been given because of the tearing action on the flesh of the runners as they crawl through the nasty blackberry briers. However, that is not why Gary so named it. The name is based on the shape of the course on a map. The outline of this new part of the course from the top of Hell hill to the Frozen Head lookout tower is shaped like a pointed projection toward the southeast. The part of the course along the New River gorge and up Hell hill is another pointed projection to the east. The angle between these two projections is similar to the outline of a rat's jaw with its mouth partly open. Hence, Gary called it the Rat Jaw.

The new Rat Jaw section of the course added about 1.5 miles to the loop. Referring to the Schematic Map on page 8, the loop sequence was 1, 2, 19, 20, 21, 22, 23, 24, 16, 17, 25, 26, 27, 8 (down), 9, 10, 11, 12, 13. To keep the three-loop race distance at the same nominal 55 miles as in the previous year, Gary shortened the third loop by having the runners take the South Old Mac trail, rather than the Chimney Top Trail, back down to the park (Schematic Map sequence 1, 2, 19, 20, 21, 22, 23, 24, 16, 17, 25, 26, 27, 8, 7, 28, 13).

On Gary's 1989 spreadsheet, the stated length of the full loop (to be run on the first two loops) was 19.13 miles. The distance for the shortened loop (loops three and higher) was 15.9 miles, with race totals given as 54.15 and 101.83 miles for the short and long races, respectively. Gary's climb and drop as given on his spreadsheet were each 26,840 and 51,080 feet for the two races. However, in the *UltraRunning* article, the stated distance and climb were 57.4 miles and 27,000 feet. In comparison, my best estimates of the new course distances and elevation changes, based on data in the Table on page 9, are as follows: for the three-loop course, 71.1 miles with 24,930 feet each of climb and drop; for the six-loop course, 133.2 miles with 47,280 feet of climb and drop. Based on my estimates, the three-loop course distance did stay about the same as in the previous year, but the climb and drop increased by several hundred feet. Furthermore, several miles of good trail were replaced by three climbs of the nasty Rat Jaw. Thus we can conclude that the 1989 course was slightly more difficult than the 1988 course.

At least one mystery arises when comparing the data in Gary's 1989 spreadsheet to that in his 1988 spreadsheet. The reported distance from the lookout tower back to the start/finish campground via the Chimney Top Trail decreased from 7.33 miles in 1988, to 6.72 miles in 1989, even though the route remained the same. What became of the other 0.61 miles? Only the devious trickster knows!

All 14 of the 1989 starters are named in Gary's *UltraRunning* article. They are: Bill Seiler, Bruce Ensign, Ken McMaster, Fred Pilon, John DeWalt, Tom Green, Dick West, Steve Bozeman, Greg Meacham, Al Montgomery, Nora Fischer, Jim Dill, Cathy Henn, and Carolyn O'Brien. Fred Pilon was starting his fourth Barkley, the only runner to do so, based on the available information. Fittingly, Fred led through the first loop, in a time of 7:45. This was 15 minutes faster than his time for the first loop last year, despite the longer and tougher loop with the Rat Jaw this year. So Fred was clearly off to a good start. He headed out on his second loop before anyone else had finished the first. Gary reported in the *UltraRunning* article that "Fred had come for the '89 run with frightening determination, and the betting line had him a sure pick to finish." But Gary had then added: "Don't ever bet against the Boundary Trail."

Apparently, John DeWalt and Dick West were the only other runners to start a second loop. However, none of the three second-loop runners finished even half the loop. Pilon and West made it, separately, to Coffin Springs before taking the Quitter's Road back to the campground to quit. DeWalt made it only the first couple of miles, and then, as Gary reported: "Bird Mountain finished him off as expected."

An interesting fact reported by Gary in his 1989 *UltraRunning* article was that Nora Fischer, 29 years old, from Tennessee, became the first woman to finish a loop within the time limit to be allowed to continue. She finished the first loop in 11:43. However, Nora chose to not continue.

Here is the list of 1989 starters, their numbers of Barkley starts, and their one-loop finishing times.

1. Fred Pilon (4)   7:45
2. John DeWalt (2)   9:01
3. Tom Green (2)   9:04
4. Dick West (1)   9:12
5. Steve Bozeman (1)   11:07
6. Greg Meacham (1)   11:07
7. Al Montgomery (1)   11:07
8. Nora Fischer (1)   11:43
9. Jim Dill (2)   12:41
10. Cathy Henn (1)   12:54* 10 minutes over the time limit.
11. Carolyn O'Brien (1) 12:54* 10 minutes over the time limit.
12. Ken McMaster (2)   Quit after Rat Jaw.
13. Bruce Ensign (2)   Lost at bottom of Hell; got ride back to park.
14. Bill Seiler (1)   Lost near Garden Spot; got ride back to park.
14 Starters

For the third time in its first four years, the Barkley Marathons had again defeated all the runners. Learning about this later, I was amazed that there were again no finishers. Furthermore, the starting field had diminished, both in numbers and arguably in quality. Not as many of the national big-name ultrarunners were there as had been in the first few years. I pondered this and came to the conclusion that I would have to return in 1990 to again prove that it could be done.

Chapter 9
1990: More Finishers

I was not the only runner to be attracted back to the Barkley in 1990. Other previous Barkley entrants Fred Pilon, Eric Clifton, Jim Dill, Dick West, Doyle Carpenter, John DeWalt, Al Montgomery, Greg Meacham, Steve Bozeman, Bruce Ensign, and Carolyn O'Brien also returned. Despite (or perhaps because of) its humiliating difficulty, the Barkley was beginning to attract a crowd of repeat customers.

This year, we were joined by several new runners who sported some strong ultrarunning credentials. David Horton, David Drach, and Dennis "The Animal" Herr were the most notable newcomers. At the time, all three of these runners, along with Eric Clifton, were regularly among the top finishers in ultras in the southeastern U.S. For example, Horton had won the Wild Oak Trail 50 Mile in March 1989, in a course record time of 8:11:22. Then in the March 1990 Wild Oak, Dave Drach had won while bettering Horton's record, with a time of 7:42:30. Clifton finished second in 1990, with Horton 5th in a new Masters (over age 40) course record. In the Massanutten Mountain Massacre, another tough 50-mile trail race in Virginia, held later in April 1990, Drach finished second and Animal Herr third. In the 1989 Massanutten race, Herr had won with a Masters course record, with Horton taking second. Thus the 1990 Barkley starting field included several of the best runners in ultrarunning at that time. I was flattered to be named among them by Gary as he wrote about this year's Barkley in the subsequent *UltraRunning* article: "Led by a plethora of big names, the likes of Furtaw, Horton, Herr, Clifton, and Drach, the biggest field in Barkley history (29) started..." However, I did not consider myself to be the equal of any of these other runners.

Significantly, we also had a couple of international runners enter the Barkley this year: Ulrich Kamm from Germany, and Milan Milanovich from Switzerland. "Ulli" Kamm at the time published one of the most comprehensive world-wide calendars of ultramarathons, the *International Fixtures List*. His participation at Barkley would ensure an international reputation for the Barkley. Ulli told me that he had completed about 100 ultramarathons without ever failing to finish. He did not run; he was a long-distance race-walker. It would be interesting indeed to see how he fared at the Barkley.

Gary's Barkley article in the June 1990 *UltraRunning* article was very interesting because this was when he first revealed the James Earl Ray connection. As mentioned in Chapter 4, Ray had escaped from Brushy Mountain State Penitentiary into the Frozen Head Natural Area behind the prison in 1977. His failure to get more than a few miles in over 54 hours had captured Gary's imagination about a race in Frozen Head. Now, after several years of Barkley races, Gary was telling the story of Ray's escapade as "the original Barkley." In his *UltraRunning* article, Gary interspersed quotes from a Playboy magazine interview of Ray, with descriptions of the 1990 Barkley race. I think this article shows Gary at his best as a writer.

Now that I lived in Nevada, nearly 2,000 miles from Frozen Head, my trip to the Barkley was more involved than it had been back in 1988.

Because of limited vacation time, I did not leave home in Nevada until after work on the Wednesday before Saturday's Barkley start. I spent two very long days driving alone to Frozen Head, not arriving until the Friday night before the start. Thus I started the race in a more tired state than I would have liked, with a three-hour time-zone difference to further impair my readiness to race. Furthermore, it had been two years since I had set foot in Frozen Head State Park, and the course now included the Rat Jaw, which was a new part of the course since I was last there. Nevertheless, I methodically prepared another written plan for the run, listing things to carry, to put in my two drop bags, and to have in my vehicle at the campground. I also made a hoped-for running schedule. This time my schedule did not include planned sleep time between loops one and two. I projected three loop-finishing times of 8:10, 17:20, and 26:20.

The course for 1990 was the same as the previous year's course. This marked the first time, in the race's fifth year, that the course had stayed the same from one year to the next. In fact, the course would now stay the same for the next several years (through 1994) as well.

As recounted in Gary's *UltraRunning* article, I led the race for the first two loops. This happened by accident. I knew that the other top runners were considerably faster than I, at least in more normal races. But a group of those faster runners had gone out together at the start, and managed to get off-course early in the race. David Horton wrote an article about this year's Barkley that appeared in the June 1990 *UltraRunning* alongside Gary's article. In his article, Horton mentioned that he, Dave Drach, and Animal Herr had come to this race planning to run together. He also stated that this group "had a great deal of difficulty finding the books on the first lap as a very heavy fog enveloped us." In part because of the fog that morning, I did not even realize that I was in the lead until I got to the first book location at the Garden Spot, and realized that no pages had been removed from the book yet. I was definitely surprised to be in the lead. I think this pushed me to run a little faster and harder than I would have otherwise; not a smart move. As I got to the top of Hell hill at the jeep road, Gary was waiting there to observe the runners getting torn to shreds in the thick stand of briers that we ran through at that location. He was surprised to see me as the first runner to emerge. As I recall, he exclaimed: "Frozen Ed! Where are all the big boys?" I told Gary that I had expected them to be ahead of me, and did not know what happened to them. I then hastened onward, enchanted by the idea of being in the lead over this pack of national-class runners, but expecting them to catch me at any time.

I finished the first loop in 7:16, well ahead of my intended schedule. Gary noted in his *UltraRunning* article that this was a course record (for this new loop with the Rat Jaw), but that it did not bode well because "The Barkley loves to eat rabbits!" Milan Milanovich was second after one loop, about 41 minutes behind me. Drach, Horton, and Herr were next, all within a minute of each other and about 12 minutes behind Milanovich. These three started loop two prior to Milanovich.

Based on the split times reported by Gary in his *UltraRunning* article, Eric Clifton had escorted his then-wife, Shelby, around the first loop; they both finished it in about 8:34. Shelby apparently then quit, while Eric accelerated and eventually caught up to Drach, Horton, and Herr early in the second loop. However, Animal Herr decided to call it a day at Coffin Springs, and took the Quitter's Road back to camp, while Drach, Horton, and Clifton continued onward together.

By the end of the second loop, I was still in the lead, finishing in 16:04. However, it was now time for me to pay the piper and become the eaten rabbit. I was so exhausted that I simply could not go on. I went to my car to get some sleep. I had several blisters on my feet, and my feet and legs were sore. Drach, Horton, and Clifton were next in after two loops, in 16:41. They prepared for loop three, while Gary came over to my car in the campground and informed me that I was about to lose my lead. He exhorted me to get up and get going. But I could only lie there and report: "I'm shot." This was probably the most exhausted and sore that I had ever been from running. I was not physically able to get up and continue. My race was over.

The triumvirate of Horton, Drach, and Clifton finished the third loop together. Gary listed them in the results in the order given, but recorded all their times as 26:22:39; a time remarkably close to my target finishing time of 26:20 that I had written on my game plan. Milan Milanovich also finished the third loop, in 33:39:01. There was also one other finisher, Fred Pilon, in 34:09:28. Fred finally had a finish after five attempts! And the Barkley finally had multiple finishers.

Gary awarded the Barkley Cup for that year to one of the three winners, presumably David Horton. David had the cup inscribed: "1990 The Three Stooges." It is worth noting that several top national runners had come to the Barkley not to compete against each other, but to work together to beat the course. This was continuing to be a recurring theme at the Barkley.

Ulli Kamm finished two loops in 23:44:07, but then retired because of swollen knees. After his 100 previous ultra finishes without a DNF (Did Not Finish), he finally knew what defeat was like. Jim Dill and Dick West were the only other two-loop finishers, both in 25:01.

Here is the list of the known starters, their numbers of Barkley starts, and their loop-finishing times for 1990.

1. David Horton (1)	8:09:32	16:41:40	26:22:39
2. Eric Clifton (2)	8:34:12	16:41:40	26:22:39
3. David Drach (1)	8:08:57	16:41:40	26:22:39
4. Milan Milanovich (1)	7:57:20	19:04:18	33:39:01
5. Fred Pilon (5)	8:35:28	20:05:53	34:09:28
6. Frozen Ed Furtaw (2)	7:16:23	16:04:05	
7. Ulrich Kamm (1)	9:48:25	23:44:07	
8. Jim Dill (3)	8:45:47	25:01:00	
9. Dick West (2)	10:10:14	25:01:00	
10. Animal Herr (1)	8:09:48		
11. Shelby Clifton (1)	8:34:34		
12. Ron Sloniger (1)	8:35:24		
13. Doyle Carpenter (3)	8:35:34		
14. John DeWalt (3)	8:42:22		
15. Jeff Gaft (1)	10:10:14		

16. Al Montgomery (2)   10:11:20
17. Greg Meacham (2)   10:11:20
18. Steve Bozeman (2)   10:11:20
19. Karl Henn (1)   10:39:28
20. Phil Hengen (1)   11:40:37
21. Tim Gross (1)   11:40:37
22. Bruce Ensign (3)   12:08:41
23. Leonard Martin (1)   12:19:44
24. Carolyn O'Brien (2)   Probably finished one loop over the time limit.
25. Ray T. Mita (1)   Probably finished one loop over the time limit.
29 Starters

In his *UltraRunning* article, David Horton made some interesting and profound statements. This national-class runner said that his three-loop finish at Barkley "may have been the best ultra performance of my career." He compared his 26:22 finishing time for the Barkley 55-mile to the 100-mile trail races he had run previously, the *slowest* of which had taken him 22:05. This comparison is similar to the impression that I had had in 1988, that the Barkley 55 should be approached as similar to 100 miles elsewhere. David also stated in his article that finishing one 19-mile loop at Barkley was equivalent to finishing a typical 50-mile trail race. I and others have observed many times over the years that this approximation is quite accurate; most of us can run other 50-mile trail races in about the same time that we can run one loop of the Barkley.

What about Gary's proclaimed 100-mile race? Interestingly, at the end of the winning trio's third loop, Clifton continued running for about another 100 meters before stopping, making a mocking start of a fourth loop. Horton waited until just before the time limit for starting the fourth loop, and then ran about 150 meters and stopped, just so that he could surpass Clifton's farthest progress. These joking attempts at a fourth loop were the closest anyone could come to making a run at the six-loop 100-mile "long race." Actually, most of us runners thought that Gary's proclaimed 100-mile race was itself a joke. Since it took several national-class trail ultrarunners all that they had just to complete three loops, clearly it was impossible for anyone to run six loops. The 100-mile Barkley remained a figment of Gary's devious trickster mind.

+++++++++++

Below is a copy of the essay I wrote, in the form of a letter to Gary, as required for entry into the 1990 Barkley.

March Fourth, 1990
Dear Gary,

This letter is my request to be allowed to once again run The Barkley Marathons. That I should be allowed to do so should be evident to even the most casual observer. After all, I am both the defending champion and the only official finisher in the event's illustrious four-year history. This claim is made notwithstanding Tom Possert's awesome performance there in 1988.

The fact remains that I alone have completed the designated course in the past holdings of the event. In fact I have learned a trick or two from Tom's techniques as well as my own ultramarathoning experiences in the last two years.

Based on my experiences and still-burned-in memories of the Barkley course, I believe that I am capable of again finishing the course. In fact, I happen to believe that my own course record is somewhat "soft," since I spent over eight hours of "down-time" in setting the existing course record. I believe that my enhanced experience and determination will enable me to establish a new course record.

In view of this seemingly cocksure attitude on my part, I believe you, as race management, owe it to the race to allow it to have another chance to "eat me." After all, I am the only runner who has never failed in an attempt to finish the race.

I must admit, however, that this apparent attitude of confidence on my part is tenuous at best. Actually, it strikes fear into my heart to face the prospect of having to attempt to run the course again. And I am obviously in need of re-humbling. This, as in 1988, constitutes the real reason why I must be allowed to run Barkley again.

Chapter 10
1991: The Soviet Invasion; Hell and High Water

After his experience at the Barkley in 1990, Ulli Kamm spread the word about the difficulty of the Barkley Marathons to the subscribers to his *International Fixtures List*. I believe that this is one of the explanations for the fact that, in 1991, the Barkley attracted even more runners from foreign countries. In his article in *UltraRunning* about the 1991 Barkley, Gary stated that he had received a large number of inquiries from overseas. The race entrants included 12 runners from Eastern Europe, including two top runners from Poland, Janicke Scigocki and Mieczyslaw Majer, and ten ultrarunners from the Soviet Union.

After my painful DNF the previous year, I again entered the Barkley in hope of redemption. In my annually required essay on "Why I Should Be Allowed to Run the Barkley Marathons," I wrote an allegory in which I represented myself as a prisoner who must escape to freedom. I wrote of "runners who are driven by an incomprehensible but irresistible need to try to overcome all obstacles to find freedom." I ended by saying that we runners must not only be allowed to try again, we were condemned to do so. Of course, this was written as humorous, but I think it represents a real psychological drive within some of us to push ourselves to find and extend our limits. That is one of the reasons for the existence of the Barkley Marathons, and why some of us keep going back again and again.

In addition to the elite European runners who came to Barkley in 1991, there were also again several top U.S. ultrarunners entered. David Horton, Eric Clifton, and Dennis The Animal Herr returned. Fred Pilon was also back again, with his co-editor of *UltraRunning*, Peter Gagarin. Notably, several years prior, Peter had won the U.S. National Orienteering Championship, and had had his picture on boxes of Wheaties cereal! Several other past Barkley DNFers also came back to try again, including Richard Schick, Jeff Gaft, John DeWalt, Cathy Henn, Jim Dill, Leonard Martin, Al Montgomery, and Steve Bozeman. In all, Gary reported 37 starters that year, the most to date.

As Gail and I drove from Nevada to Tennessee for this year's Barkley, we noticed that our progress of moving several hundred miles eastward per day was being closely tracked by a storm system moving at about the same direction and speed. Sure enough, when we got to Frozen Head, so did the wet weather.

At the pre-race campground, many of us made primitive efforts to verbally communicate with our fellow entrants from overseas. We all tried to be as friendly as possible toward each other. One of the Soviets gave me a small banner that was presumably an award from an ultramarathon in the Soviet Union. It was interesting to meet these athletes from the country that was supposedly the United States' nemesis in the "Cold War." It gave me a good feeling to see that, like we Americans, they were intelligent and friendly people who loved running. I remember talking with one of the Soviets, barely able to understand each other. But he made clear that he had run about 150 miles in a 24-hour run! According to Gary, several others had similarly impressive credentials, such as 100 kilometers in sub-7 hours, and 100 miles in 13 hours. Clearly, the Soviets and Poles who were there were among the best that Europe had to offer. This was going to be an interesting race, to say the least.

As Friday night wore on, an eerie and ominous note was cast over the site when, at about 10 PM, a park ranger drove through the campground announcing on a loudspeaker that a tornado warning had just been issued for the area. We were advised to evacuate! I don't know which was worse: being there and comprehending this warning, or being one of our foreign guests and not understanding the warning. In any case, to the best of my knowledge, no one evacuated the campground. We were all there for an important purpose, so we hunkered down in our tents and rode out the storm, which brought heavy rain and wind, but fortunately, no tornado. Gail later noted in her log book that the bottom of our tent got wet that night. In my third Barkley, the weather was keeping up its perfect record of rain each of the years that I was there.

Things could have been worse if the storm had hit during the race rather than before it. The rain had virtually stopped by the Saturday 6 AM start of the race, but the consequences of the heavy downpour would be felt by us runners in several ways. The dirt road that the race starts on was awash with water. If the inch-deep water on the road was not enough to soak all the runners' shoes before the start, then the stream literally flowing down the first stretch of trail, going up Bird Mountain, was. By the time we got to the first real (waist-deep) stream-crossing at Phillips Creek, we had waded through about a dozen temporary streams that could normally be rock-hopped across without getting one's feet wet. But the worst water crossing of the day was in the middle of the loop at the New River as we runners approached the bottom of Hell. This raging stream was at least waist deep. On the first loop, I picked a location to cross and jumped in. The rapid current pushed me over and downstream, submerged to my chest in water. I struggled toward the other side and grabbed a rock to pull myself from the water. On the other side, I immediately checked the small disposable camera that I was carrying in my fanny pack. Fortunately, the zip-locked baggie that I had the camera in kept it dry. I was thus able to take some pictures of that area. One of those pictures appears on the next page.

I later learned from Rich Schick of an easier place to cross, slightly upstream from where I had first crossed, where the river was wider and hence not flowing as swiftly. I also learned that a group of several runners, including Suzi Thibeault, had formed a "human chain" by linking arms to cross the river. Talking to Suzi later, she told me: "I came to Barkley to finish, come hell or high water, but I didn't expect to have both at the same time." Gary subsequently used the phrase, "Come Hell *and* High Water," in the title of his article in *UltraRunning* that year.

Gary reported that Eric Clifton, allegedly determined to "seriously challenge the 100-mile," led the field after the first loop. He finished the loop in a course record 6:19:43, an incredible time given the condition of the course. A group of six runners, including Horton, Herr, one of the Poles, and three Soviets, came in next. Twenty runners eventually started loop two. Clifton

also led after two loops, in 15:05:04, the two-loop record on the then-current course. However, he then quit. Another rabbit was eaten by the Barkley. I finished two loops in 18:31:30, almost two-and-a-half hours slower than my two-loop time the previous year. This slow-down was due to a combination of the slower course conditions this year, and my trying to hold back to save myself for the third loop. In my game plan for this year, I had intended to not sleep after loop two. However, I changed plans and went to sleep after my second loop. But unlike last year, this year I was able to get up after a couple of hours sleep and head out for a third loop.

As I was preparing to begin my third loop, Gary told me that three runners—Herr, Pilon, and Gagarin—were already *out there* on the third loop. He said that he was pretty sure no other runners would attempt a third loop, so he asked me to remove the books at the checkpoints and bring back the non-biodegradable plastic baggies that the books were in. So as I trudged around the course, with mixed feelings of success but resigned to an apparent last-place finish, I dismantled the book-checkpoints and carried out the plastic bags. Little did Gary and I realize then that the run was not yet over for several more runners.

Gary attributes what happened next to the combination of two tough American women, and several male egos. Suzi Thibeault and Nancy Hamilton, both veterans of numerous other 100-mile trail races, were running together. They became the first-ever women to finish two Barkley loops, in a time of 23:27:33. This put them within Gary's time limit to continue, and continue they did. This phenomenon was observed by several of the male contestants, who did not like the idea of being bested by these two women. Thus, several other runners headed out on their third loop. These other runners included David Horton, who had decided to drop out after two loops. But when he learned that Suzi and Nancy were doing a third loop, he took off in an attempt to catch them. He eventually did catch them, allegedly stopping to kiss their shoes, and then passed them. Little did I know it at the time, but he almost caught me too.

In all, eleven runners started loop three. Eventually ten finished. Animal Herr lived up to his nickname by running like an animal and winning, in a new course-record time. The team of Fred Pilon and Peter Gagarin was next. Fred thus became the first two-time Barkley finisher. I, and then David Horton, soon joined Pilon as two-time finishers. Suzi and Nancy became the first women to ever finish the Barkley. They beat the two surviving Soviets by about 29 minutes. And lastly, Dick West finally earned a finish after many attempts at the Barkley, beating the cut-off time limit by about 26 minutes, thus becoming the longest-endurance (i.e., slowest) finisher yet.

The known entrants for 1991, their numbers of Barkley starts, and loop-finishing times as reported in Gary's *UltraRunning* article, were as follows:

1. Animal Herr (2)	7:00:19	15:53:40	25:53:13
2. Fred Pilon (6)	7:31:20	17:45:57	28:21:38
3. Peter Gagarin (1)	7:33:45	17:45:57	28:21:38
4. Frozen Ed Furtaw (3)	7:54:19	18:31:30	30:42:50
5. David Horton (2)	7:00:05	15:53:40	30:49:04
6. Suzi Thibeault (1)	10:10:27	23:27:33	34:32:34
7. Nancy Hamilton (1)	10:10:27	23:27:33	34:32:36
8. Valeri Hristenok (1)	7:21:11	17:50:25	35:01:00
9. Viktor Dobryansky (1)	7:21:11	17:50:25	35:01:00
10. Dick West (3)	8:08:44	24:25:02	35:33:39
11. Eric Clifton (3)	6:19:43	15:05:04	
12. Nikolai Safin (1)	6:47:50	15:53:40	
13. Janicke Scigocki (1)	8:45:07	17:15:05	
14. Rich Schick (2)	7:56:14	18:10:05	
15. Jeff Gaft (2)	7:36:00	19:08:30	
16. Nick Williams (1)	10:10:27	23:27:33	
17. John DeWalt (4)	8:41:20	24:33:24	
18. Al Montgomery (3)	10:15:05	25:20:13	
19. Steve Bozeman (3)	10:15:05	25:48:29	
20. Andrei Fyodorov (1)	6:45:31		
21. Mieczysław Majer (1)	6:48:55		

22. Vladimir Konoplev (1)   6:50:34
23. Jim Musselman (1)   9:59:00
24. Vladimir Novikov (1)   10:10:27
25. Nancy Drach (1)   10:15:29
26. Lou Peyton (1)   10:15:40
27. Bill Simms (1)   10:46:45
28. Jim Hunter (1)   10:46:45
29. Cathy Henn (2)   12:09:57
30. Jim Dill (4)   12:13:56
31. Leonard Martin (2)   12:34:08
32. Lidia Chalaya (1)   12:35:23
37 Starters

Below is a picture of Gary Cantrell (left) and Animal Herr, taken just after Animal won the 1991 Barkley Marathons in a new course-record time. This picture was sent to me recently by Bill Losey after Quatro Hubbard scanned it and put it on a website. Animal Herr provided the photo to Quatro.

Ten finishers was the largest such number in the Barkley's six-year history. I believe that the race's growing international reputation and the resulting world-class starting field this year were factors in this relative success. The female runners and male egos played a role, too. But the 10 finishers of 37 starters is only a 27% finishing rate, still in a class by itself compared to other ultramarathons.

In a post-race conversation with Gary, one of the Soviet runners made a profound observation that captures much of the essence of the Barkley. He was quoted by Gary as having said, as he gestured toward the mountains: "It isn't man against man out there, it is men against *that!*"

This running of the Barkley occurred on March 23, 1991, only a few months before the break-up of the Soviet Union in December 1991. Just as the Soviets realized that they could not surpass the American system of democracy and capitalism, they also saw that their best runners could not beat the American runners. Only two of their elite male runners finished the Barkley, and even those two were beaten by a pair of American women. Could this defeat of the Soviets at the Barkley have been a contributing factor in the collapse of the Soviet Union later that year? We can only wonder.

For me personally, this was again one of my best ultrarunning performances, bettering my 1988 Barkley finish by over an hour and a half, despite the inclusion of the Rat Jaw and the tougher weather conditions. I was pleased to finish so well among a world-class field. I rank this run with two other specific race performances as the best of my life. The other two were my September 1988 run of 118.8 miles in the 24-Hour National Championship in Atlanta, and my 1990 finish of the Wasatch 100-mile in 29:09:11. I completed both of these latter races without sleep, whereas both of my Barkley 55-mile finishes had included a period of sleep during the race. Thus I felt that I could do even better at Barkley, by not stopping to sleep. I was determined to try again.

And what of the purported 100-mile Barkley race? As usual, none of the three-loop finishers had any inkling of going on for more loops. Also as usual, Gary taunted the runners of the world by stating in his *UltraRunning* article that, next year, "once again, no one will finish 100 miles!"

++++++++++

Below is a copy of the essay I wrote that was required for entry into the 1991 Barkley Marathons.

Why I Should Be Allowed To Run The Barkley Marathons (Again)
An Allegory (1991)

Once upon a time there was a sadistic, cold-hearted Taskmaster in charge of the prison. And it wasn't just any old prison, either. This Taskmaster lorded over the world's most fearsome prison, one which was surrounded by an utterly impassable wilderness which held such terrors as to make men's hearts and bowels quiver. No prisoners dared to attempt escape, for the legends said that some who once had tried to escape had been devoured in the wilderness.

One day, while in a particularly foul mood, the cruel Taskmaster caught some prisoners acting rather cocky and boastful. So the Taskmaster decided to have some fun. He told the prisoners that they would be set loose into the wilderness, and if anyone could make it out to freedom on the other side of the wilderness, they would be free from the prison forever! However, the cruel Taskmaster also warned that any survivors who could crawl back to the prison must promise to be quiet and humble and lick his boots forever. The prisoners were then herded with prods out into the wilderness. Of course, none came even close to finding a way out of the desolation, but most managed to come crawling back to the prison where they had to lick the boots of the Taskmaster. The Taskmaster grinned evilly.

From then on, the Taskmaster had an annual event in which he required the toughest and meanest prisoners to try to escape through the wilderness. Finally, after several years of only unsuccessful attempts, one prisoner did succeed in finding a way out of the wilderness to freedom! This only spurred on the other prisoners, but, alas, on the following year, again no one succeeded in escaping. This made the one ex-prisoner who had successfully escaped start to feel cocky and boastful. So on the next year, he decided to go back and join the other prisoners in the annual attempt to find a way to freedom. The Taskmaster grinned evilly. Of course the ex-prisoner failed to find freedom on this second attempt, although a few of the other prisoners did succeed. The unsuccessful ex-prisoner was sentenced to remain in prison until he could again escape to freedom through the wilderness. The Taskmaster grinned evilly and prepared for yet another freedom run-attempt for the prisoners.

Now the time is approaching for the next attempted escape to freedom from the prison. Can anyone succeed? Only time will tell, as the Taskmaster grins evilly.

The above story is an allegory for The Barkley Marathons. The prisoners represent the runners who are driven by an incomprehensible but irresistible need to try to overcome all obstacles to find freedom (i.e., their limits, bragging rights, fame, ego, etc.). Any resemblances between the evil Taskmaster and race director Gary Cantrell are strictly coincidental. Will any of us runners succeed and find freedom? The race director grins knowingly. He knows that the re-humbled ex-escapee, among others, must not only be allowed to try again to gain their freedom; they are condemned to try again!

Chapter 11
1992: Needless Suffering

For the 1992 Barkley, things returned to more of a norm. Apparently the rest of the world was mostly scared away by the relative thrashing that the Barkley had delivered to our foreign runners in the past couple of years, as there was only one international entrant in 1992, named Bodo Rasberg of West Germany. However, the now-usual contingent of repeat runners was there again for another round of punishment. Returning runners included myself, David Horton, Animal Herr, John DeWalt, Dick West, Jim Dill, Steve Bozeman, Lou Peyton, Nick Williams, and Leonard Martin. One other runner, a Barkley neophyte, who was there this year was Dave Cawein from Arkansas. He was a friend of Lou Peyton and Nick Williams.

Several months prior to the 1992 Barkley, I was contacted by Wendell Robison of Wyoming. Wendell was a good ultrarunner whom I had met at the Wasatch 100. He was interested in running the Barkley, and Gary had suggested that Wendell contact me for some information. I was happy to share my knowledge of the Barkley with him, and I mailed him some information, probably a map of Frozen Head and a course description.

In my required essay, I wrote that I thought that I could finish the Barkley again, and that I should be punished for my arrogance by being allowed to run the Barkley again. I also stated my intention "to not wimp out and sleep due to fear of being 'out there' in the dark, as usual."

Gary's course description this year, subtitled "A Complete Guide for the Entrant," noted that the race would start "by 8:00 AM," with attention drawn to "by" rather than "at 8 AM." Gary was starting to employ another tactic to mess with runners' heads by not stating a definite starting time, thus putting pressure on runners to camp out at the park rather than staying in a motel. As best I can reconstruct the time, the 1992 race did start at about 8 AM. I was glad that Gary was moving away from the 5 or 6 AM starting times of previous Barkley races. I have always found the very early morning starting times, especially those before daylight, that many ultramarathons have, to be one of the least enjoyable aspects of running ultras.

On race day, March 28, 1992, twenty starters began the trek around Frozen Head. Five of these starters failed to finish the first loop, largely due to straying off the course. This unfortunate group included Bodo, the German runner. Interestingly, Wendell Robison led after the first loop, in a time of 6:38:30. He led the current Barkley record holder, Animal Herr, and the previous course record co-holder, David Horton, by just over three minutes. I finished the first loop in fourth place, well over an hour behind the three front runners, at 7:54:50. I was holding back my pace somewhat, after injudiciously going too fast on the first loop in some of my previous Barkley races. I was trying to save myself so that I would not need sleep between the second and third loops.

Gary notes that while I was in camp between loops one and two, I "threatened an anti-Barkley letter-writing campaign proclaiming the race to be 'Needless Suffering Without a Point!'" I remember this episode quite well. It was not the race per se that I was commenting on, it was Gary's in-

sistence in the course directions that runners stay within the clearing beneath
the powerline on the Rat Jaw. I had found that because of the thick brier
growth in the clearing, it was more difficult and torturous to stay in the clearing. The briers weren't so bad off to the side in the trees. But Gary's rules
required us to stay in the clearing. This is what I was protesting and declaring to be "needless suffering." An adaptation of this statement would, in a
later year, become the saying on the Barkley t-shirt. It is also worth noting
here that Gary's use of rules requiring runners to stay on a route through briers, even when there was a nearby parallel route that was not so brier-
infested, would lead to a major controversy in the 2001 Barkley race.

In his Barkley article in *UltraRunning* that year, Gary gave many of the
runners nicknames. I was Frozen, Wendell Robison was Wyoming, David
Horton was Gumby, and Dennis Herr was Oogie. Gary noted that Gumby
"bagged it at 19 miles," saying: "I sure hope I never come back here again."
Oogie is quoted as saying: "But you know you will." Later chapters will reveal that both Gumby and Oogie returned in later years. But this year, they
called it quits after completing only one loop.

Twelve runners started loop two, but only six finished that loop. First in
was Wendell, in 16:47, at about 1 AM Sunday. In his *UltraRunning* article,
Gary goes into great detail about Wendell's arrival in camp after his second
loop. In his characteristically colorful writing style, Gary wrote: "When the
leader finally dragged in, he was pale and staggering. He collapsed into a
chair beside the fire and sat weeping softly, his face in his hands. At last he
looked up and spoke. He told us that it had been a death march since 'Hell.'
That he could scarcely move, that he was sick and hurt. And that at least one
runner must be worse off than he was. 'I saw his light at the bottom of Hell
when I got to the top. I've been waiting on him to catch me ever since. I
don't see how anyone could not catch me the way I've been moving! He
must really be hurting.' Then our once proud leader slumped to the ground,
face down beside the fire and began weeping in earnest. Other than check
that his jacket wouldn't melt from the heat, we left him alone. After a half
hour, he finally clambered to his feet, staggered out to the road, and began to
vomit violently." Wendell then went to get some sleep to try to recover
enough to continue.

I guess I was that other runner that Wendell referred to as possibly worse
off than he, because I was the second runner to complete two loops, about an
hour and 13 minutes behind Wendell. However, I was not nearly as bad off
as Wendell. Gary wrote that I arrived after loop two "absolutely ecstatic. He
felt great coming in, and finding out that he would be the first out on loop
three brightened his spirits even more. Frozen charged into the darkness at
18:03:09." At this point it appeared that I was successfully controlling my
pace to be able to complete three loops without stopping to sleep. As Gary
noted, I was feeling good, and elated to be back in the lead. This marked the
third race of my four to date at the Barkley when I had led the race. However, this is not the end of this year's story.

In the first paragraph of Chapter 1, I started the story of what happened
next. When I got to Phillips Creek, just two "Barkley miles" into the third
loop, it was about 3 AM. I had never been on this part of the course in the

dark before. Furthermore, I don't think I realized yet just how exhausted I was. I was about to provide an example of one of the lessons that I have painfully learned at the Barkley over the years: fatigue makes me stupid. My mind and coordination become much less effective. As I was crossing the creek on the rocks that I could normally hop across without getting my feet wet, I lost my balance and fell into the creek. This caused me to become very cold. I then tried to follow the North Boundary Trail up from Phillips Creek toward Jury Ridge. This part of the trail was very faint, and I could not stay on it in the dark. I lost the trail, and went back down to the creek to try again to find my way up the trail. Again I got off the trail and wandered around some more. I remember that I wandered around in that area for nearly two hours, never able to find the trail out of there. I was afraid to try to go onward off-trail. The dark woods were too forbidding to try to advance without knowing where the trail was. I finally decided to wait there until daylight when I hoped to be able to find the trail. It was about 5 AM by then, and I estimated that I would have to wait about an hour for daylight.

I sat on a log near the point where the trail seemed to disappear, but it was too cold to sleep. After I had been sitting on the log for a few minutes, I saw a flashlight in the distance approaching the area where I was. I think I was somewhat surprised to realize that another runner was approaching. In a few minutes, the runner got to the log where I was sitting. It was Wendell. He had made a miraculous recovery after getting some sleep, and was now hiking strongly up from Phillips Creek. As he approached I greeted him and told him I had fallen into the creek, and then been unable to find the trail. I asked him if he would mind if I followed him for a while. He didn't mind, and continued hiking up the hill. As he crossed the log on which I had been sitting, he started counting steps. He went several steps and then announced: "turn left." Sure enough, the faint pathway was there, just where he had paced off. I was amazed that, even though this was his first time at the Barkley, he knew the course so well. He had literally memorized the number of steps from that log to the obscure turn in the trail!

I followed Wendell up Jury Ridge as daylight gradually dawned. However, I was so weak and fatigued that I had difficulty keeping up with Wendell's hiking pace. On one occasion, I fell and slid a little ways down the steep slope off to the side of the trail. I then realized that I did not have enough strength to safely continue to the finish of the third loop. I had reached my limit of endurance. So when I got to Bald Knob, I bushwhacked over the ridge to Quitter's Road, and sadly walked back down to camp. I had lost my gamble that I could do three loops without sleep.

I did not realize it at the time, but this was to be a turning point in my races at the Barkley. Thus far, in four races at the Barkley, I had finished or led the race at some point in each of them. I would continue to attempt the Barkley many more times in future years. However, as the reader will see in later chapters, my rapid demise in 1992, from leading the race at the beginning of the third loop, to DNFing before the second book on that loop, would mark the turning point when I would no longer be able to contend with the top Barkley runners.

Meanwhile, another runner, Nick Williams, whom Gary had nicknamed "Mid-Terminator," was not finished with his run at Barkley either. Nick was an Assistant Principal at a High School in Little Rock, Arkansas. I think he had mentioned needing to get back to Little Rock on Monday to administer mid-term exams. Gary had used that phrase to coin the nickname for Nick. Nick was there with his friend from Little Rock, Lou Peyton. Lou "Old Gristle" Peyton and Leonard "Butt" Martin finished loop two shortly before the time limit to start a third loop. They then decided to head out on their third loop. Seeing this, Mid-Terminator couldn't let his friend Old Gristle show him up. So after several hours of rest between loops two and three, and with just a minute to spare before the cut-off time to begin loop three, Mid-Terminator took off after Old Gristle and Butt. There was that male ego again! This appears to be another example, as had happened the previous year, when a male contestant, seeing a woman start a third loop, mustered the strength to go on, when he otherwise would not have. Old Gristle and Butt both soon quit and returned to camp, but Mid-Terminator belied his nickname and refused to terminate in the middle of his third loop.

I do not know how Gary came up with "Old Gristle" as a nickname for Lou, but it was probably a tribute to her toughness as an ultrarunner. At that time, she was one of the few women ultrarunners to have finished the Grand Slam of four 100-mile trail races in one year. Leonard Martin's nickname of "Butt" was apparently earned when Leonard had been with Gary earlier in the year as Leonard slid on his butt down the extremely steep hillside from the coal road toward the New River. Henceforth, that part of the course became known as "Leonard's Buttslide," and Leonard's nickname morphed to "Buttslide" among many of the Barkley regulars. Leonard is a dentist who lives in Oak Ridge, Tennessee, just a few miles from Frozen Head State Park. He had trained regularly on the course, and had helped Gary and Karl set out the books prior to this year's race.

Wendell went on to win the three-loop race, finishing in 28:01:36. Nick Williams finished second in 34:44:31. No one else finished three loops. No one started a fourth loop. Gary delivered his annual taunting in his *UltraRunning* article about no one being able to run his mythical 100-miler: "What is wrong with you people? Isn't there even one *real* man out there?"

Below are the known starters, their numbers of Barkley starts, and their loop-finishing times for 1992.

1. Wendell Robison (1)	6:38:30	16:47:15	28:01:36
2. Nick Williams (2)	8:43:53	20:58:00	34:44:31
3. Frozen Ed Furtaw (4)	7:54:50	18:00:22	
4. Dave Cawein (1)	8:44:07	20:58:00	
5. Lou Old Gristle Peyton (2)	10:30:30	25:15:25	
6. Leonard Buttslide Martin (3)	10:55:42	25:17:25	
7. David Horton (3)	6:41:40		
8. Dennis the Animal Herr (3)	6:41:40		
9. Joe Riddle (1)	8:22:36		
10. John DeWalt (5)	8:37:47		
11. Dick West (4)	8:44:18		
12. Jerry Dunn (1)	9:40:27		

13. Jim Dill (5)   9:40:41
14. Steve Bozeman (4)   9:40:43
15. David Phillips (1)   10:13:49
16. Bodo Rasberg (1)   Lost on loop one.
20 Starters

++++++++++

Below is a copy of my essay that was required for entry into the 1992 Barkley Marathons.

Why I should Again Be Allowed To Run The Barkley Marathons
(March 7, 1992)

I am again sentenced to attempt The Barkley Marathons in 1992. This penance is being inflicted because, having finished it in 1988 and 1991, I actually think I'm tough and wily enough to complete it again. Desiring this claim to fame and ego-gratification, I am being punished for my arrogance.

I have a chance to become the first (and perhaps only) three-time finisher in the history of the event! I have a strong chance to run a personal-best time and to finish under 28 hours, a time that less than a handful of elite, national-class trail runners has bettered. Therefore, I predict that it will take an elite runner to beat me this year. I have a chance to extend my ultramarathon winning streak to two, as I actually won my last ultra, the 1992 Four Peaks 50-mile in Arizona last weekend. I intend to brave whatever conditions nature and the race director condemn me to, and I plan to not wimp out and sleep due to fear of being "out there" in the dark, as usual. I plan to put on a performance that will further enhance my reputation as an ultrarunner. Obviously, by now, my boastful arrogance is plain for all to see. I need humbling. Bring on The Barkley!

As the annual running of The Barkley Marathons again approaches, I must prepare for one of the toughest challenges I will face this year: writing another damned essay on why I should be allowed to run The Barkley Marathons. As if the run weren't humbling enough, the sadistic race director requires us would-be sufferers to try to explain why we do this outrageous event. But there may be something important philosophically here. Indeed, the B.M. has in recent years attracted runners from literally around the world. Why do we do it? What is this overpowering, global-scale lure that the event has for us?

I think the basic answer to why runners attempt Barkley is to test themselves against some hypothetical "limit." As the sadistic race director has put it: "So what the hell is The Barkley for? For all you hardasses who just gotta know how much you can take. It is here." Since I am one of the few who has passed The Barkley test, I can say there is a great amount of satisfaction from having accomplished something which has proven so difficult to so many top-notch athletes.

The satisfaction seems to be proportional to the extremity of the "limit" against which we test ourselves. In addition to the self-satisfaction, is the adulation I receive, and the reputation I seem to have acquired among the small number (about three or four) of people I know who are aware of my Barkley accomplishments.

Thus, we run Barkley to plump our egos, but only at the equivalent risk of getting them deflated.   The Barkley has also left many whimpering, crushed egos in its wake.

So please, Mr. Race Director, let me in again!   I need to get my ego plumped and/or crushed!

Great essay, huh?

Chapter 12
1993: Another Mass Finish; The Purloined Cup

This was a year in which I did not run Barkley. Hence, I have little information about this year's event, other than the *UltraRunning* articles that appeared in the June 1993 issue, and a newsletter issued by Suzi Thibeault in June 1993 that had some articles about the Barkley. There were two articles about Barkley in the *UltraRunning* issue: the usual descriptive article written by Gary, and a supplementary article written by Fred Pilon, who was still a co-editor of *UltraRunning* at that time. Fred's article was titled: "Surviving the Barkley: Some Advice from a Veteran." Since Fred had been to most of the previous Barkley races, and he had finished in 1990 and 1991, he was in a good position to write such an article. As the reader will soon find out, he was about to get even more experience at Barkley this year.

The Barkley had 32 starters this year, in what Gary described as "another overflow field of runners wanting to see how they stacked up against the hardest race available." The start was at 9 AM on April 3, 1993. Gary's trend of moving the start time to later and later in the morning, as the years progressed, was becoming evident.

As was becoming the norm for the Barkley, the starting field included several top runners. Notably, Animal Herr, a former Barkley course record holder, was there. Throughout his *UltraRunning* article, Gary referred to him as "Animal Hair." Last year's winner, Wendell Robison, was also there again. Another top nationally reputed ultrarunner, but who was at Barkley for his first time this year, was Dana "Mud'N'Guts" Miller, the multiple-year winner of the Wasatch 100-mile race in Utah. The numerous Barkley returnees included previous three-loop finishers Fred Pilon, Suzi Thibeault, Nancy Hamilton, Nick Williams, and Dick West. Suzi and Nancy were there with their husbands, Gene and Rick, respectively, both of whom were well-established ultrarunners. Also starting this year were were several multi-DNF runners from previous years, including Steve Bozeman, John DeWalt, Al Montgomery, Jim Dill, Bill Seiler, and Buttslide Martin. There was also a relatively large contingent of ultrarunners from the Hawaiian Ultra Running Team (HURT), to whom Suzi T had provided encouragement and copies of the Barkley entry form. HURT runners at the Barkley were Kawika Spalding, Jim Budde, the husband-and-wife team of John and P.J. Salmonson, Randy Havre, and Vernon Char. A pair of good ultrarunners who had come as a team were Ike Hessler and Gene "Fatboy" Trahern, from the Seattle, Washington, area. Another pair of compatriots were Evan James and Ron Hart from Ohio. Yet another pair of friends, Titian "Teeter" Benedetti and Cliff Hoy, was here from New Jersey. Dale Sutton, an accomplished Californian ultrarunner, was also here, as were Tim Oates from Indiana and Gerry Agin from Pennsylvania. Thus this year's field was well-populated with noteworthy runners from across the United States. However, there were no runners from other countries this year, unless you count Jurgen Ankenbrand, who was born in Germany but was then living in California.

Gary reported that it snowed on the upper mountains of Frozen Head the day before the race began. However, it appears that the weather was good during the race, including a reportedly beautiful full moon. This good fortune for the runners undoubtedly contributed to their relative success that was about to occur.

Animal Herr and Mud'N'Guts Miller took a short lead at the start, but promptly missed a turn and were suddenly doing extra distance off-course. This resulted in Wendell Robison and Fred Pilon moving into the lead, which they retained through the end of the loop, finishing within a couple minutes of each other, in very close to 7 hours. Gary reports that Wendell "spoke boldly of 100 miles (six loops)." The last runner about whom Gary reported hopes of the 100-miler was Eric Clifton, two years ago. But recall that Clifton finished only two loops that year.

Mud'N'Guts Miller and Animal Herr were next, about 25 minutes behind the leaders, with the team of Ike Hessler and Fatboy Trahern just about a minute behind them. It is interesting to see the first-loop finishing times listed in Gary's *UltraRunning* article. Most runners were in obvious groups, reflecting the strong trend for Barkley runners to run in small teams. This tactic allows runners to pool their collective knowledge of the course and route-finding abilities, as well as providing comfort in the face of the potential fear of being *out there* in rugged, unmarked, mountain terrain in deep woods.

Not everyone had such good results on the first loop. Vernon Char got turned around, ended up going in the wrong direction on the right trail, and ended up back at camp after only a couple of hours. Jurgen Ankenbrand got off-course in the New River section, and ended up on a highway from which he hitchhiked and walked back to the Frozen Head State Park campground. As Jurgen himself wrote in an addendum to Gary's *UltraRunning* article: "Stay home unless you are prepared to get lost in the Tennessee mountains and have your ass kicked, or wind up in the next county like I did." This was one of several times that a Barkley runner had gotten so lost that he took roads back to camp, frequently with a ride from some locals who, I am sure, were highly amused by the stories of the stray runners.

Pilon and Robison remained together after two loops, in 17:05, with Miller and Herr also still together, almost exactly one hour behind the lead team. Incredibly, another eleven runners completed two loops, all within two hours and four minutes of each other, but all more than five hours behind the front four.

Of the top four runners after two loops, only Mud'N'Guts Miller retired. He noted that it was his wife's birthday, so he had to go entertain her. The other three ran the third loop, as did eight others. Pilon was the first to finish, in 26:55:26. He became the first three-time finisher of the Barkley. Robison was second, Herr third, Williams fourth, Nancy Hamilton seventh, and Dick West eighth; these five runners thereby joined the ranks of the two-time finishers. Barkley multi-time attempters who finally succeeded this year in finishing the three-loop race for the first time were Steve Bozeman and John DeWalt. Also finishing were newcomers Kawika Spalding, Rick Hamilton, and, Gerry Agin.

The known starters, their numbers of Barkley starts, and their loop-finishing times for 1993 are listed below.

1. Fred Pilon (7)	7:00:40	17:05:00	26:55:26
2. Wendell Robison (2)	6:58:20	17:05:00	27:17:50
3. Dennis the Animal Herr (4)	7:25:04	18:05:35	30:34:11
4. Nick Williams (3)	9:32:42	23:30:49	34:59:01
5. Kawika Spalding (1)	11:29:32	24:27:27	35:17:06
6. Rick Hamilton (1)	9:32:42	23:32:45	35:18:24
7. Nancy Hamilton (2)	9:32:42	23:32:56	35:18:24
8. Dick West (5)	9:37:30	24:36:34	35:21:28
9. Steve Bozeman (5)	10:02:08	23:5425	35:21:47
10. Gerry Agin (1)	11:29:32	24:47:43	35:30:40
11. John DeWalt (6)	8:39:55	23:16:17	35:30:53
12. Dana Mud'N'Guts Miller (1)	7:25:04	18:05:35	
13. Evan James (1)	9:57:20	23:46:21	
14. Ron Hart (1)	9:57:20	23:46:21	
15. Buttslide Martin (4)	11:34:31	25:19:30	
16. Ike Hessler (1)	7:26:01		
17. Gene Fatboy Trahern (1)	7:26:01		
18. Dale Sutton (1)	8:39:55		
19. Gene Thibeault (1)	8:57:55		
20. Al Montgomery (4)	10:02:08		
21. Tim Oates (1)	10:02:08		
22. Jim Dill (6)	10:33:40		
23. Teeter Benedetti (1)	11:48:55		
24. Bill Seiler (2)	11:53:02		
25. Cliff Hoy (1)	11:53:02		
26. Jim Budde (1)	11:59:16		
27. P.J. Salmonson (1)	11:59:16		
28. John Salmonson (1)	11:59:16		
29. Randy Havre (1)	11:59:16		
30. Suzi Thibeault (2)	11:59:16		
31. Jurgen Ankenbrand (1)	Lost on loop one; hitchhiked back to park.		
32. Vernon Char (1)	Lost on loop one; returned after two hours.		
32 Starters			

Fred's victory was a tribute to his persistence and determination. He had been to seven of the eight Barkley races held so far. His first finish was in his fifth attempt in 1990. Then he finished again the following year, and now he had won the race outright, and become the first three-time finisher in the history of the event. In Gary's *UltraRunning* article, he described Fred Pilon's strengths that made him a good candidate for success at the Barkley: "Fred is the prototype for the Barkley. He walks like a demon, always knows where he is (at least in the woods), has an uncanny knack for picking a clear track through bad places, and climbs hills like a billygoat." In the article that Fred wrote in *UltraRunning*, he listed the attributes that he used to succeed at the Barkley: slow pace and steady effort; eating early and drinking plenty in the race; running with someone else, especially someone who knows the course; having a good lighting system; being prepared for varying weather conditions; and using a comfortable pack.

For his hard-earned victory, Fred was awarded the Barkley Cup, ostensibly for him to keep for one year, and then return it for the next winner, as the previous winners had done. However, when his year was up, Fred refused to surrender the Cup. He later told me that he was using the Cup as a pencil holder on his desk. Despite Fred's great achievements as a Barkley runner and co-editor of *UltraRunning*, I think his purloining of the Barkley Cup, and his refusal to allow it to continue to be awarded to each year's winner, is rude and unsportsmanlike. It diminishes my respect for Fred. Because of this transgression, throughout the remainder of this book I will refer to him as Fred Purloin.

Sometimes I fantasize about a caper to retrieve the Cup. I also like to visualize what the Barkley Cup could look like today and in the future, if all the winners' names were listed. There are now so many names that there is not room for all to be inscribed on the Cup itself. Therefore, the Barkley Cup would have to be adapted, as professional hockey's renowned Stanley Cup is, by mounting the original Cup on a pedestal that holds the winners' names on engraved plaques that are added each year.

Chapter 13
1994: A New Course Record; End of an Era

1994 was another year that I did not enter the Barkley. The only information I have on the proceedings at this year's Barkley is the article that Gary wrote about it in the June 1994 issue of *UltraRunning*.

Several past Barkley winners and finishers were back again in 1994. In his post-race *UltraRunning* article, Gary again used nicknames for several of the runners. The starting field included then-current course-record holder Animal Herr, former course-record holder and two-time finisher Gumby Horton, and the reigning champion from last year, three-time finisher Fred Purloin. Other past Barkley finishers running in 1994 were two-time finishers Nancy Hamilton and Nick Williams, and one-time finishers Milan Milanovich, Rick Hamilton, Suzi Thibeault, and John DeWalt. Prior DNFers back for another chance at redemption included Eraserback Dave Cawein, Trail Dale Sutton, Lou Old Gristle Peyton, Cliff Hoy, Teeter Benedetti, Jim Budde, and P.J. and John Salmonson. So, as usual by now, there was plenty of Barkley experience in this year's field.

Gary stated that there were 34 starters, of whom 16 were Barkley first-timers. He named only 26 of the runners in the list of one-loop finishers. Based on this list, the newcomers included Mike Devlin, Wayne Stiles, brothers Wilson and Wayne Brasington, Harry Smith, Roger Allison, Sarah Lowell, Mike Wood, and Steve Frankum. Only nine of the 16 reported first-timers are given credit for finishing loop one. From the numbers and names given, we can surmise that seven of the neophytes and one returning runner didn't complete the first loop, at least not within the time limit.

The leader after one loop, not unexpectedly, was David Horton, in 6:53:55. Animal Herr was second, over half an hour behind. The biggest surprise among the leaders was that Dave Cawein was only three minutes behind the Animal. Purloin was fourth, another seven minutes behind Cawein. Mike Devlin, from California, and Milan Milanovich, the Swiss runner who had finished the Barkley three-loop in 1990, were next, in 8:44:52. Gary remarked in *UltraRunning* that when Horton finished the first loop, it was the first time in any Barkley race that the first-loop leader arrived back at camp before the first returning DNFer. It looked like the crowd of runners was becoming collectively better over the years at navigating the course and persisting for at least one loop.

Several past finishers, including Herr, Purloin, and Milanovich, capitulated before completing the second loop. There is no further mention of any of these three after their finishing of loop one. However, loop two was relatively successful for many runners. Horton again led, in a two-loop record time of 15:40:46, and rapidly headed out on his third loop. He was more than two hours ahead of Dave Cawein in second place. Cawein then "just flat out refused" to continue. Dale Sutton had moved into third in 21:28:40 after two loops. He was among the few who then started a third loop. Ten other runners finished the second loop between 23:01 and 26:16.

The two-loop finishers included four women: Nancy, Lou, Suzi, and P.J. The first two then retired, but Suzi and P.J. headed out on their third loop with seconds to spare before the cut-off time.   Besides Horton and Sutton, they were the only other runners to start a third loop.

Gary reported that the weather was nice on the first day and night of the race.   However, by early Sunday afternoon, soon after the pair of women had begun their third loop, it got colder and began to rain.   After another hour, Dale returned.   He had decided that he had had enough sometime during his third loop, and returned to camp without completing the third loop.   He reported high wind, hail, and freezing cold up in the mountains.   The bad, but typical for Barkley, weather continued throughout Sunday afternoon and into the night.   The 36-hour time limit came and went at about 10 PM, but Suzi and P.J. were not to be seen.   Concern for the pair grew in camp among the remaining race officials and family members.   However, just before Gary and John Salmonson began to initiate a search party, Suzi and P.J. returned.   They had lost time on loop three near the Garden Spot, and finished the loop about 30 minutes over the time limit.   Gary did not consider this finish official. However, they became the first reported runners to finish three loops *over* the time limit.   To me, that is a notable accomplishment.   Most of us quit before we finish three loops, frequently using the approaching time limit as a justification for premature withdrawal.   So I was impressed to learn that Suzi and P.J. were tough enough to finish the third loop, even though they were over the time limit.

This left David Horton as the only official finisher this year.   He finished his third loop in a stunning new course record time of 23:49:40.   Gary's statement, made way back after the first Barkley in 1986, that "it is still impossible to run 50 miles on that trail in a day," had finally been proven wrong.   But it took a world-class ultrarunner in his fourth attempt to accomplish that feat.   The inevitable result was that Gary would again make the course more difficult.

Here is the list of the known starters, their numbers of Barkley starts, and their loop-finishing times for 1994.

1. David Horton (4)   6:53:55   15:40:46   23:49:40
2. <u>Suzi Thibeault</u> (3)   10:38:35   26:15:36   ~36:30* Finished loop three
                           over the time limit.
3. <u>P.J. Salmonson</u> (2)   10:35:30   26:15:37   ~36:30* Finished loop three
                           over the time limit.
4. Dave Cawein (2)   7:32:31   17:50:35
5. Trail Dale Sutton (2)   9:11:14   21:28:40
6. Wayne Stiles (1)   9:10:34   23:01:09
7. Rick Hamilton (2)   9:43:28   23:10:00
8. Nick Williams (4)   9:43:02   23:31:36
9. <u>Nancy Hamilton</u> (3)   9:43:42   24:02:34
10. Roger Allison (1)   9:43:48   24:02:36
11. Harry Smith (1)   9:41:56   24:02:38
12. <u>Lou Peyton</u> (3)   9:42:29   24:07:56
13. Wilson Brasington (1)9:23:46   26:15:48
14. Animal Herr (5)   7:29:08
15. Fred Purloin (8)   7:39:19
16. Mike Devlin (1)   8:44:52

17. Milan Milanovich (2)   8:44:52
18. Wayne Brasington (1)   9:25:03
19. Sarah Lowell (1)   9:45:12
20. John DeWalt (7)   9:45:25
21. Cliff Hoy (2)   9:47:12
22. Teeter Benedetti (2)   9:47:14
23. Mike Wood (1)   9:48:16
24. Jim Budde (2)   10:34:24
25. John Salmonson (2)   10:34:24
26. Steve Frankum (1)   11:20:52
34 Starters

In his 1994 *UltraRunning* article, Gary wrote that the Frozen Head State Park had been surveyed in the past year, that many sections of the course had been accurately measured, and a new map produced. He stated that the recent measurements had revealed the surprising fact that the Barkley was actually *less* than 55 miles. Comparing information on the old park map (undated, but from pre-1988) and the newer one (dated April, 1993), I see that a few of the listed trail lengths changed slightly, but not all became shorter. For example, the South Old Mac Trail length decreased from 2.8 miles to 2.4; the Panther Branch Trail increased from 2.0 to 2.1, and the Spicewood Trail stayed the same at 2.5 miles. The trail lengths given are not typically for the same route as the Barkley, so in any case it is not possible to determine the Barkley course length from the park listings of trail lengths. I have written more extensively in Chapters 2 and 27 about the controversial issue of the true length of the Barkley course. I continue to believe that it is and always has been longer than Gary says, by several miles per loop.

As usual, this year no one had an interest in attempting Gary's mythical 100-mile. At the end of his *UltraRunning* article, Gary quotes Lou Peyton as saying, as she quit after two loops: "It's too much. It's too much. You have to understand, it's just too much." I think that is a good summary of the Barkley experience for most runners.

+++++++++++

This year marked the end of what I call the Early Years of the Barkley Marathons courses. In the following year, the course would be changed so significantly that comparisons of results from 1994 and earlier to those of 1995 and later would be difficult.

Chapter 14
1995: Gone Too Far This Time; Doing the Impossible

The reader may recall that the Rat Jaw was added to the course in 1989. At the same time, Gary made the third loop shorter than the first two loops, in order to keep the three-loop race distance at a nominal 55 miles. The hypothetical 100-mile race consisted, on paper at least, of six loops, but that was a moot point because no one had ever attempted to finish more than three loops. This course configuration remained the same from 1989 through 1994.

At some point in those years, I told Gary that I thought having the later loops shortened, compared to the first two loops, was awkward. I suggested that he could add just a little distance to the loop, and call it 20 miles rather than the 19.13 that he called it in his course-description spreadsheet. I remember saying that he could just have the runners run around the "jug handle" road through the campground, and that would probably be enough additional distance to make the loop 20 miles. Then he could call the three-loop race 60 miles, and the 100-mile race would be five identical loops rather than six loops of two different lengths. From what he did in 1995, it appears that Gary found something he liked in my suggestion.

My running log book shows that I received a phone call from Gary Cantrell on January 12, 1995. He excitedly informed me that he was making a change to the Barkley course that I would like. He was adding what he called the "Nun-da-ut-sun'y" trail. He said that was the Native American name for "the trail where they cried," or "the trail of tears." Clearly he was trying to entice me back to the Barkley after my two-year hiatus. I told him I was interested, and started working on another essay on Why I Should Be Allowed To Run The Barkley. Gary mailed me a fragment of the Frozen Head map with the new course change highlighted.

The course change was a partial re-route of the South Section of the course. Instead of following the Chimney Top Trail (CTT) from Frozen Head Mountain through Mart Fields to Chimney Top, the new Barkley route would go roughly parallel to and south of the CTT. It would first go on an old overgrown trail to Indian Knob, and then cross-country southwesterly down the mountainside to the confluence of two streams—Beech Fork and Lowgap Hollow. On his course description, Gary called this steep, downhill, non-trail section the "Zip Line Trail." I think the name referred to the fact that the heavy growth of briers on that stretch would tear the runners legs so badly that they looked like they had zippers on them. From the stream confluence at the bottom of the Zip Line, the course went northwesterly straight up the southeast face of Chimney Top Mountain, a climb of 1,600 feet in a little less than a mile. This climb would eventually come to be called Big Hell. Near the capstones at the top of Chimney Top, the route rejoined the CTT and continued as before down to the park and the campground. This new route replaced a portion of the CTT, what Gary calls "candy ass trail," (i.e., good, maintained trail), with a very rugged cross-country, off-trail traverse with a significant descent and climb.

On the form that he sent to those of us selected for entry, Gary stated that this was "the easiest, and shortest Barkley Marathons in history. We have extended the course slightly, to make the big loop 20 miles. This way, it will only require 5 loops to make an even 100!!!" On this information sheet, he used the term "fun run" to refer to the three-loop, 60-mile race. As far as I can tell, this was the first year that he used that specific phrase to refer to the three-loop race. The name *Fun Run* subsequently has become commonplace for the three-loop race, and it will be used as such throughout the remainder of this book. Gary established a time limit of 40 hours for the 60-mile, and 60 hours for the 100-mile. However, a 36-hour time limit (12 hours per loop) was imposed on the three-loop Fun Run to "entitle" the runner to continue on subsequent loops.

On the Schematic Map on page 8, the new course sequence was 1, 2, 19, 20, 21, 22, 23, 24, 16, 17, 25, 26, 27, 8, 9, 10, 29, 30, 31, 12, 13. Using distance and elevation-change data from the Table on page 9, this new route has an estimated loop distance of 26.0 miles. At least Gary he was being consistent about systematically understating the course length. The new set of hills that comprise the Trail of Tears also added approximately 1,100 feet each of climb and descent per loop. Again using data from the Table on page 9, the elevation gain and drop per loop are each about 9,800 feet. Based on my estimates, the Fun Run was now about 78.0 miles with 29,400 feet of climb, and the 100-mile was actually about 130 miles with 49,000 feet of climb. This course configuration, with minor variations to be described in their respective years, was to be used for 1995 and several subsequent years. I will refer to these hereafter as the Two Hells courses, because in addition to the old Hell, they now also had an even bigger climb known as Big Hell.

Gary created an elevation profile graph of the new 20-mile loop. A copy of it is shown on the next page. This graph includes the interesting names of many of the landmark locations along the course.

The essay I wrote for this year's Barkley was perhaps one of the most interesting of my numerous Barkley essays. I titled it: "Please Let Me Run The Barkley Marathons Again." In it, I stated my belief that the Barkley Marathons was "highly interesting as a psychological phenomenon." I then presented a hypothesis on this aspect of the race. I had done an analysis of the results for each year, and presented the results as a graph of the percentage of starters who finished each year. A so-called "linear regression analysis" of these results showed that the percentage of finishers was increasing over time. This graph and the statistical linear regression (dashed) line showing the increase is reproduced, along with the full essay, at the end of this chapter.

I went on to note that there was also an obvious up-down trend to the percentage of finishers. I attributed this pattern to psychological factors. Past-year success created over-confidence, which resulted in failure. Past failure led to humility, which increased the probability of finishing in the next year. I then went on to predict that, because the previous year (1994) had had a relatively low finishing success, with just one finisher, 1995 would have a relatively large finishing rate. I specifically predicted that between 23% and 40% of the starters, including myself, would finish. Of course, it

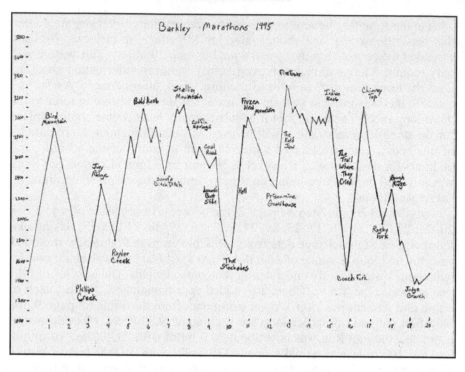

goes without saying that in all this, I was referring to the three-loop race, not the 100-mile, which in my mind was impossible. These analyses and predictions were made with my awareness of the major course change for 1995, described above. However, I was not aware of just how difficult that new part of the course was.

In addition to a tougher course this year, Gary added a new element of difficulty: no drop-bags for the runners on the course. He would continue to place bottled water at two course locations—Coffin Springs and the top of Frozen Head Mountain near the base of the lookout. But he would no longer take runners' supplies to those checkpoints. The only aid that runners could get now, other than water, would be at the campground between loops. Not only was the loop now longer and with more elevation change, but also runners would have to carry more supplies with them because of the lack of on-course aid. Clearly, Gary was ratcheting up the level of difficulty.

The 1995 starting field was another strong one. Notably, Tom Possert was there for the first time since 1988, when he had unleashed a great run but was disqualified for inadvertently short-cutting the course. Three past winners were there: myself, Animal Herr, and Fred Purloin. Other past finishers who were there again were Milan Milanovich from Switzerland, Nancy and Rick Hamilton, John DeWalt, and Nick Williams. Other returners included Trail Dale Sutton, Gene Fatboy Trahern, Harry Smith, Teeter Benedetti, Cliff Hoy, Wilson and Wayne Brasington, Lou Peyton, Wayne Stiles, and Buttslide Martin. In addition, newcomers included: Heikki Ingstrom, an ultrarunner from Utah with strong credentials from the Wasatch 100; Reid Lanham, a fast young runner from Virginia who was being coached by David Horton (although David did not enter this year); Craig Wilson from Maine; Kim Goosen, a fast woman runner from Arkansas; and a runner from England, Mark Williams, who was relatively unknown to most of us Americans, but who had twice finished the prestigious 154-mile Spartathlon race in Greece, in a best time of 32:40.

Others who are named in Gary's *UltraRunning* article in June 1995 are Greg Shoener, Ken Solakian, Richard Schuler, Bill Kendall, Phil Pierce, Steve Eubanks, Stuart Gleman, Matt Mahoney, David Hughes, and Claude Sinclair. Gary stated that there were 39 starters this year, the most in race history.

As noted above, Matt Mahoney made his first appearance at the Barkley this year. Subsequently, Matt has run the Barkley many times and has become one of it primary chroniclers by writing articles and compiling information about the Barkley for each year from 1995 and later, and posting them on a website. This website is <http://www.mattmahoney.net/barkley/>. As of the writing of this book, Matt's website is probably the Internet site which has the most comprehensive information about the Barkley Marathons. I have used some of the information from Matt's website in writing this book.

Piecing together some statements from Gary's *UltraRunning* article, it appears that the 1995 race started at about 6 AM, on April Fools Day. Tom Possert and Heikki Ingstrom were the first to finish the first loop, in about seven and a half hours, a remarkable time for the newly lengthened loop. They prepared for the second loop before checking in with Gary. Just before they checked in with Gary and headed out on loop two, Mark Williams and Craig Wilson checked in at 8:02. Fred was fifth after one loop, in 8:33, followed soon by Wayne Stiles and Reid Lanham. Animal Herr was eighth in 8:53, Milan Milanovich was ninth in 9:07. I was tenth in 9:45 as my departure time for loop two. My logbook notes show that I had finished the first loop in about 9:05, so I spent about 40 minutes in camp between loops. For most of us returning runners, these times reflect the longer loop. For example, Fred had run the first loop last year in about 7:39; this year he was about 54 minutes longer. The Animal had run the first loop last year in 7:29, about 1:24 shorter than his time this year. I had last run the first loop, in 1992, in about 7:55, about 1:10 faster than this year.

Clearly, the addition of the new Trail of Tears, with its Zip Line and Big Hell, was taking a toll on us in time and effort, adding about an hour to the first-loop times. I remember trudging up that long, steep, brier-infested climb up to Chimney Top, and as I approached the book near the top, I came upon Animal Herr. He was sitting on a log, resting. As I approached, he expressed his fatigue and frustration, saying: "Gary's gone too far this time!" This statement summed up what many of us would come to realize about the tougher course.

One important aspect of the longer loop was that more runners would now be *out there* on the North Boundary Trail (NBT) in the dark on loop two. Whereas I used to be able to "get the hell out of Hell on loop two before dark," now darkness occurred while I was still early in loop two. This is significant, because the NBT is notoriously difficult to follow in the dark. Recall the problem that I had had in 1992, getting lost on the NBT near Phillips Creek in the dark on loop three. So it appeared that Gary was achieving what he had intended with the increased course difficulty in 1995. This change was putting the race beyond the ability of many of us. Old Gristle Peyton is another runner who later told me that the course changes of 1995 put the three-loop run out of her hopeful reach. For her, the first loop took 1:43 longer.

Below is a picture of me running on the NBT on loop one in the 1995 Barkley. This picture was taken by Old Gristle with a disposable camera that I carried around the first loop.

Possert and Ingstrom ran loop two together, finishing it first in 18:06. Ingstrom then retired, but Possert headed out on loop three after a short break. Mark Williams and Craig Wilson were likewise together after loop two, in 19:19. They rested for about an hour before beginning loop three together. They were doing remarkably well, especially considering that they were both "Barkley Virgins," i.e., this was the first Barkley race for both of them. Mark had never trained on the course, and had seen only a small part of it the day before the race. In all, ten runners completed two loops, and seven of them continued on to a third loop.

Tom Possert was the first to finish the three-loop, 60-mile Barkley, in a time of 28:52:57. Incredibly, this impressive time still stands (through 2009) as the 60-mile course record. As he had done in his ill-fated 1988 perform-ance, Tom had again proven that he was an unexcelled runner in the difficult conditions of the Barkley. One of Tom's innovative methods this year was the use of trekking poles. He said that the poles helped him maintain balance on the steep parts of the trails.

Mark Williams had pulled away from Craig Wilson on the third loop. Mark was the second to finish the Fun Run, in 31:02:53. Wilson was third, about an hour and 25 minutes behind Mark. Milan completed his second Barkley three-loop race in fourth place. Fatboy Trahern and Greg Shoener were the final three-loop finishers, bringing the total to six finishers of the three-loop race. Thus the finishing rate this year was 6 of 39, or 15.4%. This was slightly above the 14.0% average for the first nine years. Thus my prediction in my essay, of a high finishing rate this year, was generally correct. However, my predicted range of 23% to 40% was too optimistic.

I had also missed my prediction that I would finish again. The new longer, slower, loop had taken its toll on me. On the second loop, as I was approaching the Garden Spot, I got off-course. This was the first time I had ever been on that part of the course in the dark. I missed the faint trail going up to the Garden Spot, and ended up wandering on old logging roads that were not shown on the map, east of and outside the Frozen Head Natural Area. I thought that I would have to spend the night waiting until daylight to find my way back to known territory. But after a short rest, I got my bearings by realizing from my elevation and compass readings that I must be up on the west side of Stallion Mountain. I then realized that the coal road going south along the 2,600-foot elevation must be below me. I headed westerly down the side of the mountain and soon came to and recognized the coal road. Exhausted and shaken by the possibility that I had nearly had to spend the night lost *out there*, I went up to Coffin Springs and took the Quitter's Road back to camp. My log book shows that I got back at about 16:45 race time. So I had been *out there* for nearly seven hours on loop two, and retrieved a page from only one book. This was by far my worst result yet at the Barkley.

However, not everyone was having the kind of problem that I was. The remarkable Englishman, Mark Williams, was not familiar enough with the Barkley to realize that the 100-mile was an imaginary joke in Gary's mind. He did not know that the 100-mile was impossible. Therefore, to him, it was not impossible. He kept right on going after finishing his third loop. Those of us who believed it was impossible thought that this was futile. Even Possert, content with his Fun Run victory, stated that he did not think anyone could finish the 100. He departed to drive home. I too left Frozen Head Sunday evening, to begin my long drive back to Nevada. I had no plans to stay at Frozen Head because there had never before been a reason to stay there past Sunday. No runner had ever still been running on Monday. Until now.

Mark was the only runner to keep going. He finished the fourth loop in 45:06, at about 4 AM Monday, and took another nap, as he had during the first night, after loop two. This time, he rested for just over two and a half hours, some of that unintentionally. He slept through his alarms, and overslept by about 40 minutes longer than intended. With just under 20 minutes to spare before the cutoff time to start the fifth loop, he headed *out there* one more time.

Mark Williams made history that day, by becoming the first person ever to finish the Barkley Marathons 100-mile race. His finishing time of 59:28:48 beat the 60-hour time limit by 31 minutes and 12 seconds. He had done what most of us really believed was impossible.

There is an interview with Mark in the June 1995 *UltraRunning*, along-side Gary's post-race article. Mark had done some incredible training for Barkley, back in England. For example, he reported having done runs in the steep fells of England of 15 and 22 miles on back-to-back days, with 13,000 and 11,000 feet of ascent, respectively, on each of the first three weekends of March. That is about 48,000 feet of vertical change within a 2-day period. It appears that his maximum mileage week was 90 miles.

Mark's breakthrough performance at Barkley in 1995 was a testimony to the power of belief. Most of us who were familiar with the Barkley from several years of experience there, did not believe that it was possible to finish the Barkley 100. Therefore, for us, it was not possible. But Mark was not limited by that self-fulfilling belief. For him it was just a challenge to be given his best effort, and to keep going until he either finished or ran past the time limit. This was one of the most amazing demonstrations that I have ever encountered about the power of our minds in determining our limits.

Not all of us were stuck in the belief that the Barkley 100 was impossible. When I was later talking to Gary about the results of the 1995 Barkley, he told me that when Mark finished the 100, Milan Milanovich jubilantly exclaimed: "I knew it! I knew it! I knew it could be done!"

Below are the known starters, their numbers of Barkley starts, and their loop-finishing times for 1995.

1. Mark Williams (1)   8:02:08   19:19:27   31:02:53   45:06:15   59:28:48
2. Tom Possert (3)   8:03:09   18:06:01   28:52:57
3. Craig Wilson (1)   8:02:08   19:19:29   32:27:12
4. Milan Milanovich (3)   9:07:04   23:38:00   36:29:37
5. Gene Trahern (1)   10:05:30   23:42:10   39:22:13
6. Greg Shoener (1)   10:05:28   24:43:43   39:22:13
7. Heikki Ingstrom (1)   8:03:09   18:06:03
8. Wilson Brasington (2) 11:14:32   25:29:40
9. Ken Solakian (1)   10:05:51   25:48:00
10. Buttslide Martin (5)   11:25:31   26:10:01
11. Matt Mahoney (1)   11:40:04   ~29:40*Finished loop two over the time limit.
12. Fred Purloin (9)   8:33:19
13. Wayne Stiles (2)   8:37:25
14. Reid Lanham (1)   8:38:04
15. Animal Herr (6)   8:53:47
16. Frozen Ed Furtaw (5)   9:45:33
17. Trail Dale Sutton (3) 10:02:58
18. Kim Goosen (1)   10:06:11
19. Richard Schuler (1)   10:06:45
20. Bill Kendall (1)   10:16:53
21. Harry Smith (2)   10:19:06

22. Teeter Benedetti (3)   10:19:53
23. <u>Nancy Hamilton</u> (4)   10:20:39
24. Rick Hamilton (3)   10:20:41
25. John DeWalt (8)   10:24:35
26. Cliff Hoy (3)   10:24:38
27. Nick Williams (5)   10:25:05
28. Phil Pierce (1)   10:29:30
29. Steve Eubanks (1)   11:23:27
30. <u>Old Gristle Peyton</u> (4) 11:25:17
31. Stuart Gleman (1)   11:25:29
32. David Hughes (1)   11:45:23
33. Wayne Brasington (2) 11:53:15
34. Claude Sinclair (1)   11:53:37
35. Don Winkley (1)   Finished loop one over the time limit.
36. Jim Jones (1)   Quit on loop one.
39 starters

++++++++++

Here is the essay I wrote for entry into the 1995 Barkley.

Please Let Me Run The Barkley Marathons Again
(January 20, 1995)

I should be allowed to run the 1995 Barkley Marathons because I have already attempted it four previous times, and have successfully finished it twice.   If that's not a good enough reason, I have a more interesting and compelling one, described below.

I find the Barkley Marathons (BM) highly interesting as a psychological phenomenon. The history of the event has demonstrated that it is one of the most difficult ultrarunning events in the world to complete. However, the history has also demonstrated that it <u>can</u> be completed, even by runners of relatively modest, non-elite capability. I myself am a good example of this. This raises the question: What is it that determines whether a runner will complete the BM in any given attempt? Another similar question is: What is it that determines how many runners will complete the BM on any particular occasion? I have a hypothesis which, if correct, may answer these questions.

The reader is referred to the attached graphs. Figure 1 shows the numbers of starters and finishers in each of the nine previous BMs (1986 through 1994). It shows that the number of starters of the BM has tended to increase gradually over the years since it was first held. The number of starters has approximately leveled off near 30 contestants per year, due mainly to the limit placed on the number of starters by the management of the race and the Frozen Head State Park. The number of finishers each year has also had a generally upward trend over the years, although this trend is less consistent. It is the pattern of variation in the number (or percentage) of finishers which most intrigues me.

Figure 2 is a plot of the percentage of starters who officially finished the BM (at least, the 55-mile portion of the BM) each year. The light dashed line

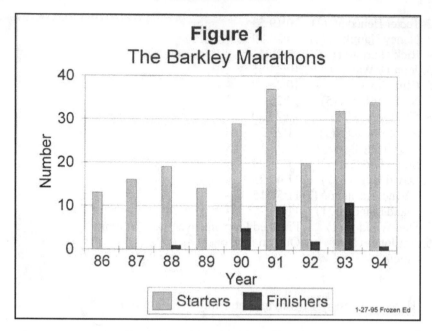

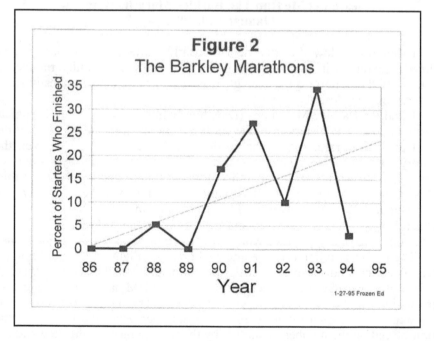

on Figure 2 is the mathematical result of a linear regression analysis of the percentage of finishers. This line shows the generally upward trend in finishers over time. I believe that this trend is best explained by the runners' better preparedness over time. As the runners have become more familiar with the course over the years, they have become better prepared for the long and difficult ordeal which finishing requires. However, it can also be seen that the actual percentage of finishers has not increased as consistently as the mathematically smoothed regression (dashed) line. The variability in the actual percentage of finishers is more difficult to explain. It is the subject of my hypothesis.

My hypothesis is best stated as follows: completing the Barkley Marathons is predominantly a psychological feat rather than a physical feat. One of the primary determinants of whether a runner will finish is the runner's expectation, which is based largely on recent past results. The more successful the recent results, the less likely is a high success rate in the next attempt. This up-down tendency is obvious in Figure 2. After the first-ever finish in 1988, there were no finishers in 1989. Then there were 5 in 1990, followed by 10 in 1991 (this is the only exception to the up-down trend in the finishing percentage). This was followed by the crash of 1992, which in turn was followed by the highest-ever success rate in 1993, followed by another crash in 1994. My own personal history is a perfect example of the up-down trend: in my four BM attempts, I have alternately finished (1988), DNFed ('90), finished ('91), and DNFed ('92).

My explanation for the apparent up-down trend is based on psychology. When the runners think that they are able to complete the BM, based on the previous year's relatively successful results, they come to the event with the attitude that that it is not that difficult to finish. That's when the BM bites them in the butt. But when the runners are reminded from the previous year's results just how difficult the BM really is, they come with a more humbled attitude that just to finish will take all they have, if they can do it at all. This attitude is more conducive to finishing than the "I can definitely finish it" attitude. In my personal case, my two DNFs both occurred in races in which I unexpectedly held the lead in the latter stages of the race. This position led me to strive to win the race, rather than to complete it. In both cases, this loss of humility led quickly to my total demise, DNF, and humiliation (which is not the same as humility). Expressed another way, I believe that if you want to finish the BM, you had better not bring a big ego to the race.

Based on these observations, I will venture some predictions for the 1995 BM:

1. I will finish again this year, because I didn't finish my last attempt. Therefore, I am properly humbled and will run it with the single purpose to finish, and not attempt to win. I also recognize that I may very well be unable to finish it. My former cockiness in believing that I could definitely do it was lost in my most recent failure.

2. There will be a relatively large number of finishers in 1995. It should be an "up" year, because 1994 was a "down" year with only one finisher. Based on extrapolation of the trends in Figure 2, I predict that between 23% and 40% of the starters will finish. Clearly this is a bold prediction, especially because Gary Cantrell has informed me that the 1995 course will be even tougher than ever before, with the addition of several new book checkpoints located in remote, trackless wilderness. However, this is largely irrelevant. The course has been made tougher before, for example by the addition of the

Rat Jaw section in 1989, but that hasn't prevented the increasing trend in finishing percentage noted above.

It may seem ludicrous to say that an event as physically grueling as the BM is not predominantly a physical competition, but rather a psychological one. Those painful muscles and joints common to all who have done even a single BM loop seem to suggest that it is a purely physical challenge. But I don't think so. Granted, all contestants will be tested to their physical limits. But the issue at Barkley is to continue onward past our normal physical limitations. It is a given that all contestants will be physically wasted long before approaching the finish line. Those who finish are those who can psychologically overcome the obvious physical torture of the BM.

Thus the Barkley Marathon is the embodiment of the essence of ultramarathon running in its most sublime expression: the attempt to transcend our perceived limits and do what we once thought was impossible.

Chapter 15
1996: The Barkley Bites Back Again

Following the landmark success of the 1995 Barkley, many of us were greatly anticipating the 1996 race. Since the 100-mile barrier had been broken, would others now be empowered to do it as well? Recall that following my first-ever 55-mile finish in 1988, 1989 had been a bad year, with no finishers of the three-loop race. Also recall that in my 1995 essay, I had identified an up-down pattern in overall finishing results from one year to the next. Would the subsequent bad year predicted by this trend occur at the Barkley in 1996? Finally the time arrived for these questions to be put to the test.

I returned for my sixth attempt at the Barkley in 1996. The theme of my essay this year was that I should be allowed to run Barkley again because I was a "Barkley Aficionado." To prove my point, I wrote about some wooded property that Gail and I had bought in 1994. This land was in northern Arizona, about a four-hour drive from our home in Las Vegas. We would go to this property on weekends to get away from the city. The land was adjacent to a steep hill with about 500 feet of elevation difference between top and bottom, over just about half a mile of distance; a Barkley-like gradient. We would go there on weekends, and I would do repetitions up and down this hill as "Barkley Training." In my essay, I stated: "Because of this devotion to specificity of training, that I bought a mountain so I could better train for Barkley, I must be allowed to run the Barkley Marathons."

The starting field was considerably smaller in 1996 than in the previous year. According to Gary's article in the June 1996 *UltraRunning*, only 24 started, compared to 39 the previous year. However, as always, the field contained numerous Barkley veterans. Most noteworthy was Mark Williams, the Englishman who had finished the 100-miler last year. It would certainly be interesting to see if he could duplicate this astounding accomplishment this year. Also returning was Tom Possert, the 60-mile winner from last year. Craig Wilson was back, after his third-place finish in 1995. Myself and John DeWalt were other former finishers. Other returning non-finishers were Jim Dill, Cliff Hoy, Teeter Benedetti, Ken Solakian, Rich Schuler, Wayne and Wilson Brasington, Matt Mahoney, and Stuart Gleman. Newcomers included DeWayne Satterfield and Craig Armstrong, both strong, young ultrarunners from Alabama who usually placed near the top of the field and who had both run sub-six-hour 50-mile races; Daniel Bellinger; Debra Moore; Will Burkhart; Todd O'Toole; Jason Poole; and Kerry Trammell, from nearby Oak Ridge, Tennessee.

The course remained the same as last year's, the Two Hells course, although at least one location name was changed. The steep uphill from the stream confluence to the top of Chimney Top was now, for the first time, called "the Big Hell Trail." Most of us have subsequently just called that climb "Big Hell." There is no actual trail there. Gary provided runners with a printout of a spreadsheet listing locations, distances, and elevation changes on the loop. He called the distance 20.00 miles, with 10,010 feet each of elevation gain and descent per loop.

In his *UltraRunning* article, Gary reported beautiful, sunny weather on the first day of the race. However, in my post-race notes, I recorded that it had rained for a couple of days beforehand, with the result that the course was wet, causing wet feet for most of the run. This in turn caused me to develop painful blisters on the soles of my feet by about 12 hours into the race.

In any case, the race-day conditions were conducive to Tom Possert running at a phenomenal pace for the first loop. He finished in the lead, in 7:09:20, a record for the Two Hells loop that was introduced last year. Tom was about 20 minutes ahead of last year's best time for the first loop, and about 54 minutes ahead of his own time for the first loop in his fun-run victory of last year. It looked like Tom was there to again put on an impressive performance. However, like so many Barkley Rabbits before him, this fast first loop proved to be nearly the end of Tom's day. He lingered in camp, and then ran only another partial loop before quitting.

Mark Williams and Craig Wilson were next in after one loop. Gary noted in his *UltraRunning* article that Mark was already 36 minutes behind his pace from last year, when he had finished the 100-mile race just 32 minutes under the cut-off time. This was not a good omen for Mark's chances of another 100 completion. He and Craig Wilson rapidly resupplied and continued onto the second loop. Craig Armstrong and DeWayne Satterfield, the fast Alabamian friends, were next into camp. Gary wrote that "upon completing loop one they threw themselves on the ground and refused to even consider continuing." I was next in, and started loop two after about 50 minutes of rest and re-stocking. In all, 15 runners started a second loop.

Not all the runners were able to finish the first loop within its time limit. Jim Dill and Cliff Hoy had an adventure on their first loop that they will probably never forget. Where the course goes down steeply from Indian Knob, on the so-called Zip Line Trail, Jim and Cliff, running together, managed to get disoriented and headed down the wrong side of that mountain. This unfortunately took them to the back side of the Brushy Mountain State Penitentiary. They were immediately apprehended by armed prison guards, who were understandably concerned about this pair of strangely-dressed men approaching the maximum-security prison. As Gary describes in his *UltraRunning* article: "After being forced at gunpoint to lay on the ground while the tower guards verified that dumb morons were in the woods this particular night, he sent them back up the now dark mountain with threats of arrest should they return. At how many ultras are runners forced to continue at gunpoint?" This story is even more amusing and ironic in view of the fact that Cliff Hoy, one of the wayward pair, was a New Jersey State Trooper!

During Saturday evening and night, as Gary stated: "loop two was turning ugly." As happens so often at the Barkley, the ugliness was in the form of bad weather. Intermittent downpours of rain, with fog in between, greatly contributed to the runners' miseries. All of us except Mark Williams and Craig Wilson quit sometime during the second loop and retreated to shelter back at the campground.

On my second loop, I was determined to stay on course. You may recall that in my two most recent Barkley adventures, I had gotten lost on the NBT in the dark. I certainly recalled it and made every effort to stay on course through this difficult North Section. I was elated to get to the Garden Spot, and then to Coffin Springs, without getting lost! I was so happy and proud of myself, that I decided to head directly back down to camp to celebrate this moral victory. In other words, I once again took that Quitter's Road back to camp and quit. I was beginning to realize that I really enjoyed hanging around the campfire on Saturday night and Sunday with Gary and the rest of the quitters. This would prove to be a habit that would be tough for me to break.

Mark Williams and Craig Wilson completed loop two together in 19:51:48, still about 32 minutes behind last year's time to this point. After about an hour of rest and refreshment, they started a third loop. Gary was adding a new twist this year: the runners were required to run their third loop in the counterclockwise direction. This was the first time since the first loop of the first Barkley, in 1986, that any runners had attempted a counterclockwise loop. The reader may recall that Gary abandoned the idea of having runners go counterclockwise after the first year because of the difficulty of navigating the NBT in that direction. That difficulty factor was now about to reassert itself. As Gary described, Mark and Craig pushed their pace to try to make up some time, but made a few wrong turns and ended up spending extra time and effort to get back on-course. The rain and fog continued, adding to their slowdown. They finally finished loop three in just under 35 hours, an excellent accomplishment, but nearly four hours behind Mark's time of last year. They still had an hour to start loop four within the time limit, but, as Gary wrote in his post-race *UltraRunning* article: "their first order of business was to declare this race over. The Barkley had its crown back." The headline title of Gary's article that year was: "Mark Williams Won in 1995; in '96 the Barkley Bites Back."

The failure of Mark to be able to return and repeat his 100-mile Barkley finish shows how tenuous the conditions are that allow a finish. The wet weather this year slowed the top runners down just enough to press them close to the time limits. The weather and their attempt to force the pace, especially while running the course in the reverse direction for the first time, contributed to them losing precious minutes by minor off-trail blunders. This further slowed their progress and sapped energy from an already razor-thin margin of ability to keep moving at the required pace. This demonstrates how close the Barkley is to the limit of possibility. Furthermore, the relatively poor overall results for this year, with only 8.3% of the starters finishing the three-loop Fun Run, tended to validate the prediction from my "updown" hypothesis. This year's results were much worse, from the runners' perspective, than last year's.

Thus Gary was able to resume his gloating at the end of his annual Barkley article, by daring runners to come and try the Barkley: "If you think you're tough enough, then come and take your shot. But I have to warn you, you'll never make it to 100 miles. The Barkley will squash you like a bug."

The known runners, their numbers of Barkley starts, and loop-finishing times for 1996 are listed below.
1. Craig Wilson (2)   8:45:11 19:51:49   34:58:06
2. Mark Williams (2)   8:42:56 19:51:48   34:58:07

3. Tom Possert (4)   7:09:20
4. DeWayne Satterfield (1)   9:03:24
5. Craig Armstrong (1)   9:03:25
6. Frozen Ed Furtaw (6)   9:32:43
7. Daniel Bellinger (1)   10:29:42
8. John DeWalt (9)   10:33:14
9. Debra Moore (1)   10:56:56
10. Will Burkhart (1)   10:56:57
11. Todd O'Toole (1)   10:56:58
12. Jason Poole (1)   10:56:59
13. Ken Solakian (2)   11:06:56
14. Rich Schuler (2)   11:06:59
15. Wilson Brasington (3)   11:07:15
16. Kerry Trammell (1)   11:07:22
17. Teeter Benedetti (4)   11:11:35
18. Matt Mahoney (2)   11:13:25
19. Stuart Gleman (2)   11:13:27
20. Wayne Brasington (3)   11:36:36
21. Jim Dill (7)   Lost on loop one; apprehended at prison.
22. Cliff Hoy (4)   Lost on loop one; apprehended at prison.
24 Starters

Later in 1996, runner Dave Biddle wrote a several-page paper about the Barkley Marathons, describing the course and the event history through the 1996 race.   This interesting paper can be found on Dave's website at <http://www.lehigh.edu/~dmd1/dave.html>.

+++++++++++

**Why I should Be Allowed To Run The Barkley Marathons
Essay #6 in a Series - Confessions of a Barkley Aficionado
(February 14, 1996)**

PROLOGUE
After a dozen years of running ultramarathons, I experienced a significant change in my ultrarunning career in the past year since my last Barkley DNF—I joined the Internet ultra lists. This has helped to revitalize my ultra life because it has given me a new source of information and support to help me pursue ultrarunning. The constant interaction with hundreds of other ultrarunners in reflecting on all aspects of ultrarunning, including why and which events to run, has stimulated my interest in and love of this sport. One of the things I have discovered about myself is that I spontaneously and joyously break into enthusiastic rantings about the Barkley Marathons. I have called myself a "Barkley aficionado" in more than one Internet conversation. The word "aficionado" means an enthusiast, or devotee. (I know because I had to look it up in a dictionary.) Thus, being on the ultra lists has helped me realize the extent of my addiction to Barkley.

EXECUTIVE SUMMARY

I should be allowed to run the Barkley Marathons because I am a Barkley Aficionado. This means several things. As I elucidate the meaning of this statement, it will become obvious that I must again be allowed to run Barkley. I will describe three aspects of being a Barkley Aficionado: history, training, and spirituality.

HISTORY

As a Barkley Aficionado, I have a long and strong historical connection with the event. I remember the first time I saw the Barkley Marathons listed in the *UltraRunning* calendar in 1986. It said 24 THOUSAND feet of elevation gain. Well, I had previously lived in eastern Tennessee, and I knew damn well that there were no mountains there of anywhere near that magnitude, so I assumed that there must have been a misprint - it must be 24 HUNDRED feet, not 24 THOUSAND. When I later saw that no one finished it that first year, my fascination with Barkley was born. Then in 1987 Gary Cantrell showed me a topographic map of Frozen Head State Park, and told me how much fun Barkley was. It was humbling to realize that I had been wrong and Gary right about the 24 THOUSAND feet. I knew I had to try it. I trained on the course to prepare myself, and on one fateful day in 1988, I visited Frozen Head State Park with Gary and Raw Dog Karl Henn. We toured a new part of the course which Gary was in the process of re-routing. Yes, in 1988 I actually climbed up Hell with the Idiot and the Raw Dog. We stopped part way up for a smoke break. I was there when the heart of Barkley was being created. I will even confess, it was my idea to use books as unmanned checkpoints to verify that all would-be finishers actually visited all the appropriate beautiful places. Dare I publicly take credit for this dubious innovation? The Barkley history clearly shows that I have a place in it, and therefore I must be allowed to run it again.

TRAINING

While I have a place in Barkley's history, Barkley also has a prominent place in my personal history. The Barkley has thoroughly infiltrated my life, such that it is now a perennial goal which helps set the entire annual cycle of my training regime and vacation plans. It orients and energizes my entire life. As part of Barkley's influence on my training, it has made me want to run more mountains, with or without trails. This in turn led to a major move in the lives of me and my wife Gail in 1994: we bought a 40-acre ranch on the side of a mountain in Arizona. My history and experience with Barkley helped create my mentality that made me want to own the side of a mountain. The result is that I now have a personal Barkley training route on which I can do 500-foot vertical hill repeats in a half-mile of bad terrain—the same average conditions as Barkley. Because of this devotion to specificity of training, that I bought a mountain so I could better train for Barkley, I must be allowed to run the Barkley Marathons.

SPIRITUALITY

I had a profound realization during the past year. Gail and I went through several major stressful changes in 1988-89. Within a two-month period, we quit our jobs, got married, moved from North Carolina to Nevada, and started new jobs. It had been my dream for many years to move to the southwest, because of my love of mountains and the sunny, dry, warm climate. It took a lot of gumption to make all those changes. But in early 1988, I had finished Barkley, the first official finisher ever. In retrospect, I believe that the sense of self-confidence which I gained by finishing Barkley that year stimulated the self-empowerment which enabled me to successfully pursue my other life-goals. Thus I think that the Barkley Marathons has indeed had a profound impact on my entire life.

Sometimes when I am lying in bed at night and want a beautiful image in which to drift off to sleep, I recall vividly the awesome beauty of Barkley's most remote spots: the Garden Spot, the New River Gorge, the stream confluence at the bottom of Worse than Hell. These images are indelibly imprinted in my memory as some of the most rugged yet serene and beautiful places on earth. With this intimacy between me and Barkley, need I say more about whether I should be allowed to run Barkley again? Oh, OK, I will say a little bit more...

The intimacy of my relationship with the Barkley Marathons transcends each of the particular aspects of it. The Barkley for me is a physical challenge, a mental challenge, a psychological challenge, a self-reliance challenge, and much more. Because it transcends all these aspects, I consider it to be within the realm of the spiritual. The Barkley Marathons has spiritual significance to me; it relates to my definition of myself and what and why I am. Surely it is obvious that I must be allowed to again run the Barkley Marathons.

EPILOGUE

Gary: if the above essay was too long and serious for you, here's a shorter version which says about the same thing: I should be allowed to run the Barkley Marathons because I am one of the few who truly realizes what the Barkley really is: it is a giant monster about to devour a runner, and I am that runner. The runner's number on the Barkley logo tells all: zero. I am zero. But accepting this, I am willing to be devoured and, like a one-way Jonah, pass through the bowels of Hell to be shat out the other end (hopefully at the finish line) feeling like fecal matter. I accept this. I embrace it. I am one with it. Therefore I must be allowed to run it.

Chapter 16
1997: Tapped Out

An interesting addition was instituted for the 1997 Barkley Marathons: the bugle. This was also the year that I first devised and used a *Pocket Guide to the Barkley Marathons*.

For 1997, the layout of the loop remained the same Two Hells course, with the same feature that was added last year, that runners would be required to run the third and fourth loops in the reverse, counterclockwise, direction. A fifth loop could be run in the direction of choice of the runner, if any were to get that far.

The starting field was an allowable-capacity crowd of 31. Several big-name returning runners were there for another shot at redemption or glory. Returning former Barkley three-loop winners were as follows: Craig Wilson, the reigning champion of the Fun Run; David Horton, the record-holder of the old 55-mile course; Fred Purloin; and myself. Additional former three-loop finishers were Milan Milanovich, John DeWalt (for his tenth time), and Nick Williams. Other runners returning with previous DNFs were DeWayne Satterfield, Reid Lanham, brothers Wayne and Wilson Brasington, Kerry Trammell, Teeter Benedetti, Ken Solakian, Rich Schuler, Matt Mahoney, Debra Moore, Lou Peyton, and Jim Dill (for his eighth time). Among the most noteworthy newcomers were Andrew Thompson, a young runner from Virginia who was a friend of David Horton, and Blake Wood, a top ultrarunner from New Mexico. Andrew would eventually (in 2005) go on to set the speed record for covering the full 2,175-mile length of the Appalachian Trail. Other newbies included Mike Dobies, Eliza MacLean, Laurie Ann Schuler (Rich's wife), Chris Ralph, Bill Johnson, Doug Barrows, and Norm Carlson.

Chris Ralph's appearance at the Barkley this year was significant because she and a colleague from the Seattle area, Tom Ripley, would later that year create and direct a new 100-mile trail race, the Plain 100. Chris later told me that the Plain 100 was inspired in part by the Barkley, and would be modeled in some ways after the Barkley. The Plain 100 subsequently has become one of the other most difficult trail races to finish, based on its historical finishing percentage. However, as will be discussed in Chapter 29, it is not as tough as the Barkley.

About this time in human history, the Internet and e-mail were booming. These relatively newer forms of communication gave us Barkley followers additional means of spreading stories and sharing advice about our favorite ultramarathon. I have print-outs of several e-mails that I exchanged with other ultrarunners about the Barkley. I believe that it was through one of the e-mail list-servers that I made the remote acquaintance of Mike Dobies. Mike was from Michigan, and was an endurance athlete in both ultrarunning and long-distance bicycle racing. I encouraged him to enter Barkley. Via e-mail, we adopted the rallying phrase RFP, the acronym for Relentless Forward Progress. This would be my mantra for my 1997 run at the Barkley. I can tell from my essay and other things I wrote prior to this year's Barkley that I was pretty serious about finishing the Fun Run again. It had now been six years since my last finish of the three-loop 55-mile Barkley. As I had done in former years, I developed a written pre-race plan with an intended schedule that would have me finish three loops in 38 hours, plus-or-minus one hour and 59 minutes.

Prior to writing my essay, I had developed a tabular summary of the Barkley course that I called "Pocket Guide To The Barkley Marathons." A copy of my 1997 Pocket Guide appears below.

Pocket Guide To The Barkley Marathons by Frozen Ed Furtaw   Revised March 1997

Barkley Mile	Location	Elev. Ft.	Up Ft.	Down Ft.	Loop 1	Loop 2	Loop 3	Directions from Location
0	Gate	1,460	-	-				Up road 200 yds, L (N) on Bird Mtn. Tr., up 14 SB, L on old trail to top
1	Bird Mtn.	2,980	1,520	0				Bear R downhill, 14 SB, N to NW boundary corner
2	Phillips Creek	1,400	0	1,580				BOOK 1. Cross creek, E uphill steep on old Boundary Tr., ~28 SB to top
3	Jury Ridge	2,340	940	0				Continue eastward on Boundary Tr., down across creek, up 16 SB
4	Jury Ridge Sign	2,780	980	540				Continue eastward on Boundary Tr., down then up 10 SB, N around Bald Knob
5	Bald Knob	3,060	480	200				SE on Boundary Tr. down 4 SB, E down 6 SB, cross SOB Ditch, up tailings pile
6	Coal Pond	2,600	160	620				NE left of ponds ~600 yds, E up to Boundary Tr., up across dirt road to NE corner
7	Garden Spot	3,140	540	0				BOOK 2. SW down old rd to dirt rd, R at L curve, down SW on old road to springs
8	Coffin Springs	2,930	50	260				SIGN LOG. E ~300 yds on old rd, then downhill S along drainage to coal road at 2600 ft. elev., S past Barley Mouth Branch ~0.3 mi. to Standing Rock
9	Standing Rock	2,600	100	430				BOOK 3. Down Leonard's Butt Slide, L at New River, down along old RR bed, cross river, SE on trail ~0.3 mi to rock wall on right
10	Bottom of Hell	1,670	0	930				BOOK 4. S across drainage, W straight up Hell Hill to dirt road
11	Top of Hell	3,000	1,330	0				BOOK 5. L down dirt rd to sharp L curve, R on old rd past powerline to guard house
12	Rat Jaw Guard House	2,300	30	730				BOOK 6. Up Rat Jaw under powerline, R around cliff near top, powerline to rd to top
13	Frozen Head Tower	3,320	1,020	0				SIGN LOG. Down rd, sharp L on Chimney Top Tr. to jct. w/Spicewood Br. Tr.
14	Spicewood Tr. Jct.	2,850	0	470				Straight on C.T. Tr. When C.T turns sharp R go straight to Indian Knob capstone
15	Indian Knob	3,050	200	0				BOOK 7. W down steep, bear L to old trail along creek, trail to creek confluence w/Lowgap Hollow, cross creek W, up steep ridge to tree W above confluence
16	Lowgap Hollow	1,500	0	1,550				BOOK 8. WNW straight up ridge to top
17	Chimney Top	3,100	1,600	0				BOOK 9. N past capstones along ridge to C.T. Tr., L on tr down steep, 7 SB to creek
18	Rocky Fork Creek	1,960	0	1,140				Cross creek on C.T. Tr., across Rough Ridge, down along boundary, 5 SB to bridge
19	Judge Branch Bridge	1,360	320	920				Cross bridge, L at trail jct, past trailhead parking lot, R on paved road, uphill to road fork, L on paved road to campground gate
20	Gate	1,460	100	0				TURN IN PAGES. Eat, rest, change socks, then continue for AT LEAST 3 LOOPS!
	TOTAL		9,370	9,370				I know I can do it. Have fun. Continue making RFP. Stretch and Smile!

In concept, this was similar to a golf scorecard. I had broken down the Barkley loop into 20 "Barkley Miles," each of those being the distance be-tween identifiable landmarks that were approximately a mile apart. In real-ity, some of those "Barkley Miles" were probably as much as two statute miles. The elevation at each mile was listed, as were the approximate eleva-tion gain and drop between each mile-point. There was a brief description of the route to follow from each mile to the next. Also, I had three blank col-umns, one for each loop, with about a half-inch space to write in my time at each mile. Finally, near the bottom, I had printed some self-encouragement, including Mike Dobies's and my rallying cheer: RFP. In retrospect, my use of the Pocket Guide in this and subsequent years at the Barkley has been a successful technique for helping me stay on course, and recording my pro-gress on each loop. I wish I had kept better notes in prior years about my times at various mile-points along the course. It is nice now, while writing this book in 2009, to have several years worth of data in these Pocket Guides that I have used in each of the years I have run the Barkley since 1997.

It is worth noting that I had included only three blank columns in which to write my times. Despite Mark Williams's 100-mile completion two years prior, I was not even thinking of attempting more than three loops. I was choosing to continue to self-limit my thinking, planning, and running ability to three loops.

However, rumor had it that David Horton was not limiting his thinking to three loops. He came to Frozen Head in 1997 with the intention of becoming the first American, and second person ever, to complete the Barkley 100. I had spoken to Gary by telephone in late March, and written a list of prospective entrants. I noted what Gary said and even put it in quotation marks: "Horton is serious." Another runner about whom I quoted Gary was a Californian, Dallas Jones, who Gary said was "doing the hundred." Dallas reportedly had run a half-marathon in 1:11. I put an asterisk in my notes beside Horton's name, and wrote: "* = I told Gary I thought these would finish the 100." I also listed my predictions of who would finish the 60-mile, and in what order: Horton, Satterfield, Wilson, Wood, Dobies, Ralph, myself, and Milan. We will soon see how these prognostications compared to reality.

Gary's post-race report this year appeared in the June 1997 issue of *UltraRunning*. He reports that on race morning, Saturday, April 5, 1995, the campground was awakened to the blare of a bugle. Davy Henn, the elder of the two sons of Karl Raw Dog and Cathy Henn, was the bugler in his Boy Scout Troop. Gary had invited Davy to come to Frozen Head and blow his bugle in appropriate tunes to note various occasions. The first such occasion was *First Call*, which Davy sounded at about 7 AM. This signified that the race would start in one hour. The bugling custom at Barkley was thus begun and would henceforth be a part of the annual Barkley tradition.

Assembly was bugled at about 8 AM. We runners gathered at the closed gate that constituted the Start/Finish line, and Gary started the race with his customary ceremonious lighting of a cigarette. The most frequent use of the bugle that weekend would be to play *Taps*, the traditional military tune signifying the end of the day, or death. But in this case, *Taps* would be played for each runner who reached the end of his or her Barkley run unsuccessfully. The phrase "tapped out" thus became synonymous with DNFing the Barkley. To add a little ego-deflating insult, *Taps* would be played even for those who successfully finished the three-loop run, but did not complete the 100-mile. Thus most of us runners could look forward to being tapped out with our own personal serenade on a bugle.

David Horton led the field back to camp after the first loop, in a time of 8:41:59, a wisely conservative pace compared to that of the previous couple of years on the Two Hells course. Running virtually with David was his friend, Andrew Thompson. Next in, only seven minutes later, were Wilson and Dobies. Then came four others between ten and 53 minutes behind the leaders: Satterfield, Purloin, Lanham, and Wood. Then after another 26-minute gap came a group comprising Milanovich, MacLean, DeWalt, Wilson Brasington, and Trammell. I was the 14th to arrive, in 10:11:29, just a little ahead of my prescribed "nominal schedule" time of 10.5 hours.

Although Craig Wilson and Mike Dobies had run the first loop together, Craig had lost one of the book pages that he had collected at one of the nine book locations. Turning in a complete set of pages to Gary at the end of each loop is a requirement to be officially counted as having completed the loop. Since Craig had been with other runners, mostly Mike Dobies, who could vouch for Craig, it was obvious that he had run the full loop. However, rules in sporting events must be followed to have meaningful competition. Gary applied the rule impartially, and technically disqualified Craig. However, Craig wanted to and was allowed to continue in an unofficial status. As Gary wrote: "Craig went on, now truly running only for the love of the run."

Gary noted in his *UltraRunning* article that the bottled water that was normally deposited for the runners' use at Coffin Springs was not there this year. This was not intentional on Gary's part. Apparently, the driver of the vehicle used to deliver the water, probably a park employee, had unintentionally left the water at the wrong location along the jeep road. I remember getting to Coffin Springs and finding no water. However, I was carrying iodine tablets just in case, and this was a case. I got some water from the spring named after Coffin, put some iodine in it, and continued on my way. I don't recall any of the runners making a big deal or complaining too much about the missing water. I think that something about most Barkley runners allows us to accept adversity and deal with it as best we can. Otherwise, we wouldn't go to the Barkley; at least not more than once.

The weather was relatively warm and dry Saturday, contributing to 24 (counting Craig) of the 31 starters finishing loop one. One runner who did not finish loop one was the speedy Dallas Jones. He got lost on the first loop and spent about 13 hours *out there* before finding his way back to camp.

Eighteen runners started loop two, with David Horton in first place. However, with the sunny weather, David had made a fateful decision to forego carrying rain gear on loop two. He soon paid a price for this bit of weight-saving, as the forecasted rain began while the leading runners were early into loop two. David, not dressed for the soaking rain and cold that visited us that night, was the first second-loop runner to quit and come back to camp to be tapped out. This was sadly ironic because so many, including myself, had expected David to show us that Americans, too, could finish the 100-mile Barkley. We would have to wait to see if anyone else could show us. But we didn't have to wait long.

With the badly deteriorating weather that seems so typical during Barkley, only six of the 18 loop-two starters, including Craig, finished that loop. Times were between 22:42 and 25:03, nearly three or more hours longer than the second-loop times of the leaders in the previous two years. The field then dwindled further, as only Dobies, Wilson, and Wood did a third loop, going in the counterclockwise direction. The added difficulty of doing the loop in the counterclockwise direction was once again about to rear its head.

Gary wrote in his *UltraRunning* article that "As a hedge against boredom, the third loop is run in reverse." This idea worked, as none of the three remaining runners appeared to get bored on their third loop. In fact, all three runners reported difficulty navigating the loop in the reverse direction. Mike and Craig, still together, had difficulty locating the book at the base of Hell, near the New River. They reported spending nearly two hours there looking for the book.   They eventually found it and pressed onward, reaching the three-loop finish with an hour and 21 minutes to spare before the 40-hour cutoff time.   This left only first-timer Blake Wood *out there* on the course alone. With just a few miles to go, on the dreaded NBT approaching Phillips Creek, Blake got off-trail in the growing dark.   This was close to the same area where I had had my race-ending problems finding the trail back in 1992. When Blake got back on trail, as Gary described: "To make the [time] limit he had to run three miles, including 1,600 feet of climb and another 1,600 of descent, at absolute top speed."   Blake raced down the final switchbacks of the Bird Mountain trail, and up to the finish gate.   He arrived with the dramatically small margin of only 2 minutes and 25 seconds remaining on the 40-hour clock.

Craig was technically disqualified but, to his great credit, he had finished the distance.   Gary compared Craig's good sportsmanship in accepting his disqualification to that of Tom Possert in 1988: "Like Tom Possert (all those years ago), Craig proved his true quality as an athlete and as a man by facing a cruelly unfair outcome without a single complaint.   For what it is worth, they each received the same award as the winner; my unqualified respect."

Recalling my pre-race predictions for this year listed earlier, I was again too optimistic.   There were no 100-mile finishers, and only two (or three) Fun Run finishers, compared to my predicted eight.   But at least I had correctly named Wilson, Wood, and Dobies among my predicted finishers.

And what about myself?   I had optimistically predicted my own three-loop finish.   I did well through the first loop, and was in my tent getting ready for loop two when the rains came.   I glumly sat there waiting for the rain to abate.   Finally I got disgusted with my own cowardice, and stepped out of the tent.   It was not raining nearly as hard as it had seemed like, with the sound amplified inside the tent.   I informed Gary that I was going to start loop two.   Soon after starting, I caught up to Ken Solakian from New Jersey, another Barkley multiple-time DNFer.   We decided to run together.   We successfully navigated the early part of the loop, including the infamous Phillips Creek crossing in the dark, and were headed up Jury Ridge when I noticed that Ken was lagging behind.   At one tricky point on the trail, I looked back and could not see his flashlight.   I called out to him, but got no response. With chagrin, I went a short way back down the trail, calling his name, until I found him going off in a slightly wrong direction on a faint game trail.   He rejoined me on the correct trail, and we continued.   We eventually caught up to John DeWalt near the Garden Spot.   The three of us continued onward together.   I recall that we got off the best line going down to the New River below Leonard's Buttslide, and wasted time skirting some too-steep terrain getting down to the New River in the dark.   For years to come, John did not let me forget that I had led our little group too far to the left on the descent into Hell.   We finally got to the right place at the bottom, went along the gorge and crossed the New River, and collected our pages from the bottom of Hell. We then started the arduous climb up.   By the time we got to the top of Hell, I had had enough fun and running.   I also feared the descent that lay ahead of us, down the Zip Line, in the dark and on wet rocks.   With this combination of fatigue and fear, I utilized my knowledge of the trails and, together with John DeWalt, took the South Old Mac trail that short-cuts back down to the park. My only minuscule shred of satisfaction was that this was the farthest I had ever gotten on the Two Hells course—about 31 Barkley Miles in 19:32, not counting the additional 1:42 it took to hike glumly back to camp to be tapped out.

Here is the list of known runners, their numbers of Barkley starts, and loop-finishing times for 1997.

1. Mike Dobies (1)   8:49:43   22:42:57   38:38:52
2. Blake Wood (1)   9:34:56   24:52:09   39:57:35
3. Craig Wilson (3)   8:49:42*22:42:56*38:38:55*DQed for missing page.
4. Fred Purloin (10)   8:56:58   23:02:55
5. Wilson Brasington (4)10:01:33   25:02:49
6. Eliza MacLean (1)   10:01:30   25:02:50
7. Ken Solakian (3)   10:36:20   Finished loop two over the time limit.
8. David Horton (5)   8:41:59
9. Andrew Thompson (1) 8:42:08
10. DeWayne Satterfield (2) 8:52:21
11. Reid Lanham (2)   9:17:00
12. Milan Milanovich (4) 10:01:06
13. John DeWalt (10)   10:01:31
14. Kerry Trammell (2)   10:01:34
15. Frozen Ed Furtaw (7)10:11:29
16. Rich Schuler (3)   10:40:53
17. Matt Mahoney (3)   10:45:15
18. Debra Moore (2)   11:30:05
19. Chris Ralph (1)   11:30:06
20. Bill Johnson (1)   11:30:07
21. Jim Dill (8)   11:44:44
22. Nick Williams (6)   11:51:27
23. Teeter Benedetti (5)   12:33:59
24. Wayne Brasington (4)12:34:00
25. Old Gristle Peyton (5)~13:40 Completed loop one over the time limit.
26. Laurie Ann Schuler (1)~13:40 Completed loop one over the time limit.
27. Greg Shoener (2)   Quit on loop one.
28. Norm Carlson (1)   Lost on loop one.
29. Doug Barrows (1)   Lost on loop one.
30. Stu Gleman (3)   Lost on loop one.
31. Dallas Jones (1)   Lost on loop one.
31 Starters

In my records from 1997, I have a copy of a page of quotes from Barkley runners that Gary had compiled over the years. Some of these sayings are hilarious, some rather poignant. The list is printed below. The last quote is one that I wrote from Gary himself, that he uttered on April 4, 1997. In an understated way, he finally admitted that the course was longer than the stated distance. But don't expect him to admit this again.

+++++++++++

The Barkley Marathons
Famous Inspirational Quotes

"This is not a trail"
"This is not a race"
"Oh God, I can't believe it hurts so bad."
"I thought this would be the toughest thing I ever did... it is much worse than that."
"Any thing that doesn't kill you (isn't the Barkley)"
"I never met a hill that didn't hurt."
"Every race has bad places, this one just doesn't have any good places."
"I think I need to go spend the rest of the weekend with my wife."
"It is not man against man, it is all the men against *that*."
"You must understand, I just can't do it."
"I have never taken over an hour to do a half mile before."
"I think I'll just wait here by the fire till my ass comes dragging in after me... then I'm gonna take what's left of it home!"
"I sure hope I never come back."
"This is just meaningless suffering without a point."
"I found the awful thing that waits in the night, and it was me."
"You cannot understand until you have been *Out There*."
"It would be better to smash my head in with that big rock."
"Anyone who doesn't think one loop is an achievement can kiss my ass."
"So I decided to go the easiest route, and in no time I was miles from the park."
"You must only not quit, then you will finish... Now, I must quit."
"I'm not sure where I was, but it was hard as hell to get to."
"Hear me, my people, my body is broken and torn. From where the sun now stands I will run no more, forever."
"It's probably a hair over a hundred." (Gary Cantrell, April 4, 1997)
+++++++++++

Below is a copy of the essay that I wrote as an entry requirement for the 1997 Barkley Marathons.

Why I Should Be Allowed To Run The Barkley
My Plan To Finish Barkley - Essay #7 in a Series
(January 31, 1997)

I should be allowed to run the Barkley for the seventh time because I have developed My Plan To Finish Barkley. Relatively few runners have finished Barkley, and I will be one of the few in 1997. This cocksure assertion is based on My Plan. I won't call it "The" Plan because I recognize that other plans may also lead others to a Barkley finish. But I am convinced that My Plan will enable me to finish Barkley in 1997.

My Plan has three aspects: physical, mental, and psychological. These aspects of My Plan will be discussed in detail in this essay.

Physical: The physical aspect of My Plan involves training, material preparation, and execution during the run.   For training, I plan to have run my highest average weekly mileage in several years.   While that level will still be low by normal ultrarunner standards, it will be higher than my previous training level for numerous years during which I have finished many ultras.   My training will also incorporate substantial effort on steep mountainsides with a similar gradient to Barkley's 1,000 feet per mile.   Material preparation will include planning and bringing all the camping and running necessities to Frozen Head State Park for a several-day effort.   During-race physical execution includes conservative pacing and nutritional intake of over 4,000 calories per loop.   Using proper lighting and apparel are also part of the physical execution for which I will be well prepared.

Mental: The mental aspect of My Plan to finish Barkley involves course knowledge and strategy.   These elements are embodied in my Pocket Guide To The Barkley Marathons, a copy of which is attached to this essay.   The essence of the Pocket Guide is to mentally decompose the Barkley loop into its 20 nominal one-mile increments.   This approach has been adapted from the wisdom of many ultrarunners who have learned to mentally see an ultra as a sequence of relatively short and achievable increments.   In the Pocket Guide, each so-called Barkley Mile is an approximation of a one-mile increment which has a distinguishing end-point.   During the run, I will merely have to continue to make Relentless Forward Progress (RFP) one Barkley Mile at a time.   The concept of RFP as a mental tool to running Barkley was adapted from the phrase "relentless forward motion" as used by Stacey Page, the director of the Bighorn Mountain ultra.   That phrase was discussed by Charles Steele, an ultrarunner from Montana, in an Internet ultra-list article about ultrarunning as a metaphor for life.   RFP will be my "ultra quote/ slogan/mantra/credo," as Charles called it in his article, for finishing Barkley in 1997 and the Pocket Guide which I will carry will be my physical reminder of this mental technique.   (Note - the Pocket Guide is based on the loop route as used in the 1995 and 1996 Barkley Marathons.   I recognize that the loop may be different for 1997.   If so I will modify the Guide accordingly after I receive updated course information.)

Psychological: I believe the psychological is the most important aspect of My Plan To Finish Barkley.   The effort required to finish Barkley is so prodigious as to seem nearly impossible.   But like "the little engine that could," I will practice positive assertion and affirmation to convince myself that I can finish.   I have done it before and I know I can do it again.   My recent string of three consecutive DNFs at Barkley has, unfortunately, conditioned me to make it psychologically easier to quit, and this represents a psychological hurdle that I must overcome.   But those same DNFs have also toughened my current resolve to finish.   I will finish Barkley this year.

I recently had a powerful insight about one's ability to do the seemingly impossible.   I was in a casual Christmas-luncheon conversation with Dr. Dean Radin, a world-renowned parapsychologist who does research on psychic phenomena, and who works in the same building where I work at UNLV.   Dean told me that one of the strongest indicators of a person's ability to manifest psychic powers in laboratory testing is that person's *belief* in their psychic abilities. When he said this, it was like a light bulb turning on above my head. Our power to do the seemingly impossible is based largely on our belief that we can do it. Of course! How elegantly simple! I immediately saw the key to my finishing Barkley. I must simply believe that I can and will do it!

Besides assertion, another psychological technique which I am already employing is visualization. This involves repeatedly practicing the mental imagery of seeing myself happily running and finishing Barkley. My Pocket Guide is very helpful in this visualization process, as it helps me to memorize the course which I frequently rehearse in my mind. This process is imprinting into my psyche the vision of my successfully using RFP to navigate and complete the course, and exuberantly sprinting to the finish line! Thus the psychological aspect links closely with the mental aspect of My Plan. They are also closely related to the physical aspect, as my awareness of my highly trained and well-prepared condition serves to further reinforce my positive belief that I will finish. Another factor which further boosts my positive attitude about finishing Barkley this year is the realization that this should be an "up" year. This relates to the theme of my Barkley Essay #5 in a Series (1995). Since 1995 was a relatively "up" year in terms of Barkley finishes, and 1996 was a "down" year, the forecast made in my 1995 essay has proven generally true. Projecting on the basis of this "up-down" theory, 1997 should be another "up" year. With My Plan, I predict that I will be one of several successful finishers in 1997.

In summary, I am sure that I will finish Barkley this year because I have developed and will follow My Plan To Finish Barkley. Therefore, I must be allowed to prove that My Plan works.

Chapter 17
1998: Quitters Countdown

After my three consecutive years of humbling by the tougher Two Hells Barkley course, I took a few years off before returning to the Barkley. So 1998 is another year for which I have little information. My sources of information for this year are the June 1998 *UltraRunning* post-race article written by Gary, and an Internet posting with the results and a few paragraphs of stories by Matt Mahoney. Matt was at this year's Barkley, for his fourth straight year. So his Internet article was based on an eyewitness and participant perspective. This article was posted on the since-defunct web site Ultramarathon World on April 7, 1998. Since the Barkley race started on Saturday, April 4 this year, these results were posted just a day after the results were known. It was nice to be able to see these results so soon after the race. This ability to acquire information on such a timely basis is certainly one of the great benefits of modern computer technology and the Internet.

Gary's *UltraRunning* article started with a few introductory paragraphs written around the theme of quitting. He stated that: "of more than 300 starters, only one has ever not quit." Of course, the "one" he was referring to was Mark Williams, the only 100-mile finisher. However, I believe that this statement involves a slight revision of history. The total number of reported starters of all the twelve Barkley events from 1986 through 1997 was 308. However, recall that in the first three years, only one race distance was offered each year, the three-loop race variously referred to as 50-some miles. In those three years, there was a total of 48 starters, with one 55-mile finisher, in 1988. I was that first finisher, and I did not "quit" after finishing those three loops. I had finished the full race distance that existed that year. After that, Gary created and announced the 100-miler. So in my opinion, Gary would have been more accurate to say that of the 260 starters *since the inception of the 100-miler,* only one had ever not quit.

In any case, Gary's point was colorfully made that nearly all Barkley starts ended with the runner quitting before reaching the finish of the 100-mile race. He noted that many race applicants made the claim to him that, "I'll never quit!" He went on to say, "It is the totality of the Barkley that must be overcome. It is not just a matter of not quitting. Barkley runners do not quit. They are beaten. Physically and mentally, the runners are beaten. Nevertheless, it is something you cannot understand until you have been 'out there'."

Gary commented that there had been torrential downpours the day before the race during the chicken barbeque, but that by the start of the race, the rainfall was only "rather modest." Colder and windy conditions with some snow, sleet, and hail up at the mountaintops would be reported later. Gary's article then became a time-series listing of events in the sequence in which they occurred. For example, he described the start of the race as follows: "**Race Time: 0:00:00:** Thirty-five runners march jauntily up the jeep road and disappear into the woods." The next entry was: "**1:18:49:** South Carolina's Claude Sinclair comes in. A late entry off the waiting list, Claude has not prepared especially well and as a semi-veteran he realizes by the top of the first climb that he is not ready. So he comes back the way he went out. One down, 34 to go."

The article continues in this fashion to describe the progress and fate of each runner. For those time-entries which describe a runner quitting, Gary gave a brief description of their proffered excuses. He then ended each such entry with a count of how many runners were out, and a countdown of how many remained in contention. By the end, all thirty-five runners' times for each loop, and reason for quitting, were accounted for.

Matt's Internet article listed 33 runners with several columns of information for each. These columns corresponded to either their time of completing each loop, or a several-word explanation of their result. Eleven of these personal results were simply the acronym RTC, for Refused To Continue. This referred to a runner who was back at camp after completing one or more loops, and who was still within the time limit to continue, but declined to do so. Many of the others' basic reason given was the word "returned" and a time. This implied that they had decided to quit somewhere *out there* on the course, rather than while in camp. These runners subsequently had to hike or run back to camp to report to Gary that they were quitting, and get tapped out. Yet another subset of runners was reported as having "missed cutoff" with a time given. This implied that the runner had finished the loop, but did so over the time limit for that loop to be counted officially.

From the names and times given in the two articles, I compiled the following lists of runners.

Returning former Barkley winners were David Horton, Mike Dobies, and Fred Purloin.

Other returning former Barkley three-loop finishers were Blake Wood, Suzi Thibeault, John DeWalt, and Greg Shoener.

Other returning former Barkley non-finishers were DeWayne Satterfield, Reid Lanham, Kerry Trammell, Matt Mahoney, Stuart Gleman, Bill Johnson, Eliza MacLean, Andrew Thompson, Dale Sutton, Jim Dill, Debra Moore, Buttslide Martin, Wayne and Wilson Brasington, Doug Barrows, Norm Carlson, and Claude Sinclair.

Barkley Virgins this year were Mark Dorion, a well-established ultrarunner of 20+ years with well over 100 ultras under his belt; David White from nearby Knoxville, Tennessee; Dink Taylor, one of the fastest ultrarunners in the southeast; Fred Vance, a well-known ultrarunner from California; Leslie Hunt, Kerry Trammell's fiancee, who would eventually become Leslie Trammell; Sue Thompson; Merrianne Brittain; Jon Basham; Steve Simmons; Tom Bennett; and Bill Andrews.

David Horton, DeWayne Satterfield, and Dink Taylor led after the first loop, in 8:06. Blake Wood and David White were next, some 51 minutes later. Eliza MacLean was next, just six minutes behind. Mike Dobies did a relatively slow first loop (for him) to show the course to Sue Thompson, his girlfriend from Michigan. Twenty-eight runners completed the first loop within its 13:20 time limit. Stuart Gleman also finished the loop, but was 16 minutes over the cutoff.

Six less-fortunate starters managed to get lost on loop one and gradually returned to camp from various directions. Gary gave a colorful description of Doug Barrows' route-finding impairment: "**10:07:25:** Floridian Doug Barrows, whose meandering is fast becoming a legend, returns from another aimless exercise in misdirection." Surprisingly, even a former three-loop finisher was not able to successfully navigate the first loop, as described by Gary: "**10:37:03:** Greg Shoener (Ohio) despite a previous fun-run finish, returns after circling the Garden Spot Checkpoint aimlessly for hours. Eight down, 27 to go."

Some runners waited until later in the race to give Gary grist for colorful descriptions of the various reasons for quitting. "**14:51:00:** Mark Dorion appears out of the darkness with one of the best stories we have heard in years. His group had stopped to rest and don warmer gear and at the end of the break, Mark forgot to put his pack back on. Doomed without his supplies, he had been unable to locate the exact spot where he had left his pack and started back to camp, only to have his headlamp die. Somehow he had made it back over the mountain and into camp in total darkness. A nice trick, but the same result. Fifteen down, 20 to go."

Gary and Matt both reported that the weather was very nice on day two, sunny and in the 60s. Horton again led after the second loop, in 18:24. Satterfield was only about 25 minutes behind, but was too tired to continue. Dobies and Wood were next, together in about 21:48; unlike Horton, they took a short nap before continuing onto loop three. Nine more runners, for a total of 13, finished loop two within its 26:40 time limit, in the following order: Lanham, White, Taylor, Purloin, Vance, DeWalt, Trammell, Hunt, and Wilson Brasington. In addition, Matt Mahoney (29:33) and Bill Johnson (31:02) finished the second loop, but over the time limit.

Seven of the 13 continued on to the third loop, in the relatively unfamiliar counterclockwise direction. Lanham and White both got lost separately near the same point approaching Chimney Top, and ended up quitting as soon as they could find their ways back to camp. The remaining five runners all finished the three-loop Fun Run.

Now the best part of the story of 1998 began. But it is a short part. After his excellent finish of the fun run, Horton did not stop. He became only the second person in Barkley history to attempt a fourth loop. Furthermore, he was about 52 minutes ahead of Mark Williams's 100-mile pace of 1995. However, Horton had not yet stopped for any significant rest time. This effort without a break surely imposed on David a level of fatigue that contributed to the subsequent turn of events. Recall that the third and fourth loops were now run in the reverse direction. As he was going down the steep Hell hill, David apparently wandered a little too far to the right. When he got to the bottom of the mountain, he came to a stream. He was expecting to arrive at the New River, which would be flowing from his left to right. Instead he presumably encountered Straight Fork, a stream flowing from his right to left. He later described his perception at the time as the stream "running uphill." He apparently took a break there to recover his senses, and took his glasses off and set them down. As Gary described it, then: "Somewhere, getting lost only a few hundred yards from the Hell checkpoint, he became convinced he could not find them [his glasses] in time to complete the last 30 miles. He had 23 hours left at the time and just like that, there were none."

He went back to camp without his glasses and without completing the fourth loop.

Despite his failure on the fourth loop, David had broken another Barkley barrier. He had become the first American to make a legitimate attempt at the Barkley 100. David's 70-mile effort was the second-longest distance run in Barkley history. Although Mark Williams remained the only 100-mile finisher, at least a little more progress had been made toward chipping into the Barkley's dominance over the runners. As we will see, others would soon follow in this quest.

Below are the runners, their numbers of Barkley starts, and their loop-finishing times for 1998.

1. David Horton (6)   8:06:15   18:24:08   30:23:00   Quit on loop four.
2. Blake Wood (2)   8:57:17   21:47:58   35:32:46
3. Mike Dobies (2)   9:06:05   21:47:58   35:32:46
4. Fred Vance (1)   10:03:10   24:41:50   39:23:45
5. John DeWalt (11)   10:00:12   24:59:50   39:23:46 (becoming the
    oldest-ever Fun Run finisher, at age 61 years 9 months and 19 days)
6. DeWayne Satterfield (3) 8:06:15   18:49:36
7. Reid Lanham (3)   9:19:44   22:58:41   Lost on loop three.
8. David White (1)   8:57:17   23:47:35   Lost on loop three.
9. Dink Taylor (1)   8:06:15   23:47:35
10. Fred Purloin (11)   9:19:44   23:47:35
11. Kerry Trammell (3) 10:11:23   25:57:26
12. Wilson Brasington (5) 10:11:25   25:57:26
13. Leslie Hunt (1)   10:11:26   25:57:26
14. Matt Mahoney (4)   11:35:05   29:33*Finished loop two over the time limit.
15. Bill Johnson (2)   11:35:06   31:02*Finished loop two over the time limit.
16. Eliza MacLean (2)   9:03:30   Quit during loop two.
17. Sue Thompson (1)   9:06:05
18. Andrew Thompson (2)10:03:10   Quit during loop two.
19. Mark Dorion (1)   10:11:22   Quit during loop two.
20. Steve Simmons (1)   10:11:24   Quit during loop two.
21. Jon Basham (1)   10:33:49
22. Suzi Thibeault (4)   11:06:13
23. Trail Dale Sutton (4)11:06:14   Quit during loop two.
24. Debra Moore (3)   11:22:22   Quit during loop two.
25. Tom Bennett (1)   11:22:22   Quit during loop two.
26. Buttslide Martin (6) 11:35:07   Quit during loop two.
27. Merrianne Brittain (1)12:15:19
28. Wayne Brasington (5)12:15:20
29. Stuart Gleman (3)   13:36:59* Finished loop one over the time limit.
30. Greg Shoener (2)   Lost on loop one.
31. Doug Barrows (2)   Lost on loop one.
32. Jim Dill (9)   Lost on loop one.
33. Bill Andrews (1)   Lost on loop one.
34. Norm Carlson (2)   Lost on loop one.
35. Claude Sinclair (2) Lost on loop one.
35 Starters

Chapter 18
1999: Barkley Racing; Ugly and Beautiful Truth

The fourteenth Barkley Marathons started on April 3, 1999. An impressive field of top runners was there. Eight former three-loop finishers started the race this year, the most ever. These eight were Horton, Herr, Dobies, Woods, Wilson, DeWalt, West, and Purloin. Other returners included Satterfield, Andrew Thompson, MacLean, Trammell, Hunt, Lanham, Sue Thompson, Gleman, White, Simmons, Mahoney, both Brasingtons, Johnson, Brittain, Carlson, Hughes, Martin, Peyton, Andrews, and Jim Dill (for his tenth start). Newcomers this year included Robert Youngren, a speedy runner from Alabama; Randy Isler, an established runner from New Mexico; Tom Smith; and Geoff Scott. Gary reported in his annual post-Barkley article in the June 1999 *UltraRunning* that 33 runners started the race this year.

Most of the above-named field was comprised of returnees, including many with multiple victories, more with multiple three-loop finishes, and even more with multiple DNFs. Fittingly, Gary wrote in the introduction of his article about the "sickos" in the ultrarunning community: "They are attracted to the genuinely impossible. It is those 'sickos,' and their amazing ability to forget last year's dismal failure before the next race, that keeps the Barkley filled up, year after year." Even though I personally was not there this year, I knew that I was one of those sickos that Gary was referring to.

Another noteworthy statement written by Gary in his *UltraRunning* article was that: "Up until Mark Williams spoiled things for everyone by completing the brutal course, it was most popular to deny that the event was even possible." This reflects my earlier statements. I was one of those who had erroneously believed that the 100 was impossible, until Mark Williams proved us wrong. But Mark didn't "spoil things" with his finish, in my opinion. He made the Barkley even better. I think it is better that the Barkley is at the edge of possible, rather than truly impossible. Anyone could devise a race that is impossible. But the beauty of the Barkley is that is possible for only about one percent of its competitors to finish it. This is how finely Gary has tuned it to correspond to the edge of possibility.

After some introductory remarks in his *UltraRunning* article, Gary described the unfolding of the race. He referred to the runners' "testosterone" that led to quite a contest among the front runners. It was interesting to note that ten miles into the race, the top ten runners were still in a pack. These ten runners were Isler, Herr, Horton, Purloin, Dobies, Satterfield, Wood, Youngren, Wilson, and Lanham. For fans of ultramarathon racing, it is a fantasy to imagine this stellar field of runners going head-to-head in a lead pack at any ultra. However, the twin climbs of Little Hell (now so-called to distinguish it from the more recently added Big Hell) and Rat Jaw served to spread out this front group. By the time the runners reached the end of the first 20-mile loop, Randy Isler led in 7:58:58, followed in order by Horton, Purloin, Dobies, Satterfield, Wood, Youngren, and Wilson all within an hour of the leader. Randy was known to be a good runner, but it was a little surprising to see him in the lead in his first tour of Frozen Head, among so many other strong runners who had been to many previous Barkleys. Following the front eight were Andrew Thompson, Animal Herr, and Eliza MacLean, all within a few seconds of each other and about 20 minutes behind Craig Wilson.

One of my favorite statements made by a quitting runner was quoted in Gary's *UltraRunning* article. Upon finishing the first loop, DeWayne Satterfield announced the end of his race by proclaiming: "Barkley BIG, DeWayne small!"

Another runner who quit after one loop was Lou "Old Gristle" Peyton. In her sixth Barkley, Old Gristle had difficulty finding the book at Beech Fork, at the bottom of the Zip Line and Big Hell. She proved her toughness and the appropriateness of her nickname by spending most of the night in the vicinity of Beech Fork. She finally finished loop one on Sunday morning, more than seven hours and 40 minutes over the time limit. This established a record for the longest time *out there* on loop one of any runner so far in the history of the Barkley. However, as the reader will see in later chapters, this record would eventually be broken in the future in other tales of failure.

Twenty-nine runners finished the first loop under the time limit, and twenty of them continued. David Horton was the first runner to start loop two. However, he did not stay in the lead for long. As Gary described, David "led the way among the second 20-mile casualties as he came back without an excuse. Simply that he did not think the 100 mile was within his reach, and he was unable to bear the suffering necessary to finish the fun run. And, as a four-time fun run finisher, David knew well what sort of suffering that entailed."

Seven runners finished the second loop, with the surprising Isler still in the lead over Wood by about 17 minutes, with Dobies another 11 minutes after. In somewhat of a departure from the typical pairing and teaming of many of the runners in most years, this year the top five after loop two were all separated by between ten minutes and over three hours. Mike Dobies led onto the third loop, with Isler about 12 minutes behind, and Wood another half-hour after Isler. However, as so often happens at the Barkley, the competition soon turned into cooperation among runners moving at similar paces. Randy and Mike paired up and ran most of the third loop together. Blake caught them about mid-loop, but declined to stay with them. He moved into the lead. As Gary wrote in *UltraRunning:* "Finally, alone in the front, Blake pursued his only remaining opponent, a 100-mile finish." Gary had earlier reported that Blake, who had finished the three-loop Fun Run in each of the past two years, was "determined to challenge the 100."

Wood subsequently won the Fun Run, with Isler and Dobies about an hour and 20 minutes behind. These were the only Fun Run finishers within the time limit. However, I was informed many years later by Mike Dobies that Leslie Hunt and John DeWalt also finished three loops this year in 47:48, nearly eight hours over the 40-hour time limit. This shows incredible determination to continue despite being well over the time to be considered finishers. Gary's *UltraRunning* article made no mention of Leslie and John's gutsy performance.

After three loops, Blake was in a good position to continue. As Gary noted, Blake was nearly two hours ahead of Mark Williams's pace from his

1995 100-mile finish.   Blake did not waste this opportunity that he had worked so hard for.   He headed out onto a fourth loop, becoming only the third man ever to do so.   Although Isler and Dobies were also still within the time limit for continuing after three loops, they declined and had to suffer the ignominy of being tapped out despite their excellent performances.

Gary then described in his *UltraRunning* article how Blake fared on his fourth loop.   "The last survivor on the trail, Blake Wood was facing a harsh reality.   Hallucinating, talking to trees and rocks, scarcely able to maintain a one-mile per hour pace, Blake repeatedly had to stop in order to remember where he was.   Valiantly he continued through the 3-mile checkpoint.   There he had to face the truth.   He could not continue this for another 36 miles.   The 100 mile was not going to happen.   More than five hours after setting out from the 60-mile mark, more than five hours for a seven-mile round trip, Blake was back.   And the Barkley was over."

Here is the list of the runners, their numbers of Barkley starts, and their loop-finishing times for 1999.

1. Blake Wood (3)   8:39:30   21:03:26   33:19:46 Quit on loop four.
2. Randy Isler (1)   7:58:58   20:46:36   34:40:04
3. Mike Dobies (3)   8:06:57   21:14:16   34:40:05
4. John DeWalt (12)   9:35:30   25:02:27   47:48* Finished loop three
   over the time limit.
5. Leslie Hunt (2)   9:35:31   25:57:48   47:48* Finished loop three
   over the time limit.
6. Craig Wilson (4)   8:57:45   25:17:21
7. Kerry Trammell (4)   9:35:32   25:57:49
8. Matt Mahoney (5)   10:58:26   28:07:34* Finished loop two over the
   time limit.
9. Steve Simmons (2)   10:33:20   29:40:02* Finished loop two over the
   time limit.
10. David Horton (7)   8:04:28   Quit during loop two.
11. Fred Purloin (12)   8:06:56
12. DeWayne Satterfield (4) 8:17:11
13. Robert Youngren (1) 8:55:13
14. Andrew Thompson (3) 9:17:01
15. Animal Herr (7)   9:17:16
16. Eliza MacLean (3)   9:17:23
17. Sue Thompson (2)   9:59:18
18. Reid Lanham (4)   10:00:09
19. Stuart Gleman (4)   10:15:42
20. David White (2)   10:24:28
21. Geoff Scott (1)   10:51:29
22. Wilson Brasington (6) 10:58:27
23. Dick West (6)   11:18:38
24. David Hughes (2)   11:21:35
25. Bill Johnson (3)   11:22:31
26. Merrianne Brittain (2) 11:24:10
27. Norm Carlson (3)   12:44:45
28. Wayne Brasington (6) 12:50:38

29. Buttslide Martin (7) 13:03:37
30. <u>Old Gristle Peyton</u> (6)   21:00:11* Finished loop one over the time limit.
31. Tom Smith (1)   Quit during loop one.
32. Jim Dill (10)   Quit during loop one.
33. Bill Andrews (2)   Quit during loop one.
33 Starters

This year Gary's *UltraRunning* article was titled: "Brushy Mountain Massacre: The Ugly Truth about the 1999 Barkley Marathons." In summarizing at the end of the article, he noted that both ordinary runners as well as exceptional runners, champions, and record holders have all failed at the Barkley. He then told what I think is one of the beautiful truths about Barkley: "But there is something more important that they did not fail. They did not fail to accept a challenge simply because success was improbable, even impossible. When they accepted that challenge, they were winners. What happened to them 'out there' was inevitable."

It was good to read that despite all his taunting and belittling of the Barkley runners over the years, Gary truly admires those runners. I certainly share that sentiment.

Chapter 19
2000: Mountains Coming Apart

It was a new millennium, and a new chance for the world to test itself against the world's toughest trail race. The Barkley attracted its now-usual strong field of runners.

Returning previous Barkley winners were David Horton, Eric Clifton, Craig Wilson, Mike Dobies, and Blake Wood. Other returning former three-loop finishers were Randy Isler, John DeWalt, and Dick West. Returning non-finishers were DeWayne "Small" Satterfield, Steve Simmons, Andrew Thompson, Robert Youngren, Eliza MacLean, Leslie Hunt, Kerry Trammell, David White, Matt Mahoney, the Brasington brothers, Stu Gleman, Buttslide Martin, David Hughes, Geoff Scott, Mark Dorion, Bill Johnson, and Doug Barrows.

Barkley Virgins this year included noteworthy runners Hans Put, Michael Tilden, Fred Brooks, and Sue Johnston. Sue was one of the best women ultrarunners in the country. Fred had reportedly said he would be disappointed if it took him longer than 50 hours to run five loops. It would be interesting to see how he would fare after this boasting. Other newcomers included Kevin Budd, Jurgen Teichert from Germany, Sean Hudson, Susan Gardner, and David Zuniga. This was a total of 35 starters.

In his June 2000 *UltraRunning* article reporting this year's results, Gary called this "the most potent assemblage of talent yet to assault the Barkley." He was probably correct in this assessment.

The race started on Fool's Day, Saturday, April 1, a warm and sunny day. With the strong starting field and nice weather, actual racing was in evidence from the start. This was reminiscent of last year's start, when the top ten runners were together for the first ten miles. This year, the lead pack of runners remained even tighter through the first loop than in last year's race. The first five runners (Horton, Put, Tilden, Clifton, and Brooks) finished the first loop within about a minute of each other, at about 7:37 race time. Four more runners (Satterfield, Johnston, Wilson, and Dobies) arrived back at camp within another half hour. Simmons and Wood were about another half-hour behind. Thirty-one runners completed the first loop within the time limit.

When most runners had begun the second loop, darkness and rain set in. Blake Wood picked up the pace relative to the faster starters, and had passed all the others by mid-way through the second loop. Blake was the first to finish loop two, in 19:13, more than 54 minutes ahead of Tilden, Dobies, Wilson, and Johnston who were staying in a tight pack. Eliza MacLean and Andrew Thompson were also together, more than two-and-a-half hours later. Randy Isler was the eighth and final finisher of loop two. Many of the other top first-loop runners and experienced Barkley runners had succumbed to the fast pace and rain before completing loop two.

Rain continued throughout Sunday. All eight runners who had completed loop two continued onto loop three, led by Blake Wood. Blake was again displaying his growing dominance over the course, following his three-year run of top-two-place finishes including last year's victory and attempted fourth loop. He was the first to finish the third loop, in 31:00:29, his best

Fun Run finish by nearly a 3-hour-and-19-minute improvement over his previous best, which was his winning time last year. After a short break, he did as he had done last year, and headed out on his fourth loop, becoming the first person to ever start a fourth Barkley loop more than once. We will soon see how Blake fared.

About two hours later, the strong duo of Michael Tilden and Sue Johnston completed their third loop. Sue's time of 32:57:56 was a new women's course record, easily bettering the previous women's best time of 34:32 that Suzi Thibeault and Nancy Hamilton had run on the old 55-mile course in 1991. Sue Johnston also became only the third woman to ever finish any Barkley three-loop race, and the first to finish the 60-mile course that was instituted in 1995.

Mike Dobies had done extremely well over the past three years, with a win and two third-place finishes. This year he was once again teaming with Craig Wilson, as they had done in 1997. Wilson had also had a recent string of three good years, from 1995 through 1997, with a win, another virtual tie with Dobies for a win (but in which he was technically disqualified for losing a book page), and a third-place finish in that span. This formidable pair of runners was the next to finish loop three in 2000, about two hours behind Johnston and Tilden. Eliza MacLean and Andrew Thompson were the next and final three-loop finishers, in 37:19. Both of these runners finally achieved hard-earned Fun Run completions in their fourth consecutive Barkley attempts. Eliza became the second-ever woman finisher of the Two Hells course. As we will see in a later chapter, Andrew set the stage for his future, further exploits at the Barkley.

The eighth runner who had started loop three this year was Randy Isler. Despite his fun-run finish last year, Randy got lost on his third loop going down Big Hell in the unfamiliar counterclockwise direction. This gaffe had sent him wandering out of the State Park, until he reached a highway on which he got a ride back to the park.

Michael Tilden spent nearly three hours after finishing his third loop before starting a fourth loop shortly before the time limit to do so. This marked another historic occurrence, as it thus became the first time in Barkley history that more than one runner started a fourth loop in the same race. Unfortunately, this distinction did not last long. The rains continued and strengthened during the second night. Gary described the weather and its effect in his *UltraRunning* article: "... by midnight the runners were 'out there' amidst bolts of lightning, crashing thunder, and heavy downpours. Michael Tilden's demise came soon thereafter. No one actually saw him return to camp, but we discovered him in his tent mumbling incoherently. Blake Wood, alone in the dark and wet, was the last hope."

Blake later wrote a report about his 2000 Barkley experience. It was published in the June 2000 issue of *UltraRunning*, immediately following Gary's Barkley article. Blake's description of what he experienced *out there* is one of the most interesting and gripping stories about running I have ever read. Regarding the counterclockwise fourth loop, Blake wrote: "This was the loop I had been dreading, having fallen apart here last year before reaching Chimney Top." However, this year he had a little more time margin, and he made it to the bottom of Big Hell before nightfall on day two. As he described it then: "Darkness fell as I headed up the trail toward where the Zipline ascent began. It seemed to be taking a very long time—had I gone past it? The trail didn't look at all familiar. I recognized this feeling from my fourth loop last year. My sense of time was messed up, so I couldn't trust the internal clock that says, 'I should be there by now.' I decided to trust my knowledge of the route, rather than my feelings..." This strategy worked, as Blake successfully reached the top at Indian Knob, and then the next checkpoint at Frozen Head. He continued writing: "It was 9:00 p.m. atop Frozen Head. The fog had condensed my entire world to a 10-foot circle around my feet." Blake thus noted something that many Barkley runners have identified as one of the worst aspects of wet weather at Barkley—fog at night. Unless you have experienced it, it is difficult to understand the sense of isolation and of being lost that you have when trying to move to a defined target in the woods, with no trail to follow, in the dark, and in the fog. In the spot of light formed by a flashlight or headlamp, you can see for only a few feet. It is difficult to know what lies ahead and if you are going in the right direction. I have experienced a little of this phenomenon at the Barkley and, as the reader will see in Chapter 27, it is a major reason why I stopped when I did in the 2008 Barkley.

Blake continued his article on his 2000 fourth loop by describing the rain and mud in terms such as "deluge," "quagmire," "drenching rain," "slippery as ice," "pounding rain," and "rivers of water ran down the road." He also described his difficulty staying awake: "I kept dozing off on my feet, and waking up to find myself just standing there. At one point I opened my eyes, and found myself standing right by the top of Little Hell. 'Lucky I opened my eyes here—I might have walked right past it!' I woke up, now that I had a difficult route to follow. This was the crux of the whole race. Dave Horton's '98 fourth-loop attempt had ended when he got lost descending Little Hell, and I had gotten lost here in broad daylight in previous years."

This latter statement points out the difficulty of doing the fourth loop in the reverse direction, and in the dark. Since most loops are run clockwise, the runners are much less familiar with the look and feel of the course on the counterclockwise loops. Many Barkley efforts have ended because of runners being unable to stay on course in the reverse direction. Adding this direction-reversal thus is part of Gary's cunning genius in gradually increasing the difficulty of the Barkley to keep it *out there* at the limit of the endurance of a handful of the best trail runners in the world—runners like Blake Wood.

Blake successfully navigated his descent of Little Hell, in what he called "surely one of my greatest orienteering feats!" However, he then spent some time and effort going back and forth at the bottom of Hell before finding the book. He then continued upstream along the New River, and was able to wade across in "muddy, knee-deep water." This is reminiscent of 1991, the year of "Hell and High Water," when the New River was similarly deep and difficult to cross. But now, in 2000, it was still raining and the river was getting deeper.

Blake continued in these difficult and slow conditions, and in a tribute to his determination and strength, he finished the fourth loop at daybreak on Monday in 46:36:21.   He thus became the second person, after Mark Williams five years prior, to finish a fourth loop at the Barkley, and the first person to ever complete a counterclockwise fourth loop.   When he arrived at camp, Blake had about an hour and 24 minutes before the time limit for beginning a fifth loop.   Incredibly, he had gone this time and distance without sleep.   Gary described him thus: "...his eyes were dull and lifeless, his movements slow and mechanical, but he still remained focused on the task at hand.   He retreated to his tent to take his first sleep break, although the time limit left him with less than an hour available to rest.   Then, he was back to tackle the final stage of his adventure.   He settled the discussion that had been going on during his rest, as to which direction he should choose for his final loop (the race has two clockwise loops, two counterclockwise and one of the runner's choice), by choosing the clockwise route."   The Barkley now had its second-ever runner on a fifth loop!

The heavy rain continued and so did Blake.   Near Coffin Springs, he had a surprise greeting from his friends from New Mexico, Randy Isler and Randy's dog Argus, who had hiked up to cheer Blake on—an awesome display of friendship and camaraderie.   Blake managed to keep going until he again got to the bottom of Hell—the New River gorge.

What happened next is the dramatic climax of this year's gripping tale from *out there*.   I will quote Blake's description from his *UltraRunning* report, which would be difficult or impossible to improve upon.   "Reaching book four, I got my first glimpse of the New River, and I knew in a moment that my run was over.   What was usually a small, clear, cascading stream was a muddy, foaming, raging torrent!   I decided to continue to the crossing, hoping to find some weakness in the barrier before me.   There was none.   I stood at the crossing for about 20 minutes, marveling at the sight, sorely wishing I had a camera with me.   A half dozen huge booming waterfalls launched into space where side streams hit the line of cliffs above me.   The crossing itself was at least 30 feet wide, a rolling, boiling flood carrying along large pieces of trees, which disappeared beneath the current and reappeared further down the rapids.   Before my eyes, the mountains were coming apart.   It was an amazing and beautiful thing to see.   I really wanted five loops, but wasn't even tempted to find a way across, and didn't think twice about turning back.   Attempting to cross would be suicide.   I was disappointed, but relieved at the same time.   The race was over, I knew I could have done it, and was stopped by the raw, naked forces of nature.   I hadn't given up, and didn't feel as if the course had beaten me."   It subsequently took Blake several hours to hike back to camp, where Gary tapped him out.

Blake's result at the 2000 Barkley was recorded as a DNF.   But those of us who follow the annual saga of the Barkley Marathons know that his valiant effort ranked right up there with Mark William's 100-mile completion, as the greatest runs ever yet seen at the Barkley.   In some ways Blake's run was more difficult than Mark's, because of the extreme weather this year, and the added difficulties of doing two of the five loops in the reverse direction.   But still, Mark remained as the only 100-mile finisher in the race's history.   At the end of his *UltraRunning* article, Gary reminded the world of this with his characteristic dare: "Come next spring we will be looking to write another chapter in the story of the Barkley Marathons. Perhaps then there will finally be a second finisher. Maybe it will be you. I doubt it, however." Blake, in ending his *UltraRunning* article, declared that he intended to try the Barkley again. The epic struggle of "man against *that*" would continue.

Below is the list of starters, their numbers of Barkley starts, and loop-finishing times for 2000.

1. Blake Wood (4)   8:37:34   19:13:02   31:00:29   46:46:31 Quit on loop five.
2. Michael Tilden (1)   7:36:42   20:07:19   32:57:27   Quit on loop four.
3. Sue Johnston (1)   8:03:10   20:07:44   32:57:56
4. Craig Wilson (5)   8:03:11   20:07:43   34:48:38
5. Mike Dobies (4)   8:07:05   20:07:21   34:48:39
6. Eliza MacLean (4)   9:07:09   22:41:28   37:19:08
7. Andrew Thompson (4) 9:07:07   22:41:29   37:19:09
8. Randy Isler (2)   8:44:32   23:14:04   Lost on loop three.
9. Steve Simmons (3)   8:37:01   ~25:48* Virtually finished loop two, but didn't touch the finish gate, so that he would be timed out rather than "quit."
10. David Horton (8)   7:36:37   Quit during loop two.
11. Hans Put (1)   7:36:38   Quit during loop two.
12. Eric Clifton (4)   7:36:44   Quit during loop two.
13. Fred Brooks (1)   7:37:40   Quit during loop two.
14. DeWayne Satterfield (5) 7:39:06   Quit during loop two.
15. Geoff Scott (2)   8:44:30   Lost on loop two.
16. Robert Youngren (2)   9:07:08
17. Kevin Budd (1)   9:18:50   Quit during loop two.
18. Leslie Hunt (3)   9:24:05   Quit during loop two.
19. David White (3)   9:24:06   Quit during loop two.
20. Kerry Trammell (5)   9:24:08   Quit during loop two.
21. Jurgen Teichert (1)   9:40:03   Quit during loop two.
22. Sean Hudson (1)   9:41:24
23. John DeWalt (13)   9:47:36   Quit during loop two.
24. Matt Mahoney (6)   9:49:57   Quit during loop two.
25. Wilson Brasington (7) 10:58:36   Quit during loop two.
26. Dick West (7)   10:58:41   Quit during loop two.
27. Stu Gleman (5)   11:02:19   Quit during loop two.
28. Susan Gardner (1)   11:26:45
29. Buttslide Martin (8)   11:31:36   Quit during loop two.
30. David Hughes (3)   12:24:01
31. Bill Johnson (4)   12:36:27
32. Mark Dorion (2)   Quit during loop one.
33. Wayne Brasington (7) Quit during loop one.
34. Doug Barrows (3)   Quit during loop one.
35. David Zuniga (1)   Quit during loop one.
35 Starters

Chapter 20
2001: Success but Controversy

Following the dramatic results of 2000, it is hard to imagine that things could be even more interesting at the next year's Barkley. But what happened next was both a historic positive and negative in the annals of the Barkley Marathons.

During the summer of 2000, I was thinking of returning for another run at the Barkley in 2001. I had missed the last three years (1998-2000), after having been destroyed by the Two Hells course in each of the three previous consecutive races. I guess I was missing it, because in July, 2000, as I was driving through Tennessee on a business trip, I detoured off of Interstate 40 to go up to Frozen Head for a training run. I knew that the race format now included the direction reversal on the third and fourth loops. I had never run any of the loop in the reverse direction during a Barkley race, and I figured that it would increase my chances of finishing three loops again if I could get in some training in the reverse direction. I ran from the trailhead southward and up to Chimney Top on the CTT, and then down Big Hell and up the Zip Line (no trails), and then on "candy ass" trails back to the trailhead. Because it was mid-summer, I hadn't worn long pants for running in recent months. I forget to bring them on this trip. As a result of running Big Hell and the Zip Line in shorts, my legs got badly scratched by briers. I also got poison ivy on my legs, something that I don't recall ever getting from my early spring visits to Frozen Head for the Barkley. A photo of my legs, taken a couple of days after this training run, is shown below. It is a grim reminder of why most runners wear long pants when running the Barkley.

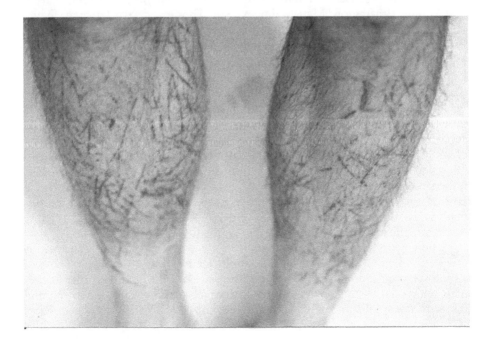

On this training run, I found what others had shown in recent years: it was harder and slower to do this part of the loop in the counterclockwise direction. When going down Big Hell, I did not arrive at the correct location at the bottom. When I got to a stream bed, I had to further navigate to get to the correct confluence. I was surprised to find the creeks dry. There was always water flowing in them when I had been there in the spring. Likewise, on the climb up the Zip Line to Indian Knob, I did not arrive directly at the correct set of capstones where the book was usually placed. When I got to the ridge I had to figure out which way to go to Indian Knob. Despite these difficulties, I was glad to have this experience in the navigational problems to be encountered if I were to ever actually attempt a counterclockwise loop during the race. I eventually entered the 2001 race, hoping that this experience would help me on loop three.

The usual suspects congregated again at Frozen Head for the 16th running of the Barkley Marathons, which started at about 9 AM on Saturday, March 31, 2001. Returning former Barkley Fun Run winners were Blake Wood, David Horton, Tom Possert (the 60-mile, three-loop course record holder), Craig Wilson, Mike Dobies (who along with Blake, had finished the past four Barkleys, at the time being the only runners to ever finish four consecutive Barkley fun runs), and myself. I suspect it is not often that an ultramarathon race has six former male winners all competing simultaneously. Also returning was the women's course-record holder and last year's women's winner, Sue Johnston.

Additional former Fun Run finishers were the following: Michael Tilden, last year's runner-up and fourth-loop starter; Andrew Thompson; Randy Isler; John DeWalt, and Dick West. Other returning runners included Hans Put, Fred Brooks, David White, Geoff Scott, DeWayne Satterfield, Wilson and Wayne Brasington, Matt Mahoney, Sue Thompson, Stu Gleman, David Hughes, Debra Moore, Bill Johnson, Norm Carlson, Jason Poole, and Buttslide Martin. First-time Barkley runners included Andras Low from Hungary, Chip Tuthill, Steve Pero, Joe Prusaitis, Stephen Miller, Rich Limacher, and a woman runner from California going by the single name Chaennnon.

This list of 35 starters was again rich in experience, both at Barkley and other ultras. In his June 2001 *UltraRunning* article, Gary called this "another superlative field." He recalled that there had been some "testosterone fests" of racing in the early loops in recent years of Barkley, and reminded us that "this was not to be a race, has never been a race, of man against man. It is rather, the men and women against the Barkley." Recognizing this, David Horton and Blake Wood, the two runners who had previously gotten the furthest at the Barkley without finishing the 100, were planning to run together in a team effort to finish the 100.

There was a lot of pre-race e-mail being exchanged about the Barkley this year. One of the topics was the qualifications of the entrants, some of which were quite impressive. Matt Mahoney posted to the "ultra list" an e-mail with a list of presumed entrants, with short statements of one or more of the ultra accomplishments of each runner. Following are some excerpts of some of the more impressive runners' credentials on Matt's list. These demonstrate the national-class level of many of the Barkley participants.

Blake Wood - Won Hardrock '99 in 30:11.

Tom Possert - Won '98 Iditasport Extreme 350 miler in Alaska winter. Has run 1,000 miles in 13 days.

Michael Tilden - Hardrock 2000 in 34:39.

Sue Johnston - Won Hardrock 2000 in 32:20 and '99 Superior Trail 100 in 23:52.

Craig Wilson - Hardrock '97 in 37:47.

Mike Dobies - Hardrock '97 in 41:31.

Randy Isler - Hardrock '98 in 31:14.

Hans Put - Hardrock '99 in 30:56.

David Horton - Hardrock '93 in 29:35. (Matt didn't mention that David had also completed a trans-America race of over 3,000 miles, and held the record for running the full length of the Appalachian Trail, over 2,700 miles.)

Fred Brooks - Won '98 Superior Trail 100 in 22:22.

David Hughes - Superior Trail 100 in 2000 in 32:12.

John DeWalt - Hardrock 2000 in 44:28.

Andras Low - 121 Km (75.1 miles) in 12 hours in 2000 in Finland.

Another e-mail subject was that Tom Possert encouraged the Barkley entrants to make monetary donations to the Friends of Frozen Head, a volunteer organization that supported Frozen Head State Park. It was an impressive act on Tom's part to spearhead this donation effort. Before the start of the race, he gave the accumulated contributions of over $1,000 to the park ranger.

Still another subject of much pre-race e-mail chatter was a course change that Gary had hinted at but did not disclose in detail until the day before the race. It was called "The Hump." It consisted of about a 0.8-mile-long detour off the Chimney Top Trail between the Frozen Head lookout tower checkpoint and Indian Knob. The detour paralleled part of the CTT to the west, along a ridge line to a peak that was nameless on the map but now called The Hump by Gary. The new route continued parallel to the CTT until re-joining it farther south. There were a few old tree blazes and traces of pathway on the ground along the ridge that indicated that this was in fact an old trail, long ago abandoned. Cleverly, this detour added about 240 feet each of additional climb and descent to the loop while adding only about a tenth of a mile of distance. It also removed about 0.7 mile of good runnable "candy ass" trail, and replaced it with the slightly longer distance of brier-covered, old overgrown trail. Gary continued to call the loop length 20 miles. Later information from my Pocket Guides suggests that The Hump added about nine minutes to my running time between Frozen Head and Indian Knob. Some other runners later estimated that the Hump added about 15 minutes to their loop times. So the Hump was a relatively minor course change, but definitely added to the effort and time required to complete the race. The trail sequence for the loop was now the same as described for 1995 in Chapter 14, except that trail segment #32 (on the Schematic Map on page 8) replaced segment #10. The new loop distance was increased to an estimated 26.1 miles (78.3 miles for the Fun Run and 130.5 for the 100-miler) with about

10,040 feet of climb and drop (30,120 feet and 50,200 feet for the Fun Run and 100-miler, respectively).

The race started in nice weather. However, the experienced field had learned its lesson from recent years, and held back a little on the early speed. The leaders arrived at the end of the first loop in 8:12:46, a slightly conservative pace, even with The Hump, compared to last year's 7:37 first-loop leading time. The lead pack, in the order recorded by Gary, consisted of Low, Possert, Horton, Wood, and Poole. Within the next hour, they were followed by Johnston, Put, Wilson, Brooks, Tilden, White, Scott, Satterfield, Dobies, Pero, Andrew Thompson, and Isler, in that order. So all the big-name runners were performing well and putting on quite a display of their collective running prowess. Thirty-one runners finished loop one within its time limit. Of those who didn't, there were some interesting stories.

Chaennnon, whom Gary had designated before the race as this year's "Human Sacrifice," had passed book one near other runners toward the back of the pack, but forgot to collect a page. When she realized this mistake, she went back to retrieve the page. This put her alone behind the rest of the runners. Unfamiliar with the course, she got lost in the New River Section. She eventually ended up on the highway down by Brushy Mountain State Penitentiary, and did a long road run to return to the park on highways.

This was not as bad as the fate suffered by Norm Carlson and Rich Limacher, who were also running near the back of the field. Rich was a Barkley Virgin, and he joined with a Barkley veteran shortly after Coffin Springs on the first loop. Norm and Rich gradually navigated successfully through the New River Section, but were moving very slowly. After 11 hours and nightfall, they were still on loop one, about at Indian Knob. Rich then tells what happened in a companion article he wrote that appeared just after Gary's article in *UltraRunning*. Rich wrote: "So anyway, sometime before midnight, Norm and I decided to cash it in and cruise the sissy trails home." However, they soon got lost by not being able to follow the tricky CTT through the capstones near its peak. You will later read more about other runners' problems in this particular area. For Norm and Rich, this was where they got off trail and onto a trackless mountainside. This was also about when it began to rain. So Norm phoned his wife on his cell phone that he happened to be carrying. She was at the campground, waiting with her cell phone around Gary's campfire with the other Barkley spectators, including myself. In a scene that was almost surrealistic, Mrs. Carlson was trying to decipher Norm's garbled and intermittent phone signal, and relay that information to Gary. Gary understood about where they were lost, and advised them to "turn right." I found this hilarious because Gary could not know which way they were facing at that moment. In any case, the cell-phone signal was soon lost, and so were Norm and Rich. They ended up spending the night huddled together under a single space blanket as partial shelter against the rain, sleet, and hail that the typical Barkley weather visited upon us that night. Gary later referred to their accommodations as "The Limacher Hilton." After daylight the next morning, they eventually found their way back to camp, arriving at 22:14 race time. They thus set a new record for the longest time to return from a first loop. They would have the distinction of holding this record for several years, but it would be surpassed in a later year in another stupendous story of a runner's defeat by the Barkley.

The observant reader may be wondering why I was one of those back in camp when Norm and Rich phoned-in the story of their travail. Earlier in the first loop, I had had a problem of my own in the same area as Norm and Rich. I was having a fairly good run through the last book, at the top of Big Hell. In fact, my Pocket Guide data show that I had reached that book in 8:44 race time, literally one minute faster than my time to that point in 1997; this was despite the slightly tougher course with The Hump. However, after collecting my book page at the top of Big Hell, I had somehow gotten headed the wrong way on the CTT, as I turned onto that trail near the Chimney Top capstones. I figure this is close to where Norm and Rich would later get off-trail. However, I wasn't off-trail. I was on the right trail moving unknowingly in the wrong direction. I remember eventually checking my compass, thinking that I should have made a right turn off the ridge by then. Strangely, the compass seemed to be pointing in the wrong direction! I was pretty certain that I had turned left onto the CTT at Chimney Top, and should be heading westerly, but my compass showed that I was eastbound. Not fully trusting that electronic compass that was built into my altimeter, I pulled a small needle compass out of my pack. Amazingly, it seemed to be reading wrong too! I continued slowly in the wrong direction, fantasizing that perhaps there were magnetic rocks on this mountain that were affecting my compass readings. But eventually, after about a half-hour on the CTT, I came to a familiar place—the campsite and ruins at Mart Fields. I was nearly sickened to finally realize that my compasses were right, and I had been heading in the wrong direction since Chimney Top. I angrily turned around and went back. This incredibly stupid error had cost me an hour. I arrived back at Chimney Top just as Sue Thompson and Chip Tuthill were heading onto the CTT near where I had turned the wrong way. I told them about the sorry mistake that I had made an hour ago. I also unleashed an angry tirade directed toward myself. I could hardly believe that I had made such an obvious blunder. I subsequently finished the first loop in 11:10, almost exactly one hour slower than in 1997. Discouraged with my getting lost, and with the rain that was starting to fall, I retired after a single loop. This was my worst Barkley result yet.

Meanwhile, while some of us were suffering those dismal failures, others were enjoying their best Barkley yet. Seventeen runners finished two loops within the time limit, led by Poole, Low, and the team of Horton and Wood. Another team of Put and Johnston, running together as last year, was next, followed by the pair of Tilden and Brooks, and then Scott, Wilson, and Dobies in yet another group. Andrew Thompson, Pero, White, Isler, Wilson Brasington, and DeWalt rounded out the two-loop finishers.

Twelve of the seventeen runners continued on to the third loop. Ten of those runners finished the third loop, the most in any year on the Two Hells course. This large number of finishers was a remarkable achievement, especially with the addition of The Hump this year. But even more amazing was the continuing performance of some of the runners. Five of them started loop four, another Barkley record. Horton and Wood headed out shortly after

finishing the third loop. Put, Johnston, and Tilden spent about an hour deciding and preparing to continue, and then headed back *out there*. This made
Sue Johnston the only woman runner to ever begin a fourth loop. However,
she and her two fellow travelers made it only about eight miles before suc-
cumbing to exhaustion and retreating, still as a team, back to camp to be
tapped out. Then, as Gary described in his article: "They repaired to their car
to drive the 50 yards to the showers. That little drive left one final Barkley
adventure. During the wind and rainstorm of the previous night, one of their
tents had blown down. A runner who had already quit decided to play good
Samaritan, and set the tent back up, tying off one end to the bumper of the
very same car in which the trio prepared to drive off. As they pulled out,
there was a loud ripping sound as the tent came right out of the ground, and
bounced along the road behind them like Charlie Brown's kite trying to take
flight. That incident provided much mirth as we awaited the arrival of the
final two survivors."

Those two survivors, David and Blake, were still in the race, not against
each other, but against the course, the clock, and fatigue. Fortunately, after
the first night, the weather had improved, and the rain had stopped. The final
duo finished loop four in 45:40:48. Taking only a brief break, and with no
sleep yet during the race, they returned to the course, having selected the
less-familiar counterclockwise direction for their fifth loop. They completed
the historic fifth loop in a little over 12 hours, finishing virtually together in
an intentional tie, but with David being recorded as the first to touch the gate
in 58:21:00, and Blake in 58:21:01. Thus the Barkley now had a new 100-
mile course record, and its second and third-ever finishers in the 100-mile.
They were the first Americans to accomplish the 100, and this was the first
time anyone had finished the 100 with loops being run in both directions. It
was also the first time that there had been more than one 100-mile finisher. It
was a truly impressive performance by these two, who were undoubtedly two
of the best ultramarathon runners in the country, and who had both worked so
hard for many years to earn this victory over the Barkley. It was a fine moment in Barkley history. Except...

David and Blake had unintentionally violated one of the rules in this
year's course directions. Near the stream confluence at the bottom of Big
Hell, on each of their loops, they had gone for about a tenth of a mile on a
parallel jeep road on the wrong (south) side of the creek. Gary's written instructions for this year had included, in bold print, six specifically emphasized locations with instructions for the required route that runners were to
follow. The instructions for the location in question read: "**We know that it
is easier to follow the new jeep road across the creek, and circle back to
the Beech Tree. That is also illegal.**" The jeep-road bypass was probably
not significantly different in length than the intended route; in fact, it may
have been slightly longer. But it was open, runnable dirt road rather than the
briers, brush, and rocks that Gary intended the runners to pass through. Tom
Possert had noticed David and Blake taking the wrong side, and pointed out
to them that they were taking a disallowed route, but they did not understand
the rule, and did not change their route. Possert subsequently reported this to

Gary and withdrew from the race, saying that he did not want to "compete against cheaters."

Horton and Wood later stated that Gary had told him that there were no course changes from the previous year. Blake later wrote that he had read the course instructions the night before the race began, and when he read the directions for this area, he thought that Gary was referring to not crossing the creek further downstream and circling back, which Blake had not done in the past, so he didn't think the emphasized rule referred to the route he had run in the past. Blake further wrote that a couple of years after this incident, he went to Frozen Head and ran both routes in question, to see how much difference there was. He reported that: "I ran up and back twice on each side of the creek, at an appropriate Barkley pace, and recorded how long it took. The result: the section in question took just over 2 minutes to cover, and the average difference between the two sides of the creek was 11 seconds." This observation puts the controversy in perspective. The difference being argued over was only a few seconds per loop.

Gary reported this controversy in his June 2001 *UltraRunning* article, writing: "An immediate protest was raised over the result, triggering a long and painful exchange between two protesting runners, the two finishers, and myself. To this day, I have been able to reach no conclusion. There was an error made. However, over the years, we have had to deal with the the the fact that a shocking number of runners intentionally cut the course. In this case, two runners that I consider to have unimpeachable ethics inadvertently made a relatively insignificant mistake. On the other hand, two runners that I consider to have unimpeachable ethics are adamant that there should be a disqualification. Frankly, the magnitude of the discrepancy is so small that I would dismiss that protest out of hand, except for one thing. In the pre-race instructions, that particular deviance from the course is specifically addressed, and the threatened penalty is....disqualification." Despite this statement, Gary listed David and Blake in his *UltraRunning* article as finishers of five loops.

In the September 2001 issue of *UltraRunning*, Tom Possert had written a letter to the editor. In it he said: "to my surprise, Gary has o.k'd the course cutting and cheating by David and Blake and counted them as finishers. It is truly a sad point in the world of ultrarunning when people's egos get in the way of fair competition. Gary has just acknowledged that cheating is o.k. at the Barkley if you can do five loops, even though you go against the rules and laugh in the face of the other competitors that have integrity." Tom's position on this was probably influenced by the memory of his own disqualification back in 1988, when he had missed a part of the required course. As reported by Gary in *UltraRunning* in 1988, and as described in Chapter 7 of this book, Tom had gracefully accepted that disqualification.

In the same *UltraRunning* September issue, Gary also wrote a letter, explaining his position. He stated that: "after all the information was in, the two finishers were disqualified." However, Gary has continued over subsequent years to refer to David and Blake as 100-mile finishers. In an e-mail several years later in 2005, when someone on the Internet ultra e-mail list asked "how many 'official' finishers have there been" at the Barkley, Gary responded that: "there is no 'official' finishers list, for reasons i would rather not get into." He listed the runners who had "made the 100 miles in 60 hours," and that list included David and Blake's 2001 finish. So Gary had resolved the controversy in his mind by counting David and Blake as 100-mile finishers, but by not using the word "official" for that status.

In his *UltraRunning* letter, Gary stated his regret for the entire incident, but that he would not criticize the ethics of any of the parties involved. Years later, as I was writing this book, I asked Gary if he still had records of all the starters and their loop times, for each year of the Barkley. Gary told me that he had thrown away his old Barkley records in 2001, in "disgust" over this episode. He also wrote in an e-mail in the summer of 2001, that he thought that the Barkley runners were "AMAZING" but that "i dont have the stomach for listening to them attack one another any more. maybe the time has come for me to spend the fool's weekend somewhere else." Gary's grief over the controversy of 2001 was so deep that he was considering ending the Barkley.

Tom's disqualification in 1988, and David and Blake's in 2001, were similar in that in both cases, the runners unknowingly failed to follow the written course instructions. I believe that in both years, for all three runners, there was no intention to cheat or break the rules. There was simply a misunderstanding of the rules. I have suggested to Gary that he could help prevent this type of problem by putting additional books in those locations where he is adamant that the runners must go.

Aside from the controversy, there is another interesting and much more positive epilogue to David and Blake's breakthrough 100-mile finish. Afterward, these two men made an agreement with each other that they would not return to Barkley. If either of them did return, he would contribute $100 to a charitable cause to be designated by the other. As the reader will see in later Chapters, both David and Blake did subsequently return to run the Barkley again. And they each made their promised contributions to the other's charitable cause. I think this reinforced Gary's judgement about these two men having "unimpeachable ethics."

Here is the list of starters, their numbers of Barkley starts, and their loop-finishing times for 2001.

1. David Horton (9)	8:12:48	19:40:19	31:18:12	45:40:49	58:21:00
2. Blake Wood (5)	8:12:49	19:40:20	31:18:13	45:40:48	58:21:01
3. Hans Put (2)	8:20:37	20:57:57	33:44:00	Quit on loop four.	
4. <u>Sue Johnston</u> (2)	8:20:36	20:57:58	33:44:01	Quit on loop four.	
5. Michael Tilden (2)	8:30:03	21:00:03	33:50:20	Quit on loop four.	
6. Mike Dobies (5)	8:35:38	21:16:30	37:03:42		
7. Craig Wilson (6)	8:21:55	21:16:29	37:03:45		
8. Andrew Thompson (5)	9:07:04	23:43:53	38:50:01		
9. Randy Isler (3)	9:07:05	24:01:15	38:50:03		
10. Steve Pero (1)	9:07:03	23:50:28	39:52:56		
11. David White (4) over the time limit.	8:30:04	23:56:57	~40:05* Finished loop three		
12. Jason Poole (2)	8:12:50	19:40:17			
13. Andras Low (1)	8:12:46	19:40:18	Lost on loop three.		

14. Fred Brooks (2)   8:21:56   21:00:04
15. Geoff Scott (3)   8:32:42   21:16:03
16. Wilson Brasington (8) 10:06:14   25:11:46
17. John DeWalt (14)   9:28:27   25:24:26
18. Matt Mahoney (7)   11:09:55   ~29:40*Finished loop two over time limit.
19. Dick West (8)   11:31:40   ~29:40*Finished loop two over time limit.
20. Tom Possert (5)   8:12:47   Quit during loop two.
21. DeWayne Satterfield (6) 8:32:43   Quit during loop two.
22. Joe Prusaitis (1)   10:06:15   Quit during loop two.
23. Frozen Ed Furtaw (8) 11:09:59
24. Sue Thompson (3)   11:15:01
25. Chip Tuthill (1)   11:15:03
26. Stu Gleman (6)   11:50:32
27. David Hughes (4)   12:03:20
28. Stephen Miller (1)   12:25:02
29. Debra Moore (4)   12:32:32   Quit during loop two.
30. Bill Johnson (5)   12:32:33   Quit during loop two.
31. Buttslide Martin (9) 12:53:26   Quit during loop two.
32. Wayne Brasington (8) Quit during loop one.
33. Chaennnon (1)   Lost on loop one.
34. Rich Limacher (1)   ~22:21* Lost on loop one; did not complete loop.
35. Norm Carlson (4)   ~22:21* Lost on loop one; did not complete loop.
35 Starters

+++++++++++

Below is the essay I wrote for entry into the 2001 Barkley Marathons.

Why I should be allowed to RUN the Barkley
An Essay by Frozen Ed Furtaw
#8 in a Series
December 2000

First, let me point out that no one has ever RUN much of the Barkley - even the one who finished the 100 and the few who have finished the Fun Run have WALKED the vast majority of it.

Aside from that minor technicality, I should be allowed to run the Barkley because I truly love it. It is my favorite ultra, because it is the most fun, if you approach it with the right attitude. Barkley is a unique and special event within the sport of ultrarunning. People who don't have a proper sense of humor and humility are repulsed by the Barkley or at least they discount it as not a real race, not in the same category as other ultras, etc. But for those of us who love it, it is the epitome of what ultrarunning is all about: extreme fun and extreme trail-running challenge.

Here are a few reasons why the Barkley is so much fun.

It is probably one of, if not THE "toughest" footrace in the world. This claim is based on the extremely low rate of finishing among starters. Only one person has ever finished the 100-mile event—Mark Williams, a British computer scientist, in 1995. The shorter "Fun Run" (55 or 60 miles in different years) has a historic finishing rate of about 12% . This is unprecedented in the sport of ultramarathoning, where even the other events that are consid-

ered among the toughest, such as the Hardrock 100, the Badwater 135, and
the Trans-America, have historical finishing rates close to 50%. Since for a
true ultrarunner, toughness is equal to fun, Barkley is the most fun of any
ultra. Where else can a runner so fully appreciate the frivolity and absurdity
of what we do?

Another reason why Barkley is so much fun is its colorful history, in
which I have participated as much as almost anyone. The Barkley was first
run as a competitive race in 1986. It has been held annually since then.
There was only one official finisher, of a 55-mile course, in the first four
years. (I was that finisher.) An average of about 30 runners per year start the
event, so there have been some 400+ attempts. These starters have included
many of America's best ultrarunners such as David Horton, Eric Clifton, Tom
Possert, Blake Wood, and Dana Miller, as well as many from foreign countries. One highlight of this history was in 1991, "The Year Of The Soviet
Invasion," when a team of about 10 elite runners from the Soviet Union attended, allegedly complete with KGB agents to ensure their return home.
Two of the Soviets finished the Fun Run, about half an hour behind two
middle-aged American women. This was also the year described as "Come
Hell and High Water" because of pre-race rains that flooded the course. The
night before the race, a park ranger drove through the campground where
most of the entrants, including the Soviets, were camped, warning of tornadoes in the area and advising people to leave!

The course has been expanded a few times over the years, to keep it at
the outer limit of attainability. Today's 60-mile Fun Run is much more difficult than the former 55-mile course that I first completed in 1988. The current course consists of multiple repeats of a 20-mile loop, with about 10,000
feet of climb per loop. (Note: that is 1,000 feet of elevation change per mile;
few if any other races even come close to this gradient.) The loop generally
circumnavigates Frozen Head State Park, an area that thankfully was set
aside to protect it from coal strip-mining. Tennessee's Brushy Mountain
State Penitentiary is adjacent to Frozen Head. This was the area into which
James Earl Ray, the alleged assassin of Martin L. King Jr., escaped from
Brushy Mountain. He managed to travel only a few miles in a couple of
days—a portentous result for the first footrace through Frozen Head.

Some of the reasons why Barkley is so tough and therefore so much fun:

The terrain is all at steep angles—up, down, and sideways. It is so steep
that normally well-trained runners have never trained on such steep angles.
The result is muscle, joint, and connective tissue damage that makes the body
ache in ways never before experienced.

Much of the route is overgrown with nasty briers. Like so many Br'er
Rabbits, runners must literally throw themselves headlong into brier patches
to follow the prescribed route. Protective clothing is highly recommended,
as I was reminded so grimly this past summer during a training run in shorts.

The course is not marked. Some of the route is cross-country, where no
real paths exist. Many runners cannot follow the course. Back-country
navigation ability is as important as running endurance. Not to mention doing this in the dark at night. Some of the most hilarious Barkley stories are
of those who have strayed from the course, and from the park itself. One of

my favorites of these stories is of the two runners who mistakenly wandered onto the grounds of the Brushy Mountain State Penitentiary, and were held at gunpoint by guards while telling their incredible story of how and why they got there!

On each loop, runners must procure, and bring back to the start/finish area, a page from each of several books that are planted at strategic locations on the course. This scavenger-hunt rule is enforced to ensure that they really did follow the prescribed course.

There are no aid stations, except water (usually) at two points on the course, and the runners' own aid at the start/finish campground. Runners must carry everything else they will need for running about 8 to 15 hours at a time.

The time limits, while nominally very liberal compared to most ultra-event time limits, tend to eliminate some of the slower but more durable contestants who could probably finish with longer time limits (say, a week or so for the 100-miler).

Weather is frequently a factor. The event is held in the rainy season, and when the sloped course is wet, progress becomes very difficult as runners slip and slide on the steep muddy slopes. In 2000, Blake Wood MIGHT have finished the 100 if heavy rains had not caused severe flooding of the New River Gorge, making it impassable.

Runners are properly ridiculed rather than encouraged by race management. Runners soon realize that what they are doing is ridiculous. Those who graciously accept this, like Sisyphus repeatedly pushing his rock up the mountain, are the ones who love Barkley and clamor to come back. The others leave in disgust and couldn't be dragged back with bulldozers. Somehow, I happen to be in the former group. Therefore, I should be allowed to run Barkley again (for the eight time), in 2001.

Another part of the fun of Barkley is the camaraderie, friendship, and humor at the campground. This is a time for renewing old friendships and forming new ones, as the participants (especially the organizers) poke fun at each other and themselves. Most of us realize that we are playing character roles in a living parody of that which we love the most. This blending of the sacred with the profane produces a memorable lesson in not taking oneself too seriously. The recent tradition of "tapping out" non-finshers by playing *Taps* on a bugle at each runner's demise, is hilarious! I can't wait to hear myself getting tapped out again! Each year the Barkley's entrants include some of the best trail-ultrarunners in the country, many of whom are extremely intent on delivering incredible athletic performances. Despite this purported seriousness, the Barkley induces a light-hearted self-deprecation among the runners, as we inevitably find our limits of endurance and how much fun we can take in one weekend. I find this exercise in humility to be spiritually renewing and downright fun. It has now been four years since I last succored my soul on this enjoyment. I crave another dose of this stupendous pleasure. Therefore I beg to be allowed to run the Barkley.

Chapter 21
2002: No Barkley; The Cantrell Marathons

For the first time since its inception in 1986, the Barkley Marathons was not held in 2002. However, its absence this year was not the result of the controversy of 2001. Rather, it was due to the debacle of a Tennessee state government financial and political crisis. The state that year had insufficient revenues to fund all of its normal functions. So certain politically selected functions were temporarily curtailed to save money while the State Legislature tried to resolve the financial crisis. One of those functions that was curtailed was the operation and maintenance of some state parks. Unfortunately for the Barkley community, one of the temporarily shuttered state parks was Frozen Head. This closure of the park resulted in the cancellation of the 2002 Barkley. Gary sent an e-mail on December 9, 2001 to many of his Barkley followers announcing the cancellation. From Gary's tone in his Barkley-related e-mails, I became concerned that maybe the days of the Barkley Marathons were over.

Meanwhile, out west where I had been living since 1989, I had gotten into organizing low-key, no-fee ultramarathon runs. Most of these were in the Spring Mountains just outside Las Vegas, where Gail and I lived. But since we also were spending a lot of our free time in northern Arizona, I was gradually becoming familiar with the mountains there. I found one in particular, Bill Williams Mountain, near the town of Williams, to have nice trails as well as some beautiful ponderosa pine forests with old logging roads and trackless backcountry. I decided in late 2001 that I would like to organize an ultra run there; a run sort of like the Barkley Marathons. After getting Gary's consent on the name, I called it the Cantrell Marathons. The idea for this run was initiated *before* the cancellation of the 2002 Barkley. So I cannot say that I held the Cantrell Marathons because of the Barkley cancellation. As it turned out however, for a couple of us Barkley regulars, it became a Barkley substitute for 2002.

To make a long story short, the Cantrell Marathons was held on October 26-27, 2002. Twenty runners signed up, ten started, and three finished in 17:30—one of the slowest 50-mile race times in the country. My goal was accomplished; I had created the toughest 50-mile trail race around. Multiple-time Barkley runner Mike Dobies, Jim Rapp (a Las Vegas running friend of mine), and I were the three finishers. But compared to the Barkley, the Cantrell Marathons was way too easy. I didn't have the heart (or lack thereof) that Gary has that enables him to create a race that eats its young.

Fortunately, the Barkley would return the following year to fill that void which I was not able to. The Barkley cancellation of 2002 extended for another year the agony that we Barkley aficionados had to endure before we could return and seek redemption from last year's bitter ending note. But the Barkley would be back.

Chapter 22
2003: Barkley Returns; A New Course Record

For the return of the Barkley on March 29, 2003, there were 33 starters. Returning past winners were Craig Wilson, Mike Dobies, and myself. Other previous three-loop finishers were Mike Tilden and John DeWalt. Other non-finishing returnees included Geoff Scott, Jason Poole, Robert Youngren, DeWayne Satterfield, Kerry Trammell, David White, Mark Dorion, Sue Thompson, Steve Simmons, Matt Mahoney, David Hughes, Buttslide Martin, Rich Limacher, and Jonathon Basham.

Among newcomers this year were a couple of notables. One was Jim Nelson, who was Mike Tilden's friend and training partner back in Utah; the other was Ted "Cave Dog" Keizer, an accomplished mountaineer from Oregon who held the record for covering all of Colorado's 14,000-foot mountain peaks within the shortest span of time. However, this was to be Cave Dog's first ultramarathon race. Other new blood presenting itself to the Barkley this year included: Todd Holmes; Michael Anderson and Gavin Harmacy, friends from Manitoba, Canada; Joe Kowalski; Julie Nelson, Jim's wife who was here from Utah with Jim and Mike Tilden; Herb Hedgecock; Sarah "Spyder" Tynes; Kevin Kepley; Michael Bur; and Neal Jamison, a writer who was working on an article about the Barkley for *Trail Runner* magazine. Neal's article was subsequently published in *Trail Runner*, in its Issue #23, in September 2003.

Thirty-one of the 33 runners are named above. I do not have a conclusive record of the names of the two remaining starters. However, the day before the race, Gary distributed a list of the 35 registered entrants. Additional entrant names that do not appear above were Eliza MacLean, Joe Prusaitis, Leslie Trammell, Luke Bartlett, and Steven Miller. Apparently three of these did not actually start the race. I suspect the no-shows included Eliza and Joe, because they had both done well enough here in the past that they would probably have finished the first loop within the time limit if they had been there in 2003, and their names would have been in Gary's post-Barkley article in the June 2003 *UltraRunning*.

Compared to the starting fields of the past few years, the number of previous Barkley finishers was clearly down. I believe this was due in part to the lingering negative aftereffects of both the controversy of 2001, and the race cancellation of 2002. Perhaps the enchantment of some of the regulars had worn off a little.

As so often was the case at the Barkley, this year there was another course change, ostensibly to make the loop just a little bit tougher. It was the addition of Stallion Mountain. This mountain is one of the highest in the area, with a peak at about 3,330 feet elevation, which is within a few feet of the highest elevation of Frozen Head Mountain itself (3,324'). Stallion Mountain lies just south of the Garden Spot, east of and outside the boundary of the Frozen Head State Natural Area. It is a mountain on which a lot of coal strip-mining has occurred, probably up until the 1980s. Recall that when I first ran the Barkley in 1988, I noted running past an old piece of coal-mine drilling equipment on the coal road after Coffin Springs. That road was on a bench cut into the west face of Stallion Mountain, at about the 2,600-foot elevation.

The new course instructions were to proceed from Coffin Springs back up the jeep road for about 0.3 miles, then to the very top of Stallion Mountain on a combination of old mining and jeep roads, and cross-country. After collecting a book page at the top, the runners were to go steeply downhill to the south into the valley drained by the Barley Mouth Branch creek. From there the runners were to proceed down along the Barley Mouth Branch to the 2,600' coal road, and then rejoin the former route on the coal road to Bobcat Rock at the top of Leonard's Buttslide, and then on down to the New River. Referring to the Schematic Map on page 8, the new loop this year replaced segment 22 with segments 21 (uphill), 33, and 34. Based on data from the Table on page 9, the new loop distance, compared to the previous route on the coal road, was slightly shorter, by about 0.1 miles. This returned the estimated loop distance to 26.0 miles, or 78.0 miles for the Fun Run and 130.0 miles for the 100-mile. But the change added about another 380 feet of climb and descent per loop. On Gary's updated spreadsheet of course data for 2003, the stated loop distance remained 20.00 miles, and the cumulative elevation climb and descent increased to 10,580 feet each, per loop. Using data from the Table on page 9, my estimate of the climb is 10,420 feet per loop (31,260' for the Fun Run, and 52,100 for the 100-mile). Gary was tightening the Barkley screws again.

There was another slight change on the course, but not to the prescribed route. This was in the area of Bald Knob, where the NBT swings north of the Knob and a little ways outside the boundary line of the State Natural Area. This area had had some logging in the past couple of years. Gary referred to it in his course instructions as a "clear cut." The logging activity had resulted in not only the removal of trees, but also the obliteration of part of the trail, for maybe a quarter-mile. This changed the appearance and increased the difficulty of navigating through this area, but did not alter the distance or elevation change.

Rain began Saturday morning prior to the race. My post-race notes show that it rained from about 4 AM until mid-morning. The result was a wet, muddy, slippery NBT. The effects of the course condition plus the Stallion Mountain detour were reflected in the first-loop finishing times. The mountaineer Cave Dog led in 8:22, with Tilden and Nelson next in 8:44 and 8:50. They were the only three runners under 10:10, compared to 20 runners better than that in 2001, and 24 runners in 2000.

It is noteworthy that although Cave Dog was a first-time Barkley runner, he was in the lead and was running alone. This was unusual compared to the typical pattern of previous neophyte fast runners staying with veterans to learn the course. Cave Dog was able to do this because he had spent the previous week-and-a-half camped out at Frozen Head, training on the course. Reportedly he had trained on the loop going in both directions, and in both daylight and darkness. So he was well prepared, and his preparation was now paying off. Some of this information was reported by Rich Limacher in a companion article that was appended to Gary's article in the June 2003 issue of *UltraRunning*.

Next to finish the first loop after Keizer, Tilden, and Nelson was a pack of five runners, all within a few seconds of each other at about 10:10. In the order recorded by Gary, these were Scott, Holmes, Poole, Youngren, and Satterfield. Following them over an hour later was a string of 14 runners within a span of 18 minutes. Three more runners in the 12+ hour range followed to bring the total to 25 runners who completed the first loop within the time limit.

I was one of those 25. However, I was also one of the majority who did not even attempt loop two. I had developed a cold starting several days prior to the race, and was running in a weakened condition. Nevertheless, I enjoyed a relatively leisurely circuit, finishing in 11:23:47, my slowest first loop ever. A few days afterward I wrote about three pages of "Post-Barkley Reflections." I stated that I really enjoyed the running experience, perhaps more than in previous years. I thought that the addition of Stallion Mountain gave back some of the excitement of wondering where I was and where to go, that had gradually diminished over the years as I had become more familiar with the course. I also had enjoyed running at various times in my single loop in the company of numerous friends, including Mark Dorion, Mike Dobies, Sue Thompson, Craig Wilson, John DeWalt, Matt Mahoney, and Steve Simmons, and some new acquaintances including Neal Jamison, Mike Anderson, and Gavin Harmacy. I ran much of the latter part of the loop with the latter two runners from Canada. I remember giving them a sort of guided tour as we progressed along the course, even pointing out the location of the fateful jeep road that was at the heart of the controversy of 2001. We had one interesting episode at the top of Chimney Top, where I had gone the wrong way in 2001. I was literally in the process of telling them how I had gone wrong there, as we came to the blazes that identify the CTT and turned what we thought was left onto the trail. To confirm that we were going the right way this time, I pulled out my compass and checked our direction. *We were heading the wrong way!* I was truly baffled, but gratified that I had had the alertness to check. We turned around and went the right way, with no more than a few seconds of lost time. By the time we reached camp, the rain had resumed and I was getting a blister forming on the instep of my right foot. I decided to take a hot shower and contemplate the decision of whether or not to start a second loop. Seeing sleet pellets bouncing on the road as I walked toward the bathhouse pretty much broke my will and clinched my decision. After showering, I went back to Gary's headquarters and asked to be tapped out.

Meanwhile back at the real race, Cave Dog spent only about five minutes in camp re-supplying after his first loop, and hurried out on loop two. Mike Tilden took about 20 minutes to start loop two. Jim Nelson started his second loop about 15 minutes after Tilden. The two friends from Utah were running within a few minutes of each other, but not together into and out of the campground.

Of the 25 loop-one finishers, fifteen continued onto loop two. However, around nightfall, the precipitation resumed, raining at the lower elevations but snowing and sleeting up on the mountains. This led to most of the runners looking for shortcuts back to camp. Three second-loop runners returned before reaching the first checkpoint at Phillips Creek. Three more apparently bush-whacked back from the north side of Bird Mountain, leaving nine runners on the course. In his *UltraRunning* article, Gary described what happened next: "Of the nine who continued, Cave Dog, Tilden, and Nelson all were past Bald Knob before the snow started to get deep on the trail. That, as it turns out, was very important, because at Bald Knob, the map-knowledgeable runner can see that there is an easy route out. Naturally, anyone surviving into loop two is going to be in the "map knowledgeable" category. The first pair to reach the easiest drop point immediately left the trail to hike out, leaving the only set of tracks in the snow. The next runner to reach that point was not confused when the tracks left the trail; he was inspired to emulate his predecessors. As each runner reached that spot, they were faced with a growing number of footprints leading off the course, and absolutely none going on. It confirmed for each of them their own wishes. In the end, Wilson, Martin, Dobies, Thompson, Mahoney, and Dorion, all cried 'no mas' at the top of Bald Knob, and trekked their way back to camp. Each of them confidently explained that trail conditions were simply too severe for a finish to be possible. However, there were three runners attempting to make liars of them all."

Cave Dog was the first of those three to finish loop two. Gary described him as "sprinting in, having finished the first 40 miles in a sizzling 19 and a half hours. After expressing his amazement that so few runners remained, he spent what was to be his longest break in camp, 50 minutes, eating, restocking, and resting, before he headed back out into the darkness." Tilden and Nelson were by now about two and a half hours behind Keizer. They arrived in camp about a minute apart. After about 45 minutes in camp, they began the third loop.

The weather got somewhat better on day two. Gary described intermittent clearing and light snow, with temperatures in the 20s in camp, and near zero at the higher elevations.

Cave Dog maintained his impressive solo run, despite some mental difficulty on loop three. As he reported later to Mark Dorion, who relayed it by e-mail to me, Cave Dog had actually turned around part-way down Big Hell on the counterclockwise third loop. He hiked back up toward the top, intending to go back to camp and drop out. But as he got back to Chimney Top, dawn broke and the weather improved. Cave Dog reconsidered his decision to quit, and turned back around and continued onward. Despite this delay, he did the third loop in a little under 12 hours. He finished the three-loop Fun Run in 32:15, the second-fastest time for the course with direction reversal, after Horton and Wood's 31:18 in 2001. Tilden and Nelson also finished the third loop, with Tilden in his characteristic short lead over his friend Jim Nelson.

After spending just another 30 minutes to refresh and re-supply with the aid of his father as his crew, Cave Dog took off on loop four. He was focussed and looked relatively strong. However, Tilden and Nelson, running much closer to the time limit, declined to go further. Cave Dog was now *out there* alone.

Keizer finished loop four in 46:31:51. Gary reported that: "the wear was obvious in his face. His stride, however, looked just as strong as it had at the start two days earlier. Barely 20 minutes later, Ted was off on loop five." Fortunately for Cave Dog (as well as for those remaining in camp), the weather had taken a turn for the better during the second night. It warmed up, and on Monday, the third day of the race, the sun shone. Cave Dog shone too. He ran the fifth loop, alone and determined, in about ten hours. His five-loop 100-mile finishing time was 56:57:52, a new course record by over an hour and 22 minutes.

Most of us Barkley followers immediately recognized that this was the most awesome performance that we had ever seen at the Barkley. Not only was it a new 100-mile record by a substantial margin, it was done as a solo effort, on the toughest course yet, by a Barkley first-timer, an athlete who was not even a regular ultramarathon runner. Not only did the course have the direction-reversal factor, it also had the Hump, and Stallion Mountain, and the Bald Knob clear cut. It had a large dose of the usual wet weather, and even a significant amount of the much less usual snow. Cave Dog had not slept during his entire race duration of nearly 57 hours, and his time in camp between loops had totaled only about an hour and 45 minutes. The 2003 completion of the Barkley 100-mile by Cave Dog Ted Keizer was clearly the best Barkley run thus far.

It is hard for me to comprehend Cave Dog's ability to do this. It was another mind-opening breakthrough that forces me to expand my belief in what is possible. This expanding of our limits is one of the most powerful lessons to be derived from the Barkley Marathons. And I am not just referring to our psychological limits. With the evolution of the Barkley over the years, the physical limit of what runners were willing and able to put themselves through to run the Barkley has expanded. In three of the first four years of the Barkley, no runners were willing to push themselves through three loops of a much easier course. But by now, seventeen years later, four runners had done five tougher loops. The runners' abilities had evolved to a new level, as epitomized by Cave Dog's incredible run of 2003. Each outstanding performance inspires others to train better, prepare better, and race better. The result is that the collective will and capability of the Barkley running community, and especially of the best within that community, has increased noticeably over the years. Thank you, Gary, for providing the inspiration and event to make that happen.

Here are the known starters, their numbers of Barkley starts, and their loop-finishing times for 2003.

1. Cave Dog Ted Keizer (1)	8:22:01	19:27:29	32:15:13	46:31:51 56:57:52
2. Mike Tilden (3)	8:44:15	21:58:03	35:04:47	
3. Jim Nelson (1)	8:50:54	21:59:03	35:05:16	
4. Geoff Scott (4)	10:10:12			
5. Todd Holmes (1)	10:10:14			
6. Jason Poole (3)	10:10:39			
7. Robert Youngren (3)	10:10:49			
8. DeWayne Satterfield (7)	10:11:01			
9. Kerry Trammell (6)	11:21:16			

10. David White (5)   11:21:17
11. Jonathon Basham (2)11:21:32
12. Michael Anderson (1)11:23:46
13. Frozen Ed Furtaw (9)11:23:47
14. Gavin Harmacy (1)   11:23:51
15. John DeWalt (15)   11:29:39
16. Neal Jamison (1)   11:29:45
17. Craig Wilson (7)   11:30:22   Quit during loop two.
18. Joe Kowalski (1)   11:30:23   Quit during loop two.
19. Mark Dorion (3)   11:30:53   Quit during loop two.
20. Mike Dobies (6)   11:31:53   Quit during loop two.
21. Sue Thompson (4)   11:31:56   Quit during loop two.
22. Julie Nelson (1)   11:39:16
23. Steve Simmons (4)   12:08:50
24. Matt Mahoney (8)   12:14:09   Quit during loop two.
25. Buttslide Martin (10)12:51:40   Quit during loop two.
26. David Hughes (5)   Finished loop one over the time limit.
27. Michael Bur (1)   ~15:30* Finished loop one over the time limit.
28. Spyder Tynes (1)   Quit during loop one.
29. Rich Limacher (2)   Quit during loop one.
30. Herb Hedgecock (1) Quit during loop one.
31. Kevin Kepley (1)   Quit during loop one.
33 Starters

++++++++++

Below is the essay I wrote for entry into the 2003 Barkley Marathons.

Why I Should Be Allowed To Run The Barkley Marathons
December 21, 2002
#9 in a series
by Frozen Ed Furtaw

The main reason why I should be allowed to run the Barkley in 2003 is that the Idiot has announced that this may be the last Barkley. Since I am so heavily involved in the history of Barkley, I must run it again to play my proper role in this possibly final edition of an important part of ultrarunning (and my) history.

A careful reading of the history of the Barkley will reveal that I am one of only two people who has officially finished the Barkley. If anyone deserves another and final run at Barkley, it is Mark Williams and I. But I wonder if Mark is even contemplating entering it again—I think he might have come to his senses in recent years. My claim that Mark and I are the only official finishers is based on the fact that when I did finish the 55-miler in 1988, that was the only official race distance. The longer Barkley distances, 110 and 100 miles in various years from 1989 onward, have been considered the official Barkley event ever since. And Mark has been the only official finisher of those longer distances, given that the last two runners to touch the gate at Frozen Head were subsequently disqualified.

Barkley is the toughest ultra in the world. The basis of this claim is Barkley's low finishing percentage. In Barkley's previous 16 runnings, there have been only two finishers of over 400 starters. Therefore, Barkley's historical finishing rate is actually less than one-half of one percent. That's over 99.5% DNFs. No other running event has such a low historical finishing rate, and this proves that Barkley is the toughest.

I have been repeatedly put in my proper humbled place with seven Barkley DNFs since my fleeting triumph in 1988, and I promise to be put there again in 2003. It is good to know that I will DNF again, because the Idiot has made us penitents agree in advance on the entry application that we will excuse our DNFs with exaggerated claims as to the difficulty of the course. In accordance with this requirement, I hereby make the exaggerated claim that it is impossible to make exaggerated claims about the difficulty of Barkley. One cannot make exaggerated claims about the difficulty of Barkley because no matter how extreme the claim, the reality is worse.

Chapter 23
2004: Race to the Finish

Following my paltry one-loop runs of the previous two Barkleys, I took off a couple more years before returning again. So for 2004 and 2005, the stories are based mainly on Gary's *UltraRunning* articles and on several related e-mails that I printed out and saved. However, I originally wanted to enter the 2004 race. I wrote the usual essay, with the first draft dated "January 2004," and the final edition dated "February 2004." As usual, a copy of my essay is included at the end of this Chapter. But then on February 25, I sent an e-mail to Gary informing him that I would not be attending that year's Barkley. I told Gary to "Please give my Barkley slot to some other deserving fool. I will get some satisfaction knowing that my absence will allow some other runner to experience the fun out there." I ended by thanking Gary "for again creating the world's toughest and most fun trail race."

One of the e-mails that I saved from early 2004 was from my friend Mark Dorion. In it he provided some closure to an old story about his run at the Barkley back in 1998, in which he had lost his backpack during the second loop. Mark wrote: "I have also heard a tall tale of Laz's and Doc Horton's that many years ago, as David clambered up the backside of Bird Mtn close to finishing his third loop, he came upon a FULLY STOCKED BACKPACK by the side of the trail. Now how could a backpack laden with food and water just appear out in the middle of the woods? HMMM. 'Bad things happen at the Barkley.'" This latter statement was actually the caption on the Barkley T-shirt from one of the years about then. And on the runners' numbers that Gary had given runners in the 2003 race, the caption "Bad Things Happen at the Barkley Marathons" had also been printed.

Based on information in Gary's Barkley article in the June 2004 issue of *UltraRunning* and on Matt Mahoney's website, the following former finishers returned and ran in the 2004 Barkley: David Horton, Fred Purloin, Mike Tilden, Jim Nelson, Andrew Thompson, Craig Wilson, John DeWalt, and Dick West. Other returners included Jason Poole, Todd Holmes, Rob Youngren, Mark Dorion, Sue Thompson, Buttslide Martin, Joe Kowalski, David Hughes, Matt Mahoney, Stu Gleman, Spyder Tynes, Herb Hedgecock, Michael Bur, Stephen Miller, and Rich Limacher. Newcomers for 2004 included Hal Koerner from Colorado, one of the top ultrarunners in the country; Hiram Rogers; Rob Hills; Rollin Perry; Hugo Walker; Janice Cahalane; Luke Bartlett; and John Bowman. This is 31 named runners. Gary stated that 32 started the race that year, so that leaves one additional unknown starter. The number of returning Barkley veterans was up a little compared to the previous year.

Gary noted the nice weather and "atypical sunshine" at the start of the race on Saturday, April 3, 2004. Early in the first loop, Luke Bartlett was the first to return without completing the loop. Next in was Fred Purloin. But he did not complete the first loop either. According to Gary, Fred decided that "his hour-long trek up the half-mile Little Hell climb satisfied his desire to suffer." This former winner, and continuing illegitimate holder of the Barkley Cup, was no longer able to make the grade at the Barkley.

The Barkley Virgin Hal Koerner was the first to finish the first loop, in 8:30:48. He was at the lead of a small pack of top runners including, in Gary's reported order, Horton, Poole, Andrew Thompson, and Holmes. Tilden and Nelson were several minutes behind, followed by Youngren, Wilson, Dorion, and Bur all under ten hours. Next in order were Rogers, Sue Thompson, Hills, DeWalt, Martin, Kowalski, Hughes, Mahoney, Tynes, Hedgecock, West, Bowman, and Limacher. Rich "The Troubadour" Limacher, who as you may recall, had spent the night in the Limacher Hilton *out there* in 2001, at last had completed a loop within the time limit. One noteworthy fact that Mark Dorion later told me was that there was no bottled water at Coffin Springs again this year. This had happened once before, several years ago. As before, the runners apparently coped without it.

Fifteen runners started a second loop, with 12 completing it within the 26:40 time limit. Amazingly, seven runners (Tilden, Nelson, Horton, Andrew Thompson, Holmes, Poole, and Koerner, in that order) were still in a tight pack at this point, finishing within less than two minutes of each other at about 19:18 race time. Also somewhat amazingly for the Barkley, the good weather had continued throughout the race thus far. Gary reported "modest temperatures and a cloudless, full-moon night," although he also noted: "the only adverse weather so far in the race, freezing gale-force winds at the tops of the hills. The veterans knew they were getting off easily."

Eight runners started the third loop—the seven listed above minus Koerner, plus Craig Wilson and Mark Dorion. Hal Koerner, the champion of many western ultras, had met his match at the Barkley, and "retired to his tent." During the third loop, Mark also met his match and returned to camp on a short-cut trail. He was quoted by Gary in *UltraRunning* as saying: "It was all I could do." The remaining seven runners (Horton, Tilden, Nelson, Thompson, Poole, Holmes, and Wilson, in that order) all finished the Fun Run within the time limit. The last four runners finished virtually together.

There was some interesting speculation in Gary's *UltraRunning* article that the final four-pack of finishers had intentionally delayed their finish to ensure that they were over the 36-hour time limit to be allowed to continue on additional loops. He wrote: "We jokingly asked, 'Did you wait out there until the time limit passed, so you wouldn't have to go on?' They just grinned sheepishly. After 36 hours, but two remained in the race." The field was down to just two because by this time, David Horton had already begun a fourth loop, and then decided to quit. He came back to camp early into his fourth loop, declaring that he "could not think of a good enough reason to continue." Thus another 100-mile finisher who later returned to attempt another Barkley, as Mark Williams had in 1996, could not pull off the repeat performance. The Barkley had gotten a measure of revenge against another alumnus. Still no one had been able to complete the 100-mile more than once.

The two remaining racers, friends Mike Tilden and Jim Nelson, were having a great run. This followed on their Fun Run finish of last year. Michael Tilden was running in his fourth Barkley, having finished the Fun Run in each previous effort. For Jim Nelson, this was his second Barkley appearance, so he too was in the distinguished ranks of those few who had not yet failed to finish at least three loops in any Barkley race that he had started. Furthermore, according to an e-mail written by Jim a couple weeks after this year's Barkley, the two of them had made an exploratory trip to Frozen Head three weeks prior to this year's race "to memorize all the tricky spots and compass bearings." Thus their running so well during the race was the product of hard-earned experience, training, and dedication.

Battling strong wind at the higher elevations, and very cold temperatures, Jim and Mike completed the fourth loop in 45:25:04 and 45:29:44, respectively. This was one of the few times that Jim led Mike into the campground. Their typical pattern, in both this year's and last year's races, was for Mike to arrive shortly before Jim. Gary described Mike as "struggling." Both runners spent only about 15 minutes in camp, and then headed out separately on loop five. Jim stated in a post-race e-mail that he had taken a five-minute nap when he came into camp after the fourth loop.

Despite his short nap, Jim was the first of the two to start a fifth loop. Mike followed about five minutes later, apparently without sleeping. However, because of a new rule this year, Mike didn't exactly "follow" Jim. The new rule required that runners on their fifth loops had to run that loop in opposite directions. Jim had chosen to go in the more-familiar clockwise direction, thus forcing Mike to go counterclockwise on his fifth loop. This marked the first time in the history of the race that this rule had been implemented. In his *UltraRunning* article, Gary quoted Mike as saying about this rule that "the cruelest thing" about this year's Barkley was "making us race that last loop." Gary had found yet another trick to make the Barkley tougher. Even though, as had been noted several times in previous years, the essential nature of the Barkley is "man against *that*" rather than man against man, Gary was now forcing the competitors to race against each other, not just against the course and the elements.

Interestingly, these two friends and competitors met each other, going in opposite directions, at just where they both had thought they would, near the bottom of Little Hell. They could both see that the race was still tight. By the end, although he appeared to be struggling the more of the two at the start of the fifth loop, and although he started five minutes later and was forced into the less-familiar counterclockwise direction, Mike Tilden was able to cover the fifth loop slightly faster than Jim. One factor in this, as Gary reported in *UltraRunning*, was that for Jim, "sleepiness had finally overcome him, he admitted he had taken a five-minute nap" during the fifth loop. Thus Jim had slept twice, but only for about five minutes each time. Jim also later reported having hallucinations during his fifth loop. He wrote: "It was here that I started mild hallucinations that would last the rest of the day. For me, both here and at Nolan's, hallucinations tend to be 'shape shifting'. I would see a shape made from trees, rocks, etc., not know what it was so my mind would assign a noun name to it. I first saw a huge structure that looked like a big deck or boat dock out towards sob ditch. As you approach, they disappear and turn into the things they really are. I saw people, chairs, and other things I can't remember. It wasn't scary, more amusing than anything."

Mike finished in 57:25:18, a mere three minutes and seven seconds ahead of Jim, in 57:28:25. Perhaps his five-minute naps had cost Jim the race. On the other hand, his ten minutes of sleep may have enabled him to run faster when he was moving. In any case, these two tough running friends had given us something that had never before been seen at the Barkley—a race to the finish of the 100-miler. In the past, the 100-mile finishers had either been the only runners on their final loops (Mark Williams in 1995, and Cave Dog Keizer in 2003) or had been running intentionally together (Horton and Wood in 2001). Now the extra element and stress of head-to-head racing between runners had been added.

A few years later I asked Jim Nelson how he and Mike, being such good friends, had felt about competing against each other on that final loop. Jim assured me that they had both strongly wanted to beat the other. I think that this was an example of racing at its finest. The word "competition" is derived from Latin language roots, with the suffix "com" meaning together, and the verb root "petere" meaning "to strive." Thus the literal meaning of "compete" is "to strive together." In 2003, Mike and Jim had competed by running the Barkley together. Now they had taken the Barkley to a higher, subtly different level of competition. I think that there should be a word "contrapetition" to indicate the man-against-man struggle against each other such as was seen at the 2004 Barkley. In my opinion, the newly added element of forced contrapetition, rather than allowing runners to run as a team on the fifth loop, enhanced the status of the Barkley as a true race. I was glad that Gary had implemented this new rule.

Here is the list of starters, their numbers of Barkley starts, and their loop-finishing times for 2004.

1. Mike Tilden (4)	8:38:09	19:17:13	31:37:38	45:29:44	57:25:18
2. Jim Nelson (2)	8:39:31	19:17:53	31:37:57	45:25:04	57:28:25
3. David Horton (10)	8:31:10	19:18:31	30:57:09	Quit on loop four.	
4. Andrew Thompson (6)	8:31:12	19:18:32	36:19:21		
5. Jason Poole (4)	8:31:11	19:18:34	36:19:22		
6. Todd Holmes (2)	8:31:15	19:18:33	36:19:23		
7. Craig Wilson (8)	8:53:12	22:25:27	36:19:24		
8. Hal Koerner (1)	8:30:48	19:18:35			
9. Mark Dorion (4)	9:11:14	24:30:06	Quit during loop three.		
10. Michael Bur (2)	9:21:00	24:59:21			
11. Buttslide Martin (11)	11:10:11	26:33:26			
12. Sue Thompson (5)	10:52:20	26:33:27			
13. Matt Mahoney (9)	12:04:59	~28:37* Finished loop two over time limit.			
14. Joe Kowalski (2)	11:41:15	~28:51* Finished loop two over time limit.			
15. Rob Youngren (4)	8:45:55				
16. Hiram Rogers (1)	10:28:32	Quit during loop two.			
17. Rob Hills (1)	10:53:32				
18. John DeWalt (16)	11:07:32				
19. David Hughes (6)	11:52:42				
20. Spyder Tynes (2)	12:41:19				
21. Herb Hedgecock (2)	12:41:20				
22. Dick West (9)	12:44:06				
23. John Bowman (1)	12:52:40				
24. Rich Limacher (3)	12:56:29				

25. Rollin Perry (1)   ~18:42* Finished loop one over the time limit.
26. Stu Gleman (7)   Quit during loop one.
27. Hugo Walker (1)   Quit during loop one.
28. <u>Janice Cahalane</u> (1) Quit during loop one.
29. Fred Purloin (13)   Quit during loop one.
30. Stephen Miller (2)   Quit during loop one.
31. Luke Bartlett (1)   Quit during loop one.
32 Starters

+++++++++++

Below is the essay I wrote for entry into the 2004 Barkley Marathons. However, I subsequently did not enter the race in 2004, and did not submit this essay to Gary.

Why I Should Be Allowed To Run The Barkley
Essay #10 in a Series
By Frozen Ed Furtaw
February 2004

I should be allowed to run the Barkley because I am lazarus lake's friend and it would be nice for us to see each other again. Besides that, I don't want to be ~~depraved~~ deprived of all the fun that I would miss if I don't run it again.

In an e-mail to an ultrarunner friend recently, I wrote about Barkley: "The experience is unforgettable, i.e., you become permanently warped. But for us fun-loving ultrarunners, it is an overindulgence in what we love to do, i.e., running in the woods and mountains without the constraint of having to stay on a "sissy trail," until you have had enough." This excerpt addresses the question of why I should run Barkley again. In a nutshell, the reason is that it is what I love to do. The fact that much of Barkley is run without having to stay on sissy trails truly is one of the factors that separates Barkley from other ultradistance races, and makes it more adventurous and fun.

Things are different now than when I was younger. Then I was confident that I could finish the three-loop fun run. Now I wimpily admit that I probably can't. Since the Barkley loop was expanded in 1995, I have not yet, in five subsequent attempts, finished even two loops. So for this year, finishing two loops is my goal. I have never admitted this before. This proves that the Barkley has reduced my ego to a mere shadow of its former self. This is good, and is a major reason why I love running Barkley.

My two most recent attempts at Barkley have ended in my quitting after a mere one loop. This weeniness is embarrassing. This year I shall attempt to salvage a little self-respect by completing two loops. When I finished the old 55-mile Barkley fun run in 1988 and 1991, I was able to do most of my running in the daylight. However, now that the loop is much tougher and slower, I have found that I can barely finish the first loop in daylight of the first day. This means that the great majority of my second loop will be done in the dark. That is pretty scary! As lazarus has said, being skeert of the dark is a major reason why many of us weenies DNF Barkley. I am man enough to admit that it is scary out there alone in the vast trackless wilderness that surrounds the Barkley course. So for this year, my challenge is to overcome my fear of what's out there in the dark, and complete loop two. I will train myself for this ordeal by watching the movie "The Blair Witch Project" to scare the crap out of me about being out in the woods in the dark.

Last year I attempted the Javelina Jundred. Lazarus knows, because he was there too. We both quit while whining about our injuries. However, a nice thing happened to me in that event—I ran for several hours in the dark. In previous years, I have not been that fond of running in the dark. However, at the Javelina Jundred, I discovered that it really can be a lot of fun. So for this year at Barkley, my goal is to have fun running my second loop in the dark. One factor that made running at night fun at the Javelina was the full moon. I notice that Barkley occurs near a full moon this year. This gives me hope that I will successfully complete the second loop.

Of course, if I can finish two loops within the unreasonably strict time limit of 26 hours and 40 minutes, I would then be faced with the next level of challenge, which would be to attempt loop three. I know I'm not man enough to do that, so I might as well end this essay before I am tempted to suggest that I could do three loops. You see what a wimp I have become. I hope you are satisfied, lazarus!

Chapter 24
2005: Barkley Terminated and Resurrected; Losing Control

The previous three runnings of the Barkley had seen relatively great successes, with five 100-mile finishers, including one or two in each year. The Barkley was beginning to lose some of its air of invincibility. However, before the next edition of the event, we followers of the Barkley would be given a new scare to worry about.

In an e-mail to his list of Barkley friends dated November 11, 2004, Gary wrote some truly dreaded words. Only this time it was not another toughening of the course or rules. This time it was more of a death threat, not to any of us, but to the Barkley itself. Gary wrote:

"While it was not made public at the time,
the state has made a move to terminate the barkley.
it is not held on trails open to the public.
i will be meeting with a bunch of state bigwigs in december,
to see if we can work out keeping the run going.
and i feel pretty good about our chances.
however, we have been asked to request that runners
not go out onto the course at this time.
we have opened up clear routes into the backcountry
that are being used by poachers.
we dont need to start a letter writing campaign.
we have been working on this carefully.
things are going good, and we dont want to rock the boat.
so please dont go train on the course at this time.
thanks,
laz"

To me it seemed preposterous to think that we Barkley runners were somehow trampling the woods to the extent that we should be prohibited from using it because poachers would follow our tracks. However, this stunning e-mail was followed by another even more dire statement from Gary to the Barkley followers on January 7, 2005. Gary now wrote: "so the meeting did not go well this morning. the state has forbidden the continuation of the Barkley." He also asked for suggestions on how we could respond. In another e-mail from Gary on the same date, he further stated that one of the arguments made against the Barkley at his meeting earlier that day, was that other groups, including mountain bikers and horse riders, had approached State officials about holding other races on the Barkley course. He then described in an eloquent but sad way what had transpired that day: "i have been going 'out there' since the '70s, when it [Frozen Head] was not even a park. i remember the first time we went, and found that it had been made a park. they were telling us how 'wonderful' it would be, now that it was a park. i told them that it was nice to have a road, and all, but i really just wanted to be in the woods... and that 'some day you will throw us out'. that day was today. laz"

These e-mails started a flurry of correspondence, both among us Barkley fans, and from some runners to state officials. Different people took different approaches. Some expressed anger. Some wanted to just go ahead and run either clandestinely or defiantly. Kerry Trammell, from nearby Oak Ridge, Tennessee, offered to work through some state legislators and officials whom he knew. I also expressed my opinions and suggestions in an e-mail to Gary, with copies to other Barkley followers. I wrote that I too was angry and pained, and called the decision to terminate the Barkley incomprehensible. I suggested moving the event to a nearby national forest and keeping it small enough, and with no fees, such that it would not be an official event. I also said: "Trying to pull political strings to get Barkley re-allowed at Frozen Head is a good idea for those who have the stomach to take that approach, which I don't". I further wrote: "Good luck with whatever you decide to do. I am still hoping to write a book about Barkley after I retire and have time to devote to it. The current situation is going to make an interesting chapter, and I have a hunch that it won't be the final chapter."

Several days later, Kerry Trammell again e-mailed the list of us Barkley aficionados, saying: "We are trying to work this thing out by working with our local legislators and contacts in Nashville. Let us try to work the system before we go too far the other direction. I have heard back from several contacts in Nashville who are 'seeing what they can do' it will take a little time. This is gary's gig. He needs to be the one deciding the direction of the protest. Civil disobedience might be the answer..but not right now." Gary followed this by stating: "i aint near giving up. it dont look so good for this year, but if we have a breakthru, we will go with anyone who can still make it."

It was 27 days later that this "breakthru" occurred. On February 16, 2005, Gary sent another e-mail to the Barkley group, this time with the good news: "ok you fine people. the word came today. we will be getting barked this fool's weekend!!!!!!!!!!!!!!!!!! the barkley has been given a reprieve for this year."

The Barkley, like Lazarus of the Bible, had been resurrected from the dead! However, there was also a warning that its new life may not last long.

Joe Kowalski, one of the Barkley runners who had written to state officials about the Barkley, shared with the group the response that he had gotten from Betsy Child, who was then the Commissioner of the Tennessee Department of Environment and Conservation (TDEC). She had sent him the following statement by e-mail: "For the past several years, our staff at Frozen Head has expressed concerns with the organizer about this type of race and the negative impact it has on the park's highly sensitive natural areas. Therefore, this is the last year that we will allow the race to be held in the park. However, we have suggested that there are at least three other State managed properties located in the same geographical area which are comparable to Frozen Head and are all more conducive to this type event." Based on news articles that two of the runners sent to the e-mail list, the three other areas referred to were the Royal Blue Wildlife Management Area, the Sundquist Wildlife Management Area, and the Chuck Swan State Forest. The first two were said to both be in an area of the Cumberland Mountains that was still mined for coal. Joe also had received correspondence from Mr. James Fyke, who was then the TDEC Deputy Commissioner for State Parks and Conservation. Fyke appeared to be one of those state officials who was convinced that we were harming Frozen Head, and who seemed determined to protect the environment by putting an end to the Barkley. We did not know it at this time, but in the following month, Mr. Fyke would be promoted to Commissioner of the TDEC. We will see in the next chapter how Fyke's name eventually became immortalized in the story of the Barkley.

Gary wrote a few days later that he had visited one of the alternate sites that the TDEC had suggested moving the race to. He displayed his dislike, saying: "i have never seen such devastation in my life. strip mines. clearcuts, jeep roads, 4-wheeler tracks, all the remainder of the mountains around frozen head are an enormous waste pit. if you could see what has become of the area, you would treasure frozen head even more. we will never be running in the wastelands."   Clearly, Gary was determined to not move the Barkley to another venue.

In another e-mail, dated March 4, 2005, Gary shed some light on how the one-year reprieve had been obtained: "this year was a particularly trying one, as the state made a concerted effort to terminate the barkley, and by early january had succeeded in having it banned. after an extended political struggle, in which there were many heroes, especially runners stu gleman and kerry trammell, along with several of our state legislators including senators randy mcnally and jim tracy, we succeeded in achieving a one year reprieve."

By late March, the focus of the Barkley-related e-mail activity had turned to the next running of the race, which began on April 2, 2005. In his post-race article in *UltraRunning*, Gary reported that 33 runners actually started the race. However, Gary named only three of the runners and did not provide many loop-finishing times in his *UltraRunning* article. Most of the information in the following list was obtained from Matt Mahoney's website and from post-race e-mails. Besides those listed below, there was one other unknown starter.

Returning former Barkley runners were the previous year's 100-mile finishers, Mike Tilden and Jim Nelson. Other returners were Andrew Thompson, Todd Holmes, Michael Bur, Craig Wilson, Mark Dorion, Chip Tuthill, Kerry Trammell, Joe Kowalski, John DeWalt, Buttslide Martin, Hiram Rogers, Matt Mahoney, Stu Gleman, Rich Limacher, David Hughes, Dick West, Sue Thompson, and Mike Dobies. Barkley Virgins this year were Davy Henn (the elder of the two sons of Karl Raw Dog and Cathy Henn), Wendell Doman, Elise Harrington, Mark Shipley, Dan Baglione, Liam Douglas, Sam Baucom, Nick Graner, Keith Dunn, Pete Ireland, Bill Losey, and Ray Krolewicz. Ray was a well-known ultrarunner who had been one of the top ultrarunners in the U.S. in the 1980s. This would be his first attempt at the Barkley. So despite the pre-race turmoil, the entry field again included many of the Barkley regulars, and another group of strong runners, including seven former Barkley Fun Run finishers and the two 100-mile finishers of last year.

Another familiar presence was also at Frozen Head this year for the Barkley: rain. It started falling the night before the race, and then stopped raining on race morning before the start of the run. However, Gary reported that just after the runners started, "the rain returned with a vengeance." Also, the temperature was close to freezing, and the precipitation was in the form of snow in the higher elevations, i.e., on most of the Barkley course. The usual horrible conditions, including the slippery side-slopes of the NBT that accompany rain at Frozen Head, were exacerbated by strong winds and cold temperatures. This harsh state of affairs led to a rapid attrition of the number of runners willing to stay out there.

Two Barkley regulars, Mike Dobies and Sue Thompson, were running together. When they got to Coffin Springs on loop one, they decided that they had suffered enough in the bad conditions, and headed down Quitter's Road to find shelter back at camp. As they headed back, they realized that the first of them to arrive back would be considered "DFL" (Dead F****** Last), a well-known acronym in the sport of ultrarunning, and one to which there is a little humorous honor attached. They thus proceeded to race each other to the finish for that honor. Mike won that race, thus becoming the first to be tapped out after a little less than six hours *out there*. Since the regular bugler, Davy Henn, was still *out there* running the race, Gary himself had to do the bugling for Mike and Sue. Gary would soon be kept busy blowing that bugle, as 15 of the starting 33 runners dropped out before finishing the first loop. Even the illustrious Ray Krolewicz did not make it past Coffin Springs. He was in a group of six runners, including Sam Baucom, Liam Douglas, Stu Gleman, Rich Limacher, and Keith Dunn. They were all near the back of the pack and trying to stay on course in part by following Stu, who knew the course. But they were so slow that it took them about five and a half hours to get to Coffin Springs. So they all bailed there and took the Quitter's Road back to camp, arriving about eight hours after the start of the race, having collected two pages. David Hughes was another starter who quit and returned from Coffin Springs. Dick West and Pete Ireland made it farther, to about the Hump, before quitting on loop one. Bill Losey was another who failed to finish the first loop.

Dan Baglione, a very experienced ultrarunner, and at 74 the oldest runner to ever yet attempt the Barkley, ran together with Nick Graner at the back of the pack. They did not even make it to the second book, at the Garden Spot, on the first loop. They got off-course on the tricky NBT, and finally managed to find their way back to the Quitter's Road and took it back to camp. They had collected only one page in ten hours *out there*. Dan later wrote: "Barkley was all I expected it to be and more. It was a miserable day; but I am very glad I was there. Met some great people. It was an experience I shall long remember." However, as we will see in the next chapter, this was not be be Dan's last run at the Barkley, and it was not to be his most memorable.

Eighteen runners did complete loop one, with Mike Bur first in at 9:12. Next were Jim Nelson at 9:17, Andrew Thompson at 9:21, Todd Holmes at 9:34, Craig Wilson at 10:23, and Mike Tilden at 10:59. Clearly the wet conditions were adding significantly to the time and effort of running. Others to complete loop one, in order, were Henn, Doman, Dorion, Tuthill, Trammell, Kowalski, DeWalt, Harrington, Martin, Rogers, Shipley, and Mahoney. Matt Mahoney had a rather humorous story to tell several days afterward. He had carried a disposable camera on this first loop, and had subsequently taken the camera to a Walmart store to get the pictures developed. But the store apparently got his photos switched with someone else's. Matt ended up with a pack of pictures of "a cute baby and some other people, but nobody I recognized. I suppose that's a happier scene than people thrashing through sawbriers, deadfalls, mud, rain and snow on monster hills, but not really what I was expecting :-(I suppose somebody somewhere is looking at my pictures, wondering who are these people and where is this place and do I want to put these in my baby album???"

Elise Harrington had a harrowing experience on this difficult first loop. While in a group of runners on the NBT, she had gotten hit on the top of the head by a branch that broke off a deadfall when another runner put his weight on it. This blow caused a gash on her head and a mild concussion. After a brief recovery, Elise wrapped a bandanna around her head and continued to finish the loop. When she arrived back in camp, Gary saw the bloody wrapping on her head and declared that she was the winner of the "Best Blood Award."

Nine runners continued onto loop two, but even though the weather turned nice at night, only four runners finished the second loop within the 26:40 time limit, in the following times: Nelson 21:37:07, Thompson 21:37:37, Holmes 24:04:53, and Bur 24:32:23. Also finishing the second loop, but over the time limit, were Craig Wilson, who had previously finished several Fun Runs, and Mark Dorion, in 31:33. These intrepid runners completed the second loop despite knowing that this loop would not be considered official. Reading Mark's post-race e-mail report, I noticed several problems he faced. He fell into Phillips Creek while trying to cross it in the dark. He got off course and tried to take a compass reading, but doubted the accuracy of his compass. He got lost trying to get up to the Garden Spot in the dark. He lost his gloves. Ironically, these were all miscues that I too had experienced in the past at Frozen Head.

Of the four two-loop finishers, only three continued on to the third loop: Nelson, Thompson, and Bur. Gary reported that: "The second afternoon was beautiful, sunny and warm. It was a shame that only three runners were around to enjoy it." Jim Nelson and Andrew Thompson finished that loop, still running virtually together, with Nelson being logged in first in 32:48:53, and Thompson in 32:48:57. They spent about 25 minutes in camp, and then headed back *out there* on loop four. About 15 minutes later, Mike Bur came in, but he was struggling and, having seen that he could not complete loop three within the time limit, "came slowly limping into camp" without having completed the loop. Thus Jim and Andrew were the only Fun Run finishers this year. And they were both now together into the rare fourth loop, the counterclockwise, nighttime loop that most who had ever gotten this far agree is the crux of the race. Would the Barkley see a second straight year with a dramatic race to the 100-mile finish?

This question was answered on the fourth loop. While on the NBT, with only about five miles to go before finishing the loop, Jim reached his limit. He told Andrew that he needed to take a nap, and that Andrew should go on ahead without him. Andrew forged ahead while Jim slept *out there* on the trail. Andrew finished the fourth loop shortly after sunrise on Monday, another day of good weather. His time to finish loop four was 47:26:59, so Andrew had just over a half hour to begin loop five. He started the loop with nine minutes to spare, going in the clockwise direction. He thus became the seventh person in the history of the race to begin a fifth loop, what Andrew later called "hallowed territory."

Andrew encountered Jim Nelson as Andrew was going down the north side of Bird Mountain, while Jim was climbing up, still heading toward camp on his fourth loop, but for which he was now past the time limit. Jim encouraged Andrew to "get going!" and never stop. Andrew continued, soon collecting his first page at Phillips Creek, and following Jim's advice to not stop. However, as he continued eastward on the NBT, he began having hallucinations of houses and neighborhoods in the surrounding woods. His exertion and lack of sleep for over 50 hours now were beginning to take their toll. By the time he got to the area of Son of a Bitch Ditch and the coal ponds, about a mile before the Garden Spot, he had pretty much lost his ability to make forward progress. As Andrew expressed it later, he experienced "a profound loss of purpose."

Several days later he wrote and e-mailed a lengthy report on what he then experienced. Like Blake's tale of his fifth-loop attempt in 2000, Andrew's is one of the most astounding and gripping stories I have ever read about the Barkley. It is best read in Andrew's own words:

"I crossed the ditch and looked for the ponds. Nothing. Just more trail. Back and forth I went, screaming like a lunatic in an evil nightmare. *Where the hell are the ponds?* The little trail that climbs the tailings, 'piled high to the outside.'—where are they? I traversed this short stretch perhaps 5 or 6 times, back and forth. Even after finding the ponds, I returned to the ditch in disbelief of the distance between. *Where is Mike Dobies' house? Who the f**k moved Mike Dobies' house?!*

I was now losing my mind in the full definition of the phrase. The Barkley would be forgotten for minutes on end although the premise lingered. I HAD to get to the Garden Spot, for...*why?* Was there someone there?

Content with finally finding the ponds, although still confused as to the whereabouts of Dobies' house, I climbed the tailings and motored around them to face the next significant climb of the Barkley Trail—Garden Spot. From the bottom I sighted the top, and I climbed in beeline fashion along the North Boundary until finally nailing the summit, and book 2. I looked at my watch—12:30. Four hours, 21 minutes for Bird Mtn. and the North Boundary Trail. This was the last time I looked at my watch. It was the last time that *time* contained any sort of significance. It was my last forward step toward the yellow gate, and the Barley 100 finish.

I sat beside Book 2 for several hours. I never collected my page. I didn't know there was a page there to collect. Loop 5 became a final exam that I could just make-up later. I was a one-hour downhill away from the halfway point in the loop. There were cars down below me in the gap. Hikers maybe? Mountain dwellers? Who knows, just people moving about. Walking in their lawns, while neighbors drove past. The race just faded away. I was ....just...there—looking around. If my mother had walked up to me at that point, I would have looked at her like she was a falling leaf.

After some time I walked down to the gap so I could hitch a ride with one of those cars, but they were all gone. (This is a profound concept. See, on a topo, it looks as if one could see the gap from the Garden Spot, and in the memory it seems so as well. But one could no more see into the gap from that position as they could see the campfires back at Big Cove. **But *I* could**.) So I stood in a shin-deep puddle for about an hour—squishing the mud in and out of my shoes. No cars. I inspected every 4-wheeler trail intersecting the gap, hoping to find a house. I walked long, up each road, but found nobody, and no houses. I walked down to Coffin Springs (the first water drop). I sat and poured gallon after gallon of fresh water into my shoes. I inspected each interesting landmark of the area, even the spring itself. The Cumberland Trail passes through here, and I marveled at the trail signs, and its white blazes. I inspected the painted trees, marking the park boundary; sometimes walking well into the woods just to look at some paint on a tree.

I had only one road left to explore, and the Cumberland Trail blazes followed it. So off I went, without any recollection of time, place, the Barkley, the people at camp, Jonboy, nothing.

I thought of Spring, and vernal pools, and spring peepers. I saw some tadpoles in the tire ruts filled with water. I expected a passing car at any moment so I could throw out a thumb. If one did stop, I would have been quite a sight. None passed. Not for 6 hours. I was on a gated road (which is now called a trail) that led directly back to camp. I could have been on numbered highway to Kentucky for all I knew, and I would have been just as content with that. I found a nice stick. It was perfect for bashing briars, which I did, on the roadside for extended periods of time. Just whipping them and bashing them. Then it was great for hitting small pebbles and hearing where they landed way down the mountainside. *Keep your eye on the f*#king pebble, man.*

When it cooled off, I had a long-sleeve shirt. When I got hungry, I had food. When it got dark, I had a light. *Wow, isn't it strange that I have all this perfect stuff, just when I need it?* Whenever I needed something else, PRESTO!, right in my pack. *Strange.*

I rounded a bend and BAM! --Big Cove Branch. Oh, shi.......

It all came flooding back in waves of sickening heartache. **The Barkley.** *Dude, you just pissed away the Barkley 100.* Ironically, I returned to camp at the precise time I was expected --just from the wrong direction. There were the bodies, lined up at the yellow gate. Jonboy called out, "Ange!" (Andrew shortened) I felt sheepish. I felt like an utter loser. I was led to the fire, to add to the annals of epic harrowing tales of failure. Mine may be the best yet, and Blake may be the only one who can truly sympathize.

I gazed into the fire and spoke for a long time--eight grown men stood around listening silently. Oh, the fire was a cacophony of voices and faces and ancient script burned into the logs. Gary's words seared

my soul when he said, "When you left here, you looked to be in total control." This is the final and most important quality of a successful Barkley runner--**being in total control**.
4/11/05
Andrew Thompson, 28, of Northern New Hampshire."

Below is a list of the known starters, their numbers of Barkley starts, and their loop-finishing times for 2005.

1. Andrew Thompson (7) 9:21:06	21:37:37	32:48:57	47:26:59 Quit on loop 5.
2. Jim Nelson (3) 9:16:58	21.37.07	32.48.53	Quit on loop four.
3. Todd Holmes (3) 9:33:54	24:04:53		
4. Michael Bur (3) 9:12:48	24:32:23	Quit during loop three.	
5. Craig Wilson (9) 10:23:10	Finished loop two over the time limit.		
6. Mark Dorion (5) 11:38:15	~31:33*Finished loop two over time limit.		
7. Mike Tilden (5) 10:59:02			
8. Davy Henn (1) 11:13:37			
9. Wendell Doman (1) 11:27:55	Quit during loop two.		
10. Chip Tuthill (2) 11:50:28			
11. Kerry Trammell (7) 11:59:39			
12. Joe Kowalski (3) 12:08:21			
13. John DeWalt (17) 12:09:15			
14. Elise Harrington (1) 12:09:51			
15. Buttslide Martin (12) 12:19:00			
16. Hiram Rogers (2) 13:10:52			
17. Mark Shipley (1) 13:11:05			
18. Matt Mahoney (10) 13:14:27			
19. Dan Baglione (1) Lost on loop one.			
20. Liam Douglas (1) Quit during loop one.			
21. Ray Krolewicz (1) Quit during loop one.			
22. Sam Baucom (1) Quit during loop one.			
23. Nick Graner (1) Quit during loop one.			
24. Stu Gleman (8) Quit during loop one.			
25. Rich Limacher (4) Quit during loop one.			
26. Keith Dunn (1) Quit during loop one.			
27. David Hughes (7) Quit during loop one.			
28. Dick West (10) Quit during loop one.			
29. Pete Ireland (1) Quit during loop one.			
30. Bill Losey (1) Quit during loop one.			
31. Sue Thompson (6) Quit during loop one.			
32. Mike Dobies (7) Quit during loop one.			

33 Starters

Chapter 25
2006: Saved By Law; Hell for the Highway

The previous year, 2005, was supposed to have been the last year of the Barkley Marathons at Frozen Head, at least if the TDEC had had its way. The Barkley's existence was still in doubt in early 2006. On January 4, 2006, Gary sent an e-mail to his distribution list of Barkley followers. One of the recipients of this e-mail was Tennessee State Senator Jim Tracy. Gary recognized Senator Tracy's role last year in resurrecting the Barkley after the TDEC had terminated it. Gary wrote: "we have a guest on the mailing list today, sen jim tracy of tenn. jim is one of the good guys, without him and senator randy mcnally, we would not have gotten to run last year. ... as of today, i am feeling fairly positive about the run. we still have a slim hope of just getting a reasonable response thru channels, if not, i will send you more information ... later. we still have a trick or two. thanks to all for your patience, i will get back to you soon. laz"

The breakthrough we Barkley lovers were all waiting for happened soon thereafter. Gary distributed another e-mail, on February 8, 2006, informing us that the Barkley was going to happen. His message was mostly teasing about what would be some course changes. The important message of Barkley's salvation was stated cryptically: "as i said in the beginning, we had to give some things up... as i said in the beginning, they had to give some things up. i will miss the parts of the course we lost. but i cant wait to try out the parts we gained... and we already have names for these new trails: fyke's folly... and engebrittson boulevard. expect them to make their place in barkley lore real soon."

What had happened was that the Tennessee legislature had passed a resolution telling the TDEC to work with Gary to let the Barkley continue at Frozen Head, with course changes as needed to protect the environment of the State Natural Area. This resolution had been introduced by Senators Tracy and McNally. The Barkley was saved! I am grateful to Kerry Trammell for providing me with a copy of the resolution. Here is what it said:

Filed for intro 02/13/2006
SENATE JOINT RESOLUTION 547
By McNally

A RESOLUTION relative to the Barkley ultra marathon held in Frozen Head Park in Morgan County.

WHEREAS, the Barkley ultra marathon, which has been held in Frozen Head State Park since 1985, is unquestionably one of the toughest 100-mile races in the world, as it features 52,900 feet of climb and an equal length of descent; and

WHEREAS, over the past 20 years, the Barkley and Frozen Head have become a Mecca for lovers of the great outdoors; the race attracts a diverse group of participants from all over the world who share in common a passionate love for the wilderness, challenge, and Frozen Head itself; and

WHEREAS, the fact that only six participants have completed the full 100 miles of the race within the 60-hour time limit during the past 20 years (over 600 attempts) speaks volumes about the unique character and extreme difficulty of the Barkley, as well as the inner fortitude, perseverance, and mental and physical discipline evidenced by its participants; and

WHEREAS, truly like no other place on earth, Frozen Head State Park provides a unique setting for this unique race; the park's monolithic mountains seem to pierce the jet stream, and temperatures can vary from 10-20 degrees or more from place to place, just as the weather can change completely within an hour from the valley to the ridgeline; and

WHEREAS, the park's perimeter trails, which were built by the Civilian Conservation Corps in the 1930s, make Frozen Head and the Barkley a perfect match; built to the park's boundary lines on the map, and ignoring completely the park's rugged terrain, the steepness of Frozen Head's northern boundary trail makes it useless for normal backpacking or hiking; however, this same feature makes the trail perfect for people who love to climb mountains, namely the Barkley's participants; and

WHEREAS, as the race has grown in popularity, the Barkley's organizers have worked closely with the Division of Parks to prevent damage to sensitive ecological areas in Frozen Head by altering the race's route; the organizers have also restricted the number of participants to 35 and ceased to post notice of the event, relying solely on word-of-mouth publicity; and

WHEREAS, the close relationship between the race's organizers and state park personnel has helped to ensure that the Barkley's participants leave behind no permanent disfigurement of Frozen Head; and

WHEREAS, after 20 years of a mutually beneficial relationship, the Department of Environment and Conservation has recently informed the race's organizers that the Barkley can no longer be held at Frozen Head, citing the race as an "inappropriate use" of the park; and

WHEREAS, this General Assembly respectfully disagrees with the Department's decision, believing strongly that not only is the Barkley an appropriate use for Frozen Head, the race is a precious jewel of Tennessee's outdoor recreation culture that is well worth preserving; now, therefore,

BE IT RESOLVED BY THE SENATE OF THE ONE HUNDRED FOURTH GENERAL ASSEMBLY OF THE STATE OF TENNESSEE, THE HOUSE OF REPRESENTATIVES CONCURRING, that this Body hereby strongly urges and encourages the Department of Environment and Conservation, Division of Parks, to reconsider its decision and permit the Barkley ultra marathon to be held in Frozen Head State Park in 2006 and annually thereafter.

BE IT FURTHER RESOLVED, that an enrolled copy of this resolution be transmitted to the Commissioner of Environment and Conservation.

++++++++++

In this resolution, the Tennessee legislators decided that the running of the Barkley was an appropriate use of the Natural Area, and called the Barkley "a precious jewel" of recreation. As a Barkley aficionado, I was elated to see this legal sanctioning of the existence of my favorite race.

An article about the "deal reached on trail race at Frozen Head," written by news reporter Morgan Simmons, appeared in the *Knoxville News Sentinel* newspaper on February 13, 2006. In that article, Mr. Mike Carlton, the TDEC's Assistant Commissioner for Parks and Recreation, said that the state wanted the Barkley tradition to continue but not at the expense of the special regulations that protect natural areas. Carlton is quoted as saying: "We recognize this event has been going on for some time, and that these people have a real passion for what they're doing. I'm pleased as punch we found middle ground we both agree on."

Talking to Gary at the Barkley in 2006, I found out that apparently the local Park Superintendent, Dave Engebretson, had been one of those who had tried to get the Barkley terminated, or at least removed from the Frozen Head State Natural Area. Dave had reportedly been the principal anti-Barkley spokesman at Gary's most recent meeting with state officials. I was surprised to learn this, as Dave had always been extremely friendly toward me and all the other Barkley participants, as far as I knew. I was not aware that he apparently had genuine concerns that the Barkley was or could be doing some actual environmental harm. I presume that Dave had what he believed were legitimate concerns. It is, after all, his professional responsibility to protect and manage the Frozen Head State Park and Natural Area in accordance with law, and to protect its environment. Fortunately, the state legislators' resolution would keep the Barkley alive, with due consideration for protecting the Natural Area.

At the meeting between Gary and state officials, they had worked out a compromise that included rerouting part of the course. Gary didn't reveal the new course description until the day before the race, but in February and March he provided several clues in e-mails to us wondering Barkley entrants. In an e-mail to Gary and others, I admitted that I was spending hours poring over the map trying to unravel the mystery, and had some hunches, but wasn't sure. I also expressed my happiness with the fact that there were to be some new navigational challenges. I stated my opinion that the Barkley should require navigation and not just running.

I was happy to be returning to Barkley, after missing the past two years. I was now retired and had moved with Gail to our new home in Pagosa Springs, Colorado. I thought I was pretty well prepared for Barkley, as I usually do before the race begins. However, consistent with my relatively low mileage of recent years, I had been running an average of only about 26.4 miles per week for the 10-week period building up to Barkley. So I was probably very inadequately trained; I would soon find out. An old Barkley friend and two-time 55-mile finisher, Nick Williams, also came back to Frozen Head this year. Nick wasn't running ultras any longer, but he was there to enjoy the company of old friends and observe the unfolding of the race. Nick was kind enough to share his pop-up camper with me while he was at Frozen Head, so I had nicer accommodations this year than my usual leaky tent.

On the day before the race began, Gary arrived and set up his camp, and then the moment we were all waiting for arrived: Gary distributed the new course instructions and made his marked "Master Map" available. Runners had to take turns copying the marked course onto their own maps. We all began studying the map and directions to decipher the course changes.

The part of the course that was now being skipped was the New River section, frequently referred to as Hell, which I had always thought was one of the most naturally beautiful parts of the Barkley course. You could say we were being thrown out of Hell. In exchange, the course was to be rerouted onto more of the coal-mined private property around Stallion Mountain. Recall that since 2003, the top of Stallion Mountain had been part of the course. Now more of it would be in play.

The new course layout would go from the Garden Spot directly to the northern peak of Stallion Mountain, without going to Coffin Springs. This is the same Stallion Mountain peak that we had gone to since 2003. The bottled water that formerly was dropped at Coffin Springs would now be placed at a jeep road slightly outside the Frozen Head State Natural Area, and close to the dirt road that the runners took from the Garden Spot to Stallion Mountain. From the northern peak of Stallion Mountain, the runners would now go to the southeastern peak of Stallion Mountain. This peak had been virtually strip mined away, such that it was now a flattened area rather than the true peak shown on the topographic map. The map shows the peak at an elevation of about 3,250 feet. The area comprising the elongated top of Stallion Mountain is laced with old mining roads and 4-wheeler vehicle tracks. It is also heavily overgrown with briers, as is so much of the area around Frozen Head. Gary referred to the southeastern peak of Stallion Mountain as Fyke's Peak. A book was placed in a plastic bag in, of all places, a rattlesnake hole on Fyke's Peak, for the runners to remove a page to prove they were there.

From Fyke's Peak, the new course went virtually straight southeasterly down a ridge of Stallion Mountain until it was a few tenths of a mile above the New River, and then dropped south down to the river, at an elevation of about 1,580 feet. Gary referred to this route as Fyke's Folly. The elevation descent on Fyke's Folly is about 1,650 feet in a distance of about 1.4 miles. Then the runners crossed the New River just below Tennessee Highway 116. The runners crossed the highway and then went up a very steep powerline cut that climbed about 860 feet in 0.8 mile to a ridge that Gary called Engebrittson Pass (spelled as such, a misspelling of Dave Engebretson's name). The powerline cut was called the Testicle Spectacle trail. Of course, as in the case of the powerline cut referred to as the Rat Jaw, this trail was also heavily grown over with briers. A book was placed in a hollow tree on Engebrittson Pass. The new names on the course, Fyke's Peak, Fyke's Folly, and Engebrittson Pass, were given by Gary in honor (or scorn) of the two people whom Gary seemed to hold responsible for the course being moved to these new locations.

How the name "Testicle Spectacle" was given to the steep climb under the powerline is an interesting and humorous story. When Gary was first out at Frozen Head earlier in the year to explore and establish this new part of the course, he was hiking with Raw Dog and Stu Gleman. When they looked up and saw this imposing climb, Stu exclaimed "Testicle Spectacle!" I asked him later why he had said this particular exclamation. He explained that he was partially quoting from the punch line of an old Vaudeville joke, that went something like this: A rabbi and his friend were walking in New York City. As they were crossing a busy street, a car came racing toward them. The friend pushed the rabbi out of its path to prevent him from being run over. The rabbi then stood up and made what appeared to be a sign of the cross on himself. The friend was astonished to see this and asked "Rabbi, you are Jewish, not Christian. Why are you signing the cross on yourself?" To which the rabbi answered, "I vas not signing the cross, I vas checking for my spectacles, testicles, vallet, and vatch!" Thus the name "Testicle Spectacle" was created and has become immortalized for this part of the course.

From Engebrittson Pass, the course continued down along the powerline cut on the other side of the ridge for about half a mile, until the runners turned off the trail and into the woods to the right. Gary called this downhill section Meth Lab Hill, because while exploring to add this new section, he and his cohorts had come upon an old shack in the woods. They speculated that it had been a meth lab, and Gary likes colorful names, so the Meth Lab name was used. Near the bottom of this hill another book was placed at the rootstock of a large fallen tree. From there, the runners were to go south-westerly to near the boundary of the Frozen Head State Natural Area, and then re-cross Highway 116, and go steeply up a rocky wash and an old road-bed to the bottom of the familiar Rat Jaw, on the old Prison Mine Trail. This steep uphill to the Rat Jaw happened to skirt near the edge of the Brushy Mountain State Penitentiary property, just outside the State Natural Area. Gary called this new trail "Rat Jaw Jr" and the old, upper Rat Jaw trail "Rat Jaw Sr." At Rat Jaw Sr the course resumed as before, going up to the lookout tower at the top of Frozen Head Mountain. One other course change this year was that the Hump was eliminated. Recall that the Hump had been added in 2001.

Gary had claimed in an e-mail on February 9, 2006, that, based on his map measurements with a string, this new course was shorter than the old one. He said that "the difference isn't much, but probably guarantees a mass finish." On a revised spreadsheet of course elevations and distances, he continued to call the loop distance 20.00 miles. Gary's new estimate of elevation change was 10,380 feet each of climb and descent per loop. This was 200 feet less than his stated climb of 10,580 feet for the 2003-2005 loop. On the Schematic Map on page 8, the new loop trail sequence was 1, 2, 19, 20, 33, 35, 36, 37, 38, 39, 26, 27, 8, 9, 10, 29, 30, 31, 12, 13. Using data from the Table on page 9, my estimate of the distance of this new loop is 25.9 miles, with 10,500 feet each of climb and descent. Thus the new Fun Run distance and elevation gain became 77.7 miles and 31,500 feet, while the new 100-mile distance and climb became 129.5 miles and 52,500 feet. My estimate corroborates Gary's claim that the loop was slightly shortened (from 26.0 miles) relative to the course of the past three years. However, my estimate of the elevation change shows a slight increase of 20 feet in the elevation gain and drop per loop. Since these changes are so small, it is fair to say that the course difficulty remained virtually the same as in recent years. Because the Barkley course was no longer allowed to pass through Hell, and forced in-stead to cross a paved highway twice, I will refer to this new loop configuration as the Hell for the Highway course.

Starters for 2006 included returning 100-mile finisher Jim Nelson, and previous fun-run finishers Craig Wilson, Mike Dobies, Milan Milanovich from Switzerland, Sue Johnston, Todd Holmes, John DeWalt, and myself. Other runners returning after prior DNFs included Leonard Buttslide Martin, Dan Baglione, Mike Bur, Wendell Doman, Keith Dunn, Elise Harrington, Pete Ireland, Bill Losey, Matt Mahoney, Stu Gleman, Sue Thompson, Chip Tuthill, Rich Limacher, Mark Shipley, and Hiram Rogers. Newcomers included Pat Costigan, Allan Holtz, Greg Eason, Scott Gala, Nick Gracie from England, Andrew Hackett, Robert Andrulis, and Flyin' Brian Robinson. Flyin' Brian was a friend of David Horton who had helped crew David on David's record-setting run of the full length of the Pacific Crest Trail in the past year. Gary stated that 33 runners started the race this year, so there were two additional unknown starters.

Gary's regular post-race article about the Barkley appeared in the June 2006 issue of *UltraRunning*. He reported that the weather this year was, unusually enough, not rainy; at least not for the first day which happened to be April Fool's Day. But it was something potentially worse: warm and humid. My notes indicate that it had rained intermittently from about 6 PM until midnight the night before the race began. I remember some fog early in the first loop, and realized going up the first climb, Bird Mountain, that sweat was dripping off my face. Daytime highs were in the 80s. This would prove to be a factor that would slow down many of us runners.

Not surprisingly, Jim Nelson was the first to finish the first loop, in about 9:27. Nick Gracie and Flyin' Brian Robinson, both Barkley Virgins, were running essentially with him. They spent about 30 minutes in camp and started loop two. Next were Holmes in 9:55, and then Wilson and Johnston in 10:10, and Dobies in 10:14. Note that these first-loop times were somewhat slower than last year when paces were slowed by the wet and muddy conditions. Times this year were considerably slower than two years ago, when the top seven runners were all under 8:40 for the first loop. So at least for this first loop on the new course, leading runners' times were about a half hour to an hour and a half slower than in 2004. The new course and heat were probably both major reasons for this slowdown.

Other first-loop finishers, in order, were Eason, Bur, Costigan, Doman, Furtaw, Losey, DeWalt, Tuthill, Thompson, Rogers, Shipley, Gala, Hackett, Harrington, and Martin. Twenty-two runners completed the first loop within its time limit. Despite my inadequate level of training, I was pleased to have finished this loop in 12th place. My time was 11:58:49, just over 35 minutes longer than my last run here, in 2003. That was the year I had wasted an hour by going the wrong way on the Chimney Top Trail. My time this year was about 49 minutes longer than my time in 2001. I think this slowing on my part was a result of several things: my low training, my inevitable continuing slowing down with age (I was 58 years old at that time), the warm weather, and the new course. I had probably wasted about 20 minutes due to route-finding delays on the new parts of the course—several minutes each between Stallion Mountain and Fyke's Peak, the top of the Testicle Spectacle, and finding the correct route, that Gary called "Pig Head Creek," to go up to the Rat Jaw from the second crossing of Highway 116. By the time I finished the first loop, I was exhausted and had little desire to continue. I ended my run after one loop. This was becoming a habit. But now I got to enjoy the banter, joking, and stories with the other runners (at least those who had also DNFed) and friends around Gary's campfire. Watching the Barkley unfold is always an interesting show.

One of my navigational delays on the new part of the course is worth mentioning. When I got to the top of the Testicle Spectacle, it took me several minutes of roaming and searching to find the book. The course instructions said: "Follow the powerlines to the top. Once you hit the jeep road crossing at the top, look to your right. There is a small point, on the same side you came up. Go to the very top of that point and look back towards the trail you came up. You will see a small tree, with a strip of duct tape around it. Behind the small tree is a big one. The big tree is hollow at the bottom, and **BOOK 4** is in that hollow." I thus proceeded to the "very top" of the hill that I thought he was referring to as a "point," but did not see a tree with duct tape or a hollow tree with a book in it. I searched around, then went back to where I had gotten to the top of the Testicle Spectacle, and tried again. I soon found the book in its hollow tree, but it was on a lower hillock on the same ridge as the higher hilltop. I thought that the description of it as at "the very top of that point" was not accurate. In any case this delay cost me several minutes.

Later in camp, I was talking to Milan Milanovich, the Swiss runner who was a past finisher of both the old 55-mile three-loop course, and the 60-mile Fun Run in 1995. Milan had chosen to spend the night in a nearby motel rather than at the campground. When he got to the park on Saturday, he found that the race had already started. Thus he started his race about 20 minutes later than the rest of us had. This put him at the back of the field, running alone in catch-up mode, while trying to navigate the new parts of the course. When he got to the top of the Testicle Spectacle, he had a similar problem to the one I had just had at the same "point." Milan's command of the English language is adequate, but his command of Gary's instructional language was less than adequate. As he explained his problem to me, he repeated: "Vhat is point?" He didn't understand Gary's terminology of going to "the very top of that point." Although I felt great sympathy for him, I realized the humorous irony of the fact that this year's T-shirt motto was: "The Barkley Marathons Meaningless Suffering Without a Point." Furthermore, the race numbers that Gary had given us this year bore the motto: "The Barkley Marathons There Is No Point."

Milan was unable to find the very top of that point, even after spending considerable time searching in the nearby area. So he continued on without retrieving a page from that book. He knew that he would be disqualified by Gary. But he was about to encounter an even bigger problem: the Brushy Mountain State Penitentiary. At the second crossing of Highway 116, Milan got too far west of the intended course, and inadvertently wandered onto the grounds of the prison. Like Jim Dill and Cliff Hoy back in 1996, Milan was promptly apprehended at gunpoint by prison guards. They do not like strangely dressed people walking onto their grounds. With his adequate but imperfect English, Milan had to convince the guards that he was not there for nefarious purposes. However, after holding and questioning Milan for several hours and verifying his story about the Barkley race, the prison guards were kind enough to give our visitor from Switzerland a ride back to the park campground.

It is hard to say whether this was the most harrowing story of the weekend. The story of Dan Baglione may deserve that honor. Recall that Dan had been here the previous year, and had managed to get lost off the North Boundary Trail (NBT) on the first loop with Nick Graner. They had spent a total of ten hours getting back to camp after collecting only one book page. This year, Dan, at 75 years the oldest Barkley runner ever, got lost again on the NBT on loop one. Only this time he was alone and couldn't find his way back in ten hours. He got lost outside the north boundary of the State Natural Area, and wandered all day trying to get back in. Although he realized that he wanted to go south to get back into the park, he had lost his compass and couldn't figure out the correct direction to go. He also lost part of his flashlight while trying to change batteries in the dark, so he was basically immobilized without a light. He spent the night alone *out there*. The next morning he got onto some dirt roads and eventually saw some local good ol' boys riding 4-wheelers. They asked Dan if he needed help, but apparently Dan happened to think at that moment that at last he was on a road to the park. Amazingly, he declined the offer of help, and kept wandering. He never did find his way back into the park. Fortunately for Dan, the same 4-wheelers happened to pass by him again later that day. This time Dan was wise or tired enough to accept their help. In turn, they were gracious enough to offer Dan a ride back, and a beer and smoke in the meantime. He took the ride and a soda, but declined the beer and smoke. Those gentlemen delivered Dan back to Frozen Head via the highway through Wartburg. They arrived back at camp in the middle of the afternoon. As Gary wrote in *UltraRunning*: "The new record for Barkley futility: 31:42:27 to cover a grand total of 2.95 miles on course. Limacher's two-hour-per-mile pace pales next to Baglione's 10:44:54-per-mile mark. Truly, this is a record that could stand forever." Here Gary was referring to Rich Limacher and Norm Carlson's overnighter at the Limacher Hilton in 2001 (Chapter 20), which had been the previous "record for Barkley futility."

While Dan was *out there* on his adventure, Gary and others in camp, including myself and several other runners who had already DNFed, were growing increasingly concerned for Dan's welfare. Finally, Gary contacted the park rangers and preparations were begun for a search party. Gary dispatched runners to go to various book checkpoints, including the first book at Phillips Creek. Another volunteer drove to the first water drop on the dirt road between the Garden Spot and Stallion Mountain. These scouts were told what page number Dan was to have retrieved from the books. They checked the books for that page. Eventually, these scouts were able to report that Dan's page had been removed from book 1, but not book 2, at the Garden Spot. Thus we were able to deduce that Dan had gotten lost somewhere along the NBT. We organized several teams of volunteers and got into park pickup trucks. Each team had a radio to allow them to communicate with each other and with a ranger at the park headquarters. Park rangers then drove us up the jeep road, also known as the Quitter's Road, and we had three parties search at various locations along the NBT. I believe Bill Losey, Chip Tuthill, and I were in the same group. We drove to Coffin Springs and hiked up to the Garden Spot, looking and calling for Dan. After perhaps an hour up there, we got the word by radio that Dan had been returned to camp. We were all relieved that Dan was apparently OK, and got back in the trucks and rode slowly back down Quitter's Road. It was quite bumpy riding down that hill in the back of a pickup truck, but we were looking forward to hearing Dan's story. Fortunately, Dan was in good health and relatively good spirits. He was appreciative of everyone's concern and help in the search. However, Dan was eventually informed by park personnel that they would not allow him to run the Barkley anymore. A couple years later, Dan again showed up at Frozen Head, but just to observe, not as a runner. He was proudly wearing a T-shirt that he had had made. It said: "I Was Banned From The Barkley."

Meanwhile, back at the 2006 race, 16 of the 22 first-loop finishers started the second loop. However, the field dwindled relatively rapidly. The heat, and the time and energy penalty that many runners incurred finding the books on the new parts of the course, contributed to the attrition. Jim Nelson was one of those whom the heat had depleted prematurely. I remember seeing Jim when he came back to camp. He had that gaunt look of dehydration and fatigue. The only 100-mile alumnus running this year was out. The Barkley still had no repeat 100-mile finishers. This left the remaining front-runners, Nick Gracie and Flyin' Brian, *out there* without the benefit of a Barkley veteran to help them navigate the course. However, a veteran of past Barkleys might not have helped them, as they soon got lost trying to find the new checkpoint on Fyke's Peak—a location that had not been on the course in past years. They spent about two hours trying to find this book, and were not able to locate it until the second group of runners, Wilson, Dobies, and Eason, caught up to them and were able to show them where the book was. These five runners then continued around the loop, and were the only runners to complete loop two within the 26:40 time limit. Gracie was the first in at 24:24:14, and Robinson was next in 24:38:12. They were followed by Wilson in 24:56:23, Eason in 25:06:24, and Dobies in 25:17:07.

Four of these five continued onto the third loop, now in the counterclockwise direction. Mike Dobies decided he had had enough after two loops. The others continued in two teams of two runners each: Gracie with Robinson, and Wilson with Eason. However, Craig also reached his limit at Indian Knob, the third checkpoint. He came back to camp on one of the "candy ass" trails. This left just three runners on the course on loop three, and all three were Barkley virgins. Greg Eason was the next to quit, at the bottom of Rat Jaw Senior. This left him with a long hike back to camp, but not as long or difficult as continuing on the course.

Now Gracie and Robinson were the sole survivors. They continued working their way around the third loop. However, with the new parts of the course and their relative lack of experience on the course, they repeatedly had difficulty finding the checkpoints. As Gary wrote in his *UltraRunning* article: "Time bled away at every turn as they searched out their route."

Then when they were about half-way around the loop, an old familiar Barkley factor intruded: the weather. Severe storms were moving toward Frozen Head. Gary noted in his article that tornadoes from this storm had killed 22 people across the state of Tennessee. This severe storm hit the Frozen Head area with heavy rain, strong wind, lightning, and thunder. This soaked the course, which, as we have noted several times before, causes the trails, especially the NBT, to become very slippery and difficult to run on. These weather factors contributed to further slowing the progress of Nick and Brian. Another factor that contributed to their slowing was that Brian was there for a bigger goal than a Fun Run finish. He had already fixed his determination on a 100-mile finish. But he realized earlier in this run that that goal would not be met this year. So he intentionally spent extra time on his third loop exploring parts of the course in more detail than was necessary to just finish three loops. He was already planning for next year.

The above factors resulted in Nick and Brian taking just a little too long to finish the Fun Run within its 40-hour time limit. They completed the third loop in about 40 hours and 7 minutes. Thus they were not considered official finishers of the Fun Run. For the first time since 1989, and the fourth time in the history of the event, the Barkley would have no official three-loop finishers. Gary declared in his *UltraRunning* article that: "The Barkley had won— again."

Here is a list of the known starters, their numbers of Barkley starts, and their loop-finishing times for 2006.

1. Nick Gracie (1)   9:27:20   24:34:14   ~40:07* Finished loop three over the time limit.
2. Flyin' Brian Robinson (1) 9:29:21 24:38:12   ~40:07* Finished loop three over the time limit.
3. Craig Wilson (10)   10:10:08   24:56:23   Quit during loop three.
4. Greg Eason (1)   10:32:05   25:06:24   Quit during loop three.
5. Mike Dobies (8)   10:14:25   25:17:07
6. Jim Nelson (4)   9:26:46   Quit during loop two.
7. Todd Holmes (4)   9:55:40   Quit during loop two.
8. Sue Johnston (3)   10:10:27
9. Mike Bur (4)   11:47:06
10. Pat Costigan (1)   11:47:13   Quit during loop two.
11. Wendell Doman (?)   11:56:54
12. Frozen Ed Furtaw (10) 11:58:49
13. Bill Losey (2)   12:03:29
14. John DeWalt (18)   12:03:30
15. Chip Tuthill (3)   12:17:38
16. Sue Thompson (7)   12:17:40
17. Hiram Rogers (3)   12:29:05
18. Mark Shipley (2)   12:29:07
19. Scott Gala (1)   12:29:15
20. Andrew Hackett (1)   12:38:49
21. Elise Harrington (2) 12:38:51   Quit during loop two.
22. Buttslide Martin (13) 12:53:19
23. Matt Mahoney (11)   ~15:56* Finished loop one over the time limit.

24. Pete Ireland (2)   ~15:56* Finished loop one over the time limit.
25. Allan Holtz (1)   ~15:56* Finished loop one over the time limit.
26. Milan Milanovich (5) Lost on loop one; apprehended at prison.
27. Keith Dunn (2)   Quit during loop one.
28. Stu Gleman (9)   Quit during loop one.
29. Rich Limacher (5)   Quit during loop one.
30. Robert Andrulis (1) Quit during loop one.
31. Dan Baglione (2)   31:42:27* Returned to camp after being lost on loop one.
33 Starters

Gary wrote some interesting things in an e-mail a couple of days after the race. Regarding Brian's and Nick's effort, he wrote: " i suspect that, with the novelty behind them, and with a normal year of cold weather, these guys could make a run at the 100. i put my money on flyin bryan getting it within the next 3 years. and i wouldnt bet against him in '07." We will soon see whether Gary's prediction was warranted.

Gary then went on to make one of his most profound statements about the Barkley, that I think sums it up pretty well: "bottom line on barkley; it is not reasonable. but if you are in this thing to find your limits.... they are to be found "out there". probably not nearly as far 'out there' as you would like to think."

++++++++++

Below is the essay I wrote for entry into the 2006 Barkley Marathons.

Why I Should Be Allowed To Run The Barkley
Essay # 10a in a series
By Frozen Ed Furtaw
February 23, 2006

I should be allowed to run the 2006 Barkley Marathons for many reasons. Perhaps the most important is that lazarus lake and I are friends, and it would be nice for us to see each other again. Another important reason is that I am foolish enough to want to run the Barkley, and for this I should be both rewarded and punished by being allowed to run the Barkley. This will be the 20th Barkley Marathons, and it will be my tenth running of the Barkley; this symmetry suggests that correct alignment of the universe ordains that I should be allowed to run the Barkley.

The observant reader will note that I have identified this as #10a in a series. "Why the 'a' after the 10?" this reader would ask. The reason for this numbering suffix is that I wrote an essay in 2004 for that year's Barkley, which would have been my tenth running if I had run it that year. However, I never submitted that essay because at that time I was too unfit to attempt the Barkley. So this current writing is the 11th Barkley essay that I have written, but it will be the 10th that I will have submitted. Hence I have numbered it #10a. (I hope the observant reader enjoyed that rare but appropriate use of the future pluperfect tense, i.e., please award bonus grammar points when grading this essay.)

The most important point of my never-submitted 2004 Barkley essay was a whining admission that I am a weenie and cannot hope to finish even the three-loop Barkley Fun Run. Since the loop was extended in 1995, in five attempts I have not been able to finish even two loops. Therefore my goal this year will be to finish two loops. To claim that I think I am able to do more would be lying. Because of my honest admission of my own limited goal and ability, I should be allowed to run the Barkley.

Another reason why I should be allowed to run Barkley is that I intend to write a book about the Barkley Marathons. By allowing me entry, lazarus will have the opportunity to tell me his side of the story before I write mine. This will hopefully help us to get the true story of Barkley out there. Without laz's input, my own version might be considered an under-exaggeration, whereas the true story of Barkley is not capable of exaggeration, because Barkley itself is the exaggeration.

Now that I am retired and have more time to run and relax, I believe I am at a higher level of running fitness than I have been in several years. Also, my wife says that I am a stud-muffin. Thus there is a good chance that I will finish two loops. If I do finish the first two loops within the secret time limit that lazarus is worrying about, I would then be faced with the next level of challenge, which would be to attempt loop three. I know I'm not man enough to do that, so I'd better end this essay before I am tempted to suggest that I could do three loops. You see what a wimp I have become. I hope you are satisfied, lazarus.

Chapter 26
2007: Another Near Miss

After the 2006 Barkley had no finishers of even the Fun Run, many good runners came to Frozen Head in 2007 to try to conquer the new, apparently more difficult course. Returning former Barkley winners were David Horton and Jim Nelson, who had both won Fun Runs and finished the 100-miler, as well as Mike Dobies and myself. Other returning three-loop finishers were: Andrew Thompson, who had had the dramatic fifth-loop collapse in 2005; Milan Milanovich, the Swiss runner who had finished both the old 55-mile and the 60-mile three-loop races; and John DeWalt who also had both 55- and 60-mile finishes.

Other returning non-finishers included: Flyin' Brian Robinson, who had come so close to a three-loop finish last year; Greg Eason; Joe Kowalski; Mike Bur; Rich Limacher; Pete Ireland; Mark Shipley; DeWayne Satterfield; Davey Henn; David Hughes; Hiram Rogers; Andras Low from Hungary, who had had a strong run but DNF at Barkley in 2001, and had also finished the Spartathlon 154-mile race an amazing 11 times; Chip Tuthill; Leonard Buttslide Martin; Allan Holtz; Stu Gleman; Wendell Doman; Bill Losey; Sue Thompson; and Pat Costigan.

Barkley newcomers this year included Steve Durbin; John Price; David Harper; Art Fisher: Paul Melzer; and Balazs Koranyi, a friend of Andras Low, who was also from Hungary, and a former Olympian 1500-meter runner. Gary reported that 35 runners started the race this year, so there were two unnamed starters in addition to those named above.

In his article about this year's Barkley in the June 2007 issue of *UltraRunning*, Gary called this "a crowd of elite runners." The race started on March 31, a warm but rainless morning. I recall that the temperatures were similar to last year's, but the humidity seemed lower. Gary wrote that the temperatures rose into the 80s as they had the previous year. He also noted that the past 100-mile finishes had been run in rain and snow, but never when the temperatures were as high as the 80s. It would be an interesting race to see if anyone could break that pattern this year.

The course this year remained virtually the same as last year, although some of the book locations were slightly relocated. For example, last year the course went right past the top of Stallion Mountain's north peak, but there was not a book there. This year a book was added at that mountain peak. The book that had been at the fallen tree beside "Meth Lab Hill" was now moved about a couple hundred meters westward, close to a small waterfall that Gary called Raw Dog Falls, in honor of Karl Raw Dog Henn. One other change in the course description was that the book location on the top of the small hilltop at the top of the Testicle Spectacle was no longer called the "point," it was now called a "peak." I wonder if that change in the description would have helped Milan find it last year when he did not understand what was meant by the "point."

One other minor rule change this year compared to last was that now runners had to immediately proceed to the gate when arriving at the end of each loop, and turn in their pages before getting aid. They then had to return to the gate to get another number from Gary before beginning the next loop. Depending on how far a runner's campsite was from the gate, this rule would add as much as a couple hundred meters to the distance the runner would travel in camp between loops.

The first drama of this year's race was a tragedy that occurred within the first few miles of the start. While going down the steep and overgrown trail on the north side of Bird Mountain, just two or three miles into the race, Balazs Koranyi, one of the Hungarian runners, impaled his knee on a broken branch while climbing over a fallen tree across the trail. The branch penetrated to bone. Balazs had to turn around and limp back to camp, where he was subsequently taken to an urgent-care medical facility for repairs. It was a tragic ending to a short adventure, for someone who had obviously put a lot of time, effort, and cost into making this trip to Frozen Head. The only good aspect of this sad tale is that later, Balazs was in camp and able to share the stories around Gary's campfire, and tell us some things about his colorful career, and about Hungary.

Flyin' Brian lived up to his nickname by being the first runner to complete the first loop, in 8:17:35. He was running alone, not relying on a partner to help navigate the course as he had last year when he ran the first loop with Jim Nelson and Nick Gracie. This year, he was an hour and ten minutes faster than last year. Brian and Wendell Doman, both from Northern California, had come out to Frozen Head a few days before to do some pre-race reconnaissance, so Brian knew the course well for the race this year. He finished loop one about 22 minutes ahead of the next runners, Andrew Thompson and Andras Low. Just another minute behind them were Dobies and Eason, with Nelson yet another minute later. Horton was ten minutes after, followed by Losey 11 minutes behind, and Doman six minutes later. Thus the top nine were all under 10 hours. Last year only four runners were under ten hours. So runners were doing a better job navigating this year. Other runners to complete loop one within its time limit were the following, in order: Henn, Fisher, Milanovich, Bur, Costigan, Furtaw, Satterfield, Tuthill, Sue Thompson, DeWalt, Shipley, Rogers, Martin, and Hughes, for a total of 23 of the 35 starters.

I had run a good first loop, with no significant navigational delays, finishing in 15th place in 10:48:47. This was an hour and ten minutes faster than last year for the virtually identical loop. This year I had been really determined to not stop after loop one. I had been reminded by my friend Mark Dorion that it was crucial to not enter camp after a loop with doubt about whether or not I was going to continue. This advice was also some that Andrew Thompson had written in an e-mail after his near-miss of the 100-miler in 2005. I had to already have my mind made up before entering camp that I was going on, and just get ready and go. I followed this good coaching advice, and made a determined effort to eat (with help from my wife, Gail), get some foot blisters taped (with the help of Nick Williams, the two-time finisher of the old 55-mile Barkley), and get back out on the course. When I headed out of camp it was just getting dark, and I had a headlight on, as well as a small LED flashlight in my fanny pack. I had intended to also carry a relatively large, 2-D-cell, hand-held flashlight, but I forgot it when I left my campsite. A few minutes later, Gail saw that I had left my flashlight on our table in camp. She grabbed the flashlight and ran up to the gate, hoping to catch me before I got too far *out there*. But Gary stopped her at the gate, and informed her that I was not allowed to accept aid outside the campground. So instead she went over to Gary's campfire and ate a piece of Barkley Chicken. I would have to go without my flashlight. Actually, that was not a problem. My headlight was adequate, and I did not even realize that I had forgotten that flashlight for a few hours. It taught me that I didn't really need to carry that big flashlight.

What finally did me in was leg weakness. I had developed a pain in one of my knees late in the first loop, and gradually this pain became worse until by the time I was approaching Bald Knob on loop two, I could barely lift my left leg to go uphill. I remembered that there were some uphills ahead, so I decided I had better quit while I was still a relatively short walk from camp. I took the Quitter's Road back and quit. However, I had achieved a minor success for me. For the first time since 1997, I had gotten beyond one loop. I had also identified a few areas where I could improve for next year, especially strengthening my leg muscles.

Even though Brian was well in the lead after loop one, he had encountered a couple of delays on the loop. He wrote a several-page-long report a few weeks after the race, in which he described his experiences. In that report, he noted that when he arrived at the top of Big Hell in the lead, he spent about five minutes there because he "had to unpeel about 10 yards of duct tape holding Book 10 to the side of a tree." The devious trickster had found yet another clever way to slow down the front runner! There is a lesson hidden here for would-be top runners at the Barkley: if you are fast enough to be the first runner to arrive at a particular book location, carry a small pocket knife to use for cutting the books out of their duct tape wrappings. We runners further back in the pack don't have to worry about that.

Another interesting delay that Brian reported on his first loop was just after this book. When he got to the Chimney Top Trail, he apparently made the same mistake that I and others had made in past years: he somehow turned and went the wrong way on the CTT! He wrote that he lost about ten minutes because of this error, and as a result wasn't sure that he was still in the lead until he arrived back in camp.

Gary reported that 14 or 15 of the 23 first-loop finishers continued onto loop two. Among those not continuing was David Horton. A couple of years prior, David had set a new record for running the full length of the Pacific Crest Trail, and that in that effort, Flyin' Brian had helped crew for David. Now David and his crew would return the favor and help Brian in his run at the Barkley, with coaching and handling assistance in the campground.

With good pre-planning and in-camp crewing, Brian spent only about 13 minutes in camp before heading out onto loop two before anyone else had finished loop one. Brian also flew around the second loop, completing it in less than ten hours, at 18:15:47. This was over six hours and 20 minutes better than his two-loop time of last year. He had now opened up a 2 hour and 16 minute lead over the nearest competitors, Dobies, Eason, and Low, who were running together and arrived in about 20:32. A couple hours later, at

22:20, was Andrew Thompson, followed a couple minutes later by Nelson. Doman finished loop two in 24:35, with Costigan barely beating the 26:40 time limit, in 26:31:32.

After his second loop, Brian spent about half an hour in camp, but he did not sleep. He began the counterclockwise third loop less than 19 hours into the race. Early in this loop, it started to rain. This was, after all, the Barkley. However, fortunately for the runners, the rain did not persist long. The cooler temperatures that came with the rain were probably beneficial to the runners. As he progressed counterclockwise around the loop, Brian encountered the oncoming runners who were completing the second loop. He completed the third loop without significant problems noted in his report, in 31:21:31, an amazing 8 hours and 46 minutes faster than his disallowed 40:07 time last year. Of the eight finishers of loop two, four others had continued onto loop three: Dobies, Eason, and Low, still running together, and Pat Costigan. However, Pat was running too close to the time limit. He ended his run early in the third loop. The other three finished the Fun Run together in 34:16.

Brian began his fourth loop, also in the counterclockwise direction, after about only 25 minutes in camp. He decided to defer any sleeping until before the fifth loop, so he began loop four with no sleep, almost 32 hours into the race. The main problem he noted in his report was sore feet. He noted that because of the intermittent rain on the third loop, his feet "pruned up and blistered, and the pain slowed me down." He carried a pair of trekking poles, lent to him by Buttslide Martin, on the fourth loop, hoping that the use of the poles would help relieve the pressure on his sore feet.

Mike and Greg started the rare fourth loop after about an hour in camp re-supplying after their third loop. However, they went only a few hours before quitting and returning to camp at about the 40-hour point. Despite their valiant attempt to tackle the fourth loop, they were tapped out just like the earlier quitters. This left Flyin' Brian alone in the race against the course, against time, and against his own limits.

Brian continued uneventfully around the fourth loop, until he got to near Indian Knob. By this time, it was foggy and beginning to get dark. Approaching Indian Knob in the uphill direction, up the so-called Zip Line Trail, Brian had some difficulty finding the book in the crevice in the capstones. He went for a while in the wrong direction on the ridge along which Indian Knob lies. Thinking he was heading south, he checked his compass and discovered that he was going toward the east. He noted that: "My gut tells me the compass is wrong, but I know better. I tell myself, 'Trust the compass. Figure out where you are.'" It is interesting to note that, like some of us other Barkley runners in the past, he had difficulty believing his compass reading. However, he wisely forced himself to go with the compass reading, and immediately figured out where he was, and found Indian Knob within minutes. He reported that this delay in finding the book at Indian Knob had cost him half an hour.

As he continued in the dark and fog, he also found that the trekking poles were a burden to carry at times when he tried to use his hands for other things such as pointing a light and eating. However, he did say that the poles helped ease his foot pain when he used them. His progress going down Rat Jaw was very slow. About this time he reported that the fog lifted, but "the fog of sleepiness in my head thickened. When I reached the penultimate road near the bottom of Rat Jaw, I followed it until I realized it wasn't the right one. My mind just wasn't working so well anymore." This was beginning to sound like some of the past years' harrowing tales of runners mentally losing control on later loops. Recall that Brian had been going for the entire race without sleep.

After Rat Jaw, his progress continued slowly, but without significant lost time finding the checkpoints. However, his sore feet and tired legs slowed him down. He finished the fourth loop in 47:49:43, with just 10 minutes and 17 seconds remaining on the time limit for starting the fifth loop. Despite his painful and weary condition, he was determined to keep going. Several other runners who were still at the campground formed a support crew, and helped get Brian ready to go back *out there* onto the course, while Gary counted down the remaining minutes. As Gary described in *UltraRunning:* "The final minute found Brian stumbling up to the start, eating eggs straight out of the frying pan as fast as he could shove them down, while the last items were stuffed into his pack and it was strapped to his waist." Dramatically, Brian began his fifth loop with *seven seconds* remaining on the time limit. Just after he left, Gary reported: "I turned and looked at a friend, who looked back with a very serious expression on his face and said; 'He's got that seven-second cushion. Do you think he'll use it to take a nap now, or keep it in the bank for later?'"

Brian had elected to do his fifth loop in the clockwise direction. He went over the first climb, Bird Mountain, "By sheer force of will," then descended to the northwest corner of the Natural Area at Phillips Creek, and collected his page from book 1. He then began the ascent up Jury Ridge. He later described what happened: "Up Jury Ridge, I really struggled. It was broad daylight, but I couldn't stay awake. I stopped for a 15 minute nap. I set my watch alarm and fell unconscious in seconds. It was a warm morning and the sleep felt so good. But when the alarm went off, I got up and started moving. I just didn't feel any better. I crested Jury Ridge and tried to run downhill on the newly maintained trail. It's good footing, but I just couldn't move fast. I stumbled with sleepiness. At the bottom I stopped for another nap. This time I didn't even set the watch. It had taken me three hours to get to Rayder Creek. On loop one, I had made it to the Garden Spot in three hours. I was barely going half that pace. I calculated that at that rate, it would be another 16 hour loop. I couldn't afford the time to sleep, but I couldn't go on without it. My race was over. I slept."

After napping along the trail, Brian continued to the familiar place along the NBT, near Bald Knob, where there is easy access to the Quitter's Road jeep trail back to camp. He took it. The walk back took him three more hours. He wrote that this year's ending was easier to take than his ending last year, when he had finished three loops just seven minutes over the time limit, because, then, "he still had some fight left and wasn't allowed to continue. This year I had the chance to give it my all."

Here are the known starters, their numbers of Barkley starts, and their loop-finishing times for 2007.

1. Brian Robinson (2)   8:17:35   18:15:47   31:21:31 47:49:43 Quit on loop 5.
2. Mike Dobies (9)   8:40:37   20:32:14   34:16:19 Quit on loop four.
3. Andras Low   (2)   8:39:35   20:32:17   34:16:20
4. Greg Eason (2)   8:40:40   20:32:16   34:16:21 Quit on loop four.
5. Andrew Thompson (8) 8:39:33   22:20:35
6. Jim Nelson (5)   8:42:47   22:25:20
7. Wendell Doman (3)   9:10:38   24:35:13
8. Pat Costigan (2)   10:40:55   26:31:32   Quit during loop three.
9. David Horton (11)   8:53:12
10. Bill Losey (3)   9:04:20
11. Davy Henn (2)   10:22:39
12. Art Fisher (1)   10:22:40
13. Milan Milanovich (6)10:37:02
14. Mike Bur (5)   10:40:46   Quit during loop two.
15. Frozen Ed Furtaw (11)10:48:47   Quit during loop two.
16. DeWayne Satterfield (8) 10:54:39
17. Chip Tuthill (4)   11:24:05
18. Sue Thompson (8)   11:34:39
19. John DeWalt (19)   11:35:10
20. Mark Shipley (3)   11:51:22
21. Hiram Rogers (4)   11:51:25
22. Buttslide Martin (14)12:18:07
23. David Hughes (8)   12:33:32
24. David Harper (1)   ~15:08* Finished loop one over the time limit.
25. Allan Holtz (2)   ~16:10* Finished loop one over the time limit.
26. Steve Durbin (1)   ~17:31* Finished loop one over the time limit.
27. Stu Gleman (10)   ~17:31* Finished loop one over the time limit.
28. Rich Limacher (6)   Quit during loop one.
29. Paul Melzer (1)   Quit during loop one.
30. Pete Ireland (3)   Quit during loop one.
31. John Price (1)   Quit during loop one.
32. Joe Kowalski (4)   Quit during loop one.
33. Balazs Koranyi (1)   Injured and quit during loop one.
35 Starters

In the June 2007 issue of *UltraRunning*, just after Gary's Barkley article, is another article about the Barkley, written by Andrew Thompson. This article provides a colorful description of several aspects of the Barkley. Andrew notes the presence this year of a crew from the *Washington Post* newspaper who were there to write a story about the race. Andrew also described some of the characteristics of the "elite six" who had finished the 100-mile in its history. He wrote: "There seems to be a common thread among the decisively small group of finishers. Of the elite six, three have masters' degrees, two have doctoral degrees. They are engineers, scientists, professors, Navy SEALs, and a former Brown University student body president. And if a Barkley finish is not a big enough crown jewel, the athletic resumes of the elite six ring with world-class qualifications: multiple Hardrock wins, Nolan's 14 wins, Badwater finishes and course records, speed records beyond count on the Appalachian Trail, The Long Trail, The John Muir Trail, peak-bagging in Colorado's 14ers, New Hampshires's Whites, New York's Adirondacks and Catskills, and North Carolina's 6,000-footers."

Andrew also noted that, at the Barkley: "A legitimate 100-mile bid is a monumental battle against sleep deprivation." And: "The universal currency at Barkley, however, is pain." At the end of his article, Andrew described the *Washington Post* reporter sitting near Brian and recording an interview after Brian's ending of his near-miss run. Andrew wrote: "In the end she had captured what she came to find: the *real* Barkley, the greatest race among men and mountains. The real Barkley doesn't end in victory. Its rare finishers are what statisticians call 'outliers.' The real Barkley chases down its strongest talent, its brightest stars, and annihilates them. It never ends the way it should. *That* is the real thing."

Of course, Andrew had tasted the bitter defeat of the Barkley on his fifth loop in 2005, just as Brian had this year. Andrew's statement, that the real thing about Barkley is failure, is almost always true. But I believe that equally real about the Barkley are those few breakthrough finishes that have forced us to expand our belief in what is possible. The elite six have shown us that a 100-mile finish is possible. The three dramatic near-miss failures that had occurred on fifth loops—Brian's in 2007, Andrew's in 2005, and Blake's in 2000—were indicators of just how difficult the 100-mile finish is. It is near the margin of what some of the best endurance runners in the world can do, but it is not impossible. It had been done before, and now Flyin' Brian seemed close to doing it again. Remember, too, that just a year prior, Gary had predicted that Brian *would* finish the 100. Brian's performance this year was significantly improved over the previous year. Could he find some yet further way to improve upon his result of this year? We would find out soon, as Brian would return to the Barkley in 2008.

+++++++++++

Below is the essay I wrote for entry into the 2007 Barkley Marathons.

Why I Should Be Allowed To Run The Barkley
Essay #11 in a series
By Frozen Ed Furtaw
February 3, 2007

I should be allowed to run the 2007 Barkley Marathons because I am so fanatical about the Barkley that I define and plan my life around it. This will be the 21st Barkley Marathons, and it will be my 11th running of the Barkley since 1988. The personal history of much of my adult life has involved the Barkley. I plan my yearly racing calendar around the Barkley. I even plan much of my travel to visit family in the eastern United States in conjunction with the Barkley.

I am obsessed with the Barkley, and I need it. The Barkley is the primary yardstick with which I measure myself as an ultrarunner. Therefore I must run it again in order to measure how far I have shrunk in the past 19 years.

In 1988 I was the first official finisher of a Barkley Marathons. At that time it was "only" a single race of three loops for a total of 55 miles, with a time limit of 36 hours. However, no one had finished it in its first two years (1986 and 1987). When I finished it in 1988, I did so in 34 hours, about 8 of which were spent resting and sheltering from rain in my car in the camp-ground. Therefore I spent about 26 hours actually on the course.

Now, 19 years later, I will be 59 years old for this year's Barkley. Admittedly age has slowed me down, and I am no longer as fast nor as durable an ultrarunner as I was back then. But how much of my former ability have I lost? One good way to estimate the loss is by running Barkley again, and seeing how closely I can approach my former performance.

Unfortunately for purposes of comparison, the Barkley has gotten bigger in the years that I have gotten smaller as an ultrarunner. Since the loop was expanded in 1995, I have not been able to finish two loops. If the time limits this year are the same as in recent years, I will have 26 hours and 40 minutes to complete two loops (40 miles). My goal this year will be to finish two loops. Based on my most recent several performances at Barkley, I estimate that it will take me near or perhaps over the 26:40 time limit to finish two loops. Since this time is similar to my on-course time of 1988, this accomplishment—two loops this year—will be a run of similar endurance to my 1988 three-loop Barkley run.

Another reason why I should be allowed to run Barkley is that I am now in the process of writing a book about the Barkley Marathons. By allowing me entry, Race Management will encourage my book-writing endeavor. Here are some excerpts from the draft which I have written so far:

- "My first reaction to seeing information about the Barkley Marathons was disbelief—I thought there must be an error in the race listing in the early 1986 *UltraRunning* magazine event calendar. It said that the 50-mile Barkley Marathons had 24,000 feet of elevation climb. I was familiar with the mountains of eastern Tennessee, and I did not think that there was a 50-mile trail there that had anywhere near that much elevation change. I actually thought that there must be a misprint in *UltraRunning*—the Barkley probably had 2,400 feet of climb, not 24,000 feet."
- "Why is the Barkley Marathons so different, and so much more difficult to finish, than other footraces? These are the questions that will be addressed in this chapter."
- ... the actual distance has not been (and probably cannot be) accurately measured, and the exact route of the loop has been changed many times over the years. These course changes will be described in greater detail in later chapters of this book. Most participants believe that the course length is actually longer than stated. For example, one runner who carried a Global Positioning System (GPS) device around the loop (before Gary prohibited their use during the race) estimated that a nominal 20-mile loop was actually about 27-28 miles.

- The Barkley course is not marked for the race; back-country navigation is required of the runners. This is one major difference from most trail ultramarathons, and one major factor why Barkley is so much more difficult than other races.
- The Barkley course really does have close to 10,000 feet of elevation climb per loop.
- Many of the cross-country (no trail) parts of the course are overgrown with briers.
- There are no aid stations on the Barkley course. This factor is again unlike other ultra races, which typically have aid for the runners every few miles. This lack of aid is another major factor that makes the Barkley both physically and psychologically more difficult than other races.
- The Barkley course and race are intentionally designed, and frequently changed, to keep it at the outer limit of human possibility. The design of the Barkley is intended to minimize the number of finishers. This is in contrast to most ultramarathon events, which have aid and course markings to help runners finish the event."

Chapter 27
2008: A New Course Record

As I write this, I have just finished unpacking my car after returning home from the 2008 Barkley. As always after an ultramarathon, and especially after another Barkley, I feel a sense of nostalgia and loss. I remember what a fun time I had, but how poorly I did compared to my pre-race expectations. This makes me miss it and regret that it will now be another 50+ weeks before I can try again for a measure of redemption at next year's Barkley.

I spent three days driving alone to Frozen Head State Park, and arrived at the Big Cove Campground on the Wednesday evening before the race, a couple of hours before dark. Some of the old familiar regulars were there already. John DeWalt, there for his twentieth consecutive Barkley, had already set up camp. Rich Limacher and Flyin' Brian Robinson were already there, and I had seen Dan Baglione, now 77 years old, as I was driving into the park. I chose the closest remaining campsite along the main road to the familiar yellow gate that marks the start and finish of the Barkley loop. I set up my campsite using a new technique that was inspired by Gary's regular practice of using a large tarp to cover his race-headquarters camping area. My experience with last year's wet tents in both the Barkley and the Boulder 24-hour race, had led me to try the tarp-over-tent method. I parked my car as close as I could to the edge of the tent-pitching area, and then tied one end of the tarp to the car. After pitching my tent alongside the car, I then stretched the tarp out and secured it to a tree and my cooler, thus suspending it above the tent. Over the next few days of my stay at Frozen Head, there would be ample opportunity of falling rain to test my new tent-tarping method. I am happy to report that the method was successful at keeping my tent dry over the five days that I was there.

I had an interesting conversation that evening with Flyin' Brian. He had arrived the previous night, and had spent some time earlier Wednesday exploring parts of the course. He reported that he had not been able to find a book at the normal place in the rattlesnake hole on Fyke's Peak, and that he had found a book on the Hump. Brian also talked about his training leading up to this year's race. He exuded an air of fitness and determination. I could tell that, after his near-miss here last year, he was going to make another serious effort at a 100-mile finish this year.

The following day, Thursday, I set out to do something that I had fantasized about for many years: measure part of the Barkley course with a measuring wheel.

The true length of the Barkley loop has always been the subject of speculation. It is widely believed by most participants that the loop length is longer than the distances given by Gary, which has been 20 miles per loop since 1995. As I have noted throughout this book, I myself have long believed that each loop is several miles longer than stated. I was a little surprised in 2007 when I carefully estimated the length of the loop with a scale on the map and found it to be only 22.48 miles. This estimate even included calculation of the hypotenuse length of a right triangle given the horizontal distance measured by scaling on the map, and the vertical distance as determined by elevation change from contour lines on the map. I had expected something more like 25 or 26 miles. This expectation was based on my awareness of my own running pace and the time it took me to run certain portions of the loop.

As an attempt to address my own lingering uncertainty of the course length, I took a Rolatape Professional model measuring wheel to Frozen Head in 2008. This device has a wheel that is designed and manufactured to roll four feet with each revolution. There is a peg in the wheel corresponding to each one foot of distance, and a counter that registers the number of times a peg passes the counter. When the wheel is pushed along the ground, the counter shows the distance that the wheel has rolled in one-foot increments. I referred to this wheel as the "truth-o-meter."

I measured from the starting gate of the Barkley course at the Big Cove Campground, to the top of the first climb along the Bird Mountain trail. Gary's spreadsheet of information on the trail segment lengths and elevations for the Barkley loop gives the distance of this first trail segment as 1.40 miles. This is the same distance, to within one one-hundredth of a mile, that I had gotten using my map-scaling and hypotenuse-calculation method, even with measuring along the 14 switchbacks that the map shows on that length of trail. My on-site wheel-measurement data confirmed the 14 switchbacks. However, the distances I measured with the wheel were 10,565 feet (2.001 miles) in the uphill direction, and 10,525 feet (1.993 miles) for the downhill return trip. Thus my measurements yielded an average of 1.997 miles with a difference between the two measurements of less than 0.4%. If this average measured distance is compared to the stated and map-scaled distance of 1.40 miles, it is found that the wheel-measured distance is about 42.6% longer than the stated distance. I believe that this difference occurs because the switchbacks on the map are not accurately shown. The true distances between the turning points of the switchbacks are farther apart on the ground than represented on the map. I have subsequently estimated the trail segment distances shown on the Schematic Map on page 8 and the Table on page 9 by multiplying map-scaled distances by a "switchback factor" to estimate the actual trail distances. I used switchback factors ranging from 1.00 to 1.42, depending on the extent of switchbacks on each trail segment.

The resulting loop-distance estimates have been given throughout this book in the chapters where new course configurations were introduced. These results support the belief among the runners over the years that the loop length is considerably longer than Gary states. Inevitably, the true length of the course is still unknown and ultimately unknowable to a high accuracy. However, I believe that an estimate of about 26 miles per loop is certainly closer to the truth than the advertised 20 miles. This, of course, adds to the magnitude of the accomplishments of those who run the Barkley and especially of those who succeed in accomplishing the ultimate goal of completing five loops. It appears that instead of 100 miles, the distance of five loops is more like 130 miles.

When I told others about this result of my measurement, most runners indicated that they too suspected that the 20 miles was a significant understatement. Leonard Martin told me that he had used two different GPS devices to attempt to measure the length of a loop in training (Gary's rules forbid the use of GPS devices during the race), and had gotten results of about 24.6 miles and 25.4 miles; he also estimated that these GPSs underestimated distance by about 3%. However, when I told Gary about the results from my "truth-o-meter" measuring wheel, he seemed to shrug off my revelation of this new measurement data. It was as if he did not think that this information was important or significant. I think he likes to understate the true distance, because that adds to the psychological difficulty of the race by building the expectation in unfamiliar runners' minds that the course is shorter and easier than it really is when running it. This is an interesting way in which much of the legend of Barkley is actually understatement rather than exaggeration. At Barkley, the reality itself is the exaggeration, not the stories about it.

Gary arrived at Frozen Head Park this year, as usual, near mid-day on Friday, the day before the race. He methodically set about putting up his tarp over the race headquarters. He then started giving out the course directions to each entered runner. He set out the Master Map on one of the picnic tables under the tarp, and runners began copying the course and checkpoint locations onto their own maps, and reading the course directions. This was when speculation about course changes ended and this year's course was revealed. Most runners were somewhat surprised that the course changes were minimal for this year. In the weeks prior to the race, Gary had sent out some red-herring information on the Barkley e-mail list, suggesting that a mountain named Big Fodderstack might be part of this year's course. However, this proved to be yet another psychological ploy by the "devious trickster" to mess with the runners' minds. Some of the books were slightly relocated, and the Hump was returned to being part of the course after a couple years of it not being on the course. But the course was basically the same as in each of the past two years. The return of the Hump to the loop increased the number of books from ten last year to eleven this year. Based on data from the Schematic Map and Table on pages 8 and 9, the new loop distance with the Hump (replacing trail segment #10 with #32) was back to 26.0 miles, and the elevation gain and drop were up to 10,740 feet each. Thus my estimated distances and elevation gain and drop for the Fun Run and 100-miler, respectively, are about 78.0 miles with 32,200 feet, and 130.0 miles with 53,700 feet.

Gary continued his customary site set-up by hanging the license plates along the front of his campsite. For many years, the collection of license plates has been growing as runners from the various states and nations bring plates from their home states. Bringing a license plate is now one of the entry requirements for Barkley Virgins. Gary also displays a Confederate flag at his campsite. This is not a racist statement but rather a statement of his own rebellious nature. I personally wish that he would not display that flag, because it is so widely perceived as a symbol of tolerance of slavery. But it is consistent with Gary's unconventional and irreverent nature. I have never seen any indication in his behavior or statements that Gary is racist. He seems to be very egalitarian in his teasing and taunting of everyone! This is not a criticism of Gary. I believe that, despite his poking fun at us, in fact Gary has a deep respect and fondness for the Barkley runners.

By Friday afternoon Gary had begun his customary cooking of the Barkley Chickens. This is one of my favorite times at the Barkley. The runners gather around Gary's campsite, and everyone is very happy and busy. Over the years, many of us who frequent the Barkley have become friends, and it is like a big party atmosphere. Many stories are told, with lots of pre-race speculation and the typical optimistic attitudes that seem to peak the day before a big race.

This year, there were many familiar faces of Barkley regulars. Returning runners were Blake Wood, Jim Nelson, Flyin' Brian Robinson, Andrew Thompson, John DeWalt (at age 71, the second-oldest Barkley entrant ever, after Dan Baglione), Jason Poole, Todd Holmes, Greg Eason, Fatboy Eugene Trahern, Andras Low (returning from Hungary), and myself, all of whom were previous finishers of three loops or more. Other returners still looking for their first finishes included Wendell Doman, DeWayne Satterfield, Stu Gleman, Matt Mahoney, Andrew Hackett, Sue Thompson, Buttslide Martin, David Hughes (who had recently completed an amazing eleven 100-mile trail races within a year), Hiram Rogers, Steve Durbin, John Price, Merrianne Brittain, and Rich Limacher. Barkley Virgins this year were Bill Goodwine, Jon Barker (an orienteering champion from England), Heather and Michael Graz, Will Harlan (a fast young ultrarunner from North Carolina who had won the Mount Mitchell Ascent race seven times), Rebecca Nelson (Jim's wife), Carl Laniak, John Tyszkiewicz from England, Byron Backer, Joe Trujillo, and Joe Decker.

This latter runner, Joe Decker, is worth further mentioning. In camp, I heard that Joe had a website billing himself as the world's fittest man! When I heard this, I was dubious that he—or anyone—would make such a claim. However, I later did an Internet search for "world's fittest man" and sure enough, I immediately was directed to Joe's website: <http://www.joe-decker.com/>. Although surprised by the fact that anyone would make such an assertion, I found this website very interesting. Joe's claim is based mostly on his having broken the record in the Guinness World Records® Twenty-four-hour Physical Fitness Challenge in 2000. This is a combination of numerous exercise events that are performed within 24 hours. Joe is certainly a very fit, accomplished, and dedicated athlete and coach. I found it motivational to read some of his blog postings. We will see later how the world's fittest man fared at the world's toughest trail race.

The list of entrants includes several of the best trail ultrarunners in the U.S., in my opinion. Jim and Blake are "Barkley Alumni" who had both completed the Barkley 100 in previous years. Flyin' Brian and Andrew Thompson are both runners who had begun the rare fifth loop in past years, but had been stopped short. A married couple, Michael and Heather Graz, had come here from South Africa for this event; they both looked very fit and seemed to have a lot of experience at ultrarunning and multi-day adventure racing. As has happened so many times before at the Barkley, this was a very high-quality field and there was a lot of speculation of how well we would do, and of how many 100-mile finishers there would be. Of course, reality was lying in wait for us *out there*, biding its time before rearing its ugly head, starting tomorrow.

Actually, reality reared its ugly head for one of us the night before the race began. A first-time entrant, Ron Jansen, received a cell-phone call from home that a dear friend had just unexpectedly passed away. He decided to forego Barkley this year, and to go home to be with family and friends. This was a grim reminder that there are more important and difficult things in life than even the world's toughest ultra. This sad happening resulted in Joe Trujillo getting to run. Joe had come to Frozen Head with no entry slot, but knowing that he was high on the waiting list. Now, at about 9 PM the night before the race, Joe was suddenly in. He hastily began studying the course directions.

After an enjoyable afternoon and evening eating and sharing stories, the party wound down and the runners went off to their campsites to get some sleep. Soon, as I was lying in my tent, I began to hear that familiar Barkley sound: rainfall. The sound seemed amplified by the tarp I had put over the tent. I was agonizingly aware of the rainfall during my intermittent sleep throughout the night, as the rain fell for most of the night. The good news for me was that the tarp over my tent was working as designed and keeping my tent and its contents dry.

Fortunately, the rain diminished to a drizzle by daybreak Saturday. I got up, ate some breakfast, and then went down to the bathhouse for a shower. Soon thereafter, I saw Gary up and about, and then shortly after that, I heard the long, loud note of the conch shell as Gary signaled that the race would start in one hour. Intermittent light rain and fog would persist for most of the duration of the event. Temperatures were in the upper 40s to mid-60s during the race. For Barkley, this weather was not too bad, but the fog was a significant difficulty factor for many runners including myself, as the reader will learn later in this chapter.

At 8:41 AM, precisely one hour after the conch signal, Gary lit his cigarette while standing beside the closed gate in front of the assembled field of runners. I immediately recognized this as the starting signal, and ducked under the gate and started running slowly uphill, in the lead! It seemed that it took a couple of seconds for most of the runners to realize that Gary wasn't going to yell "GO" or any other signal besides lighting the cigarette. After a few-second delay, runners headed under or around the gate and began passing me. Within less than a minute I had settled into a fast walking pace somewhere in the middle of the pack. Flyin' Brian took off running and moved into the lead just a few yards past the gate. The 22nd running of the Barkley Marathons was underway!

The Bird Mountain trail was in pretty good shape this year, despite the rain the night before. However, parts of the North Boundary Trail (NBT) were quite muddy. Much of the NBT had been maintained in the previous two years, and despite the mud, most of the NBT was in the best condition for running that it had been in for the history of the Barkley Marathons. I ran much of these first few miles with Bill Goodwine, who was here for his first time. Gary had identified Bill as the "Human Sacrifice" for this year. But Bill had wisely decided to stay with runners, including myself and Leonard

Martin, who knew the course (or at least, thought we did). I kept telling Bill how good the trail condition was compared to past years. Eventually, we got to Bald Knob, about five "Barkley Miles" into the race, and entered the "clear cut" section of trail that was hard to follow, overgrown with briers, slippery with mud, and with numerous dead trees fallen across the trail. I noted to Bill that this was the way the entire North Boundary Trail used to be. He commented that he was glad to be able to see a section of the trail in the old state of disrepair. I admire him for this attitude, instead of complaining about the poor trail conditions. We got to the Garden Spot, the second book checkpoint on the loop, in about 3:33. This is within a few minutes of my time to that checkpoint in each of my previous few Barkley runs, so I felt that we were progressing OK but not fast. As we approached the book, we came upon Matt Mahoney. Matt was sitting on the ground performing surgery with a pocketknife on one of his shoes. I had noticed earlier that Matt's shoes, which were rather lightweight-looking British racing flats, had had some sections cut away where his ankle bones protruded. I guess he needed to whittle away a little more shoe material!

Matt, Bill, and I proceeded to the water-drop location a fraction of a mile down from the Garden Spot, and refilled our bottles. We then continued up to the top of the northernmost peak of Stallion Mountain for book 3. This was easy to find because it is right at the very top of the mountain along a faint old dirt jeep road. However, from there, the course got problematic for me.

From the north peak of Stallion Mountain, the course goes to the southernmost peak of Stallion Mountain, called Fyke's Peak by Gary. This was the third consecutive year I was to attempt this traverse. I had had problems navigating this section alone in 2006, and gone through lots of briers. In 2007 I had been with Sue Thompson and Chip Tuthill. Chip seemed to know a good sequence of roads and cross-country sections, and we did this section easily last year. However, now in 2008 I was about to have more navigational problems.

Everything on Stallion Mountain looked different to me this year, and I could not remember which way we had gone last year. Adding to the difficulty was the fact that it was foggy this year, and we could not see Fyke's Peak. I was still with Matt and Bill at this point. Matt seemed to know which way to go. But to me, the way we were going seemed wrong, and different than the way I had gone in the two previous years. We stopped to check our maps and written directions, and I got out my nice new leather gloves, recalling that we would soon be going through an area overgrown with briers. Based on reading the map, we kept going generally eastward on an old road. However, a couple minutes later, in an area that I noted did not look familiar to me, I realized that I had dropped my gloves back where we had checked our maps. I told Matt and Bill to go ahead without me, and I went back to get my gloves. After retrieving my gloves (a delay of several minutes), I then went back to where I had left Matt and Bill, and continued alone in what seemed the generally right direction, although I was really quite unsure of the best way to go. After heading easterly for a while, I checked my altimeter and realized that I had dropped several hundred feet from the first Stallion Mountain peak. I was down to around 2,600 feet elevation, but I knew that Fyke's Peak was up at about 3,200 feet. Farther downhill from me I could see a trailer or mobile home alongside what looked like a waste treatment pond. I knew that was not on the course, and was well outside Frozen Head Natural Area. Through patchy fog, I could also see that a mountain peak was west of me. I figured that I must have gotten too far down on the eastern slope of Stallion Mountain, so I headed uphill in a westerly direction. I went through some terrible stands of thick and tall briers. At one point, I got cut along my nose by a sawbrier. I soon tasted blood.

I kept climbing back toward the top of the Stallion Mountain ridge, and eventually reached the top and started following some old dirt roads in a southerly direction. I soon recognized the final section of dirt road to Fyke's Peak, and went on up to the top. At the top, I saw Bill and another runner, David Hughes. They told me that no one had been able to find the book, that they had been there half an hour, and that Matt had gone on without finding the book. We checked our written directions, which said that the book was at the root ball of a fallen tree 90 feet due west of a stump and rock. We found the stump and rock, and paced off about 90 feet due west. There we found a baggie of some white candy mints and a water bottle, but no book. We methodically checked all the fallen trees in the area, and after several minutes, David shouted that he had found a book in a baggie. It was in a hole by a dead tree maybe 100 feet north of where it should have been, and the baggie the book was in looked aged, dirty, and tattered. As I was getting my page, I thought I recognized the title of that book from a past year. Ironically, it was "The Endless Game." It turns out that that book was indeed from 2006. However, we took our pages and began to head in the southerly direction. As we were leaving, Rebecca Nelson arrived and went to get her designated page 60 out of the book. I heard her say that her page was missing. To me, this confirmed my suspicion that that was a previous year's book. We continued onward anyway, deciding not to waste more time in the endless game of looking for the missing book.

Based on data that I recorded on my Pocket Guides, I had reached the north peak of Stallion Mountain in 3:51 this year, compared to 3:54 in 2007. But this year I got to Fyke's Peak in 4:48 compared to 4:17 last year. Thus my misadventure finding Fyke's Peak and looking for the missing book this year had cost me 34 minutes compared to my time for the same section last year. I later learned that Jim Nelson, one of the first runners through Fyke's Peak, had intentionally left that bag of mint candies where the Fyke's Peak book should have been, thinking that if runners took a mint and gave it to Gary in lieu of a book page, Gary would know that they had been to the correct location. This was pretty smart thinking on Jim's part, but it did not occur to me or the others I was with at Fyke's Peak to take a mint from the bag. Gary later told me that several runners did bring him a mint from the bag as proof that they had reached Fyke's Peak. Why the book was missing remains a mystery. The most likely speculation I heard is that an animal, such as a pack rat, carried it off from where Gary and Karl had placed it several weeks prior. This wild-animal did-it theory would also explain how the 2006 book got relocated to where David Hughes found it this year, a few hundred feet from the rattlesnake-hole location where it had originally been placed for the 2006 race.

On the long and tortuous downhill from Fyke's Peak, I fell behind Bill and David, and eventually got to the New River alone. I spent a couple minutes looking for a place to cross on rocks without getting my feet wet, but finding none, I just waded across in a place where the water was about shin-deep. I then headed up the paved road on the other side a short distance until I recognized the small waterfall on the left, and went uphill along the stream. I soon came to the next book, while Bill and David were still there. We then began the slow trudge up the Testicle Spectacle powerline cut. Going up the Testicle Spectacle, I counted a line of nine runners all within sight on the hill. I was a little surprised that this many of us, over one-quarter of the starting field, were so close together at this point.

I had no trouble navigating or finding books the rest of the way to the top of Frozen Head. The briers on the Rat Jaw section had been cut down recently, so going up the Rat Jaw was easier and a little faster than last year. I got to Frozen Head in about 7:33 this year, compared to 7:17 the previous year, and 7:58 in 2006. I was gradually gaining back some of the time I had lost at Fyke's Peak.

When I left Frozen Head I was in a small group that included Bill and Fatboy Trahern. Fatboy and I have met each other at numerous ultras over the years, and we talked a lot about some of our past runs. We both agreed that one of the most memorable runs of our lives, besides Barkley, was the 1997 Sawtooth Wilderness Odyssey, a 55-mile adventure run in Idaho, much of which we had run together. We both recalled the "snow enema," as Fatboy had called it at the time, that he got while butt-sliding in running shorts down a steep snow-covered slope at the Sawtooth. Unfortunately, this enjoyable social chatting as we were heading toward the next book made us overlook the faint turnoff to go up the ridge to the Hump. This mountaintop lies only a few hundred feet beside the trail we were on, but it is up an extremely steep cliff from where we were when we realized that we had missed the turnoff. So we had to backtrack for a couple of minutes. We then turned and climbed the steep slope. This diversion again resulted in several precious minutes of wasted time. It was a reminder of the need for constant navigational vigilance at the Barkley. Once on the ridge to the Hump, we met Sue Thompson, Buttslide Martin, and Andrew Hackett. We continued and soon found the book at the top.

From the Hump, we had no trouble finding the rest of the books and making our way back to camp. However, the climb up Big Hell took a toll on me. I seemed to be very tired and unable to move fast, but most importantly and sadly, I was starting to want to quit. I lagged behind most of the group as we climbed this intimidating hill. I told Sue I was having a problem with my attitude, that maybe it was time for me to recognize that Barkley had outgrown me and I should stop taking up a slot every year. She commiserated that she too was not feeling strong or optimistic about a second loop at this point. However, we eventually made it to the top, and our group re-formed. Someone noted that we had done the Big Hell climb in 44 minutes. That seemed a few minutes faster than my normal, so my attitude started to turn around and I felt better about things. In reviewing my Pocket Guide data, I see that the Big Hell climb had taken me 48 minutes in 2007 and 58 minutes in 2006. So indeed I was moving well at this point compared to previous years, despite my wavering mental state.

Buttslide Martin led us through the tricky section around the capstones at the top of Chimney Top and onto the Chimney Top Trail. This was probably the easiest I had ever done this part, in the area where I had gotten off-course for an hour in 2001. The route Buttslide knew was to go to the right of the first capstone, then to the left of the second, bigger set of stone peaks. This quickly put us onto the trail just to the west of the cliff area where there is a small campsite in a shallow cave in the capstone. In recent years, based on my interpretation of what Gary's instructions allowed, I had gone to the right of the second capstone formation, and thus had gone out of the way somewhat. It was good to finally learn the best allowable way through this section. This is the area where many runners, including myself, have gone the wrong way on the Chimney Top Trail in past years.

I ran with Bill and Sue the rest of the way back to camp. We got to the gate and Gary recorded my time to complete the first loop as 11:18:19. This was almost exactly 30 minutes longer than my time to finish the first loop last year. The lost time at Fyke's Peak was my major difference in time from last year to this year. When we arrived at the gate, I told Gary that I would get ready for a second loop, but that I was not certain that I was actually going to go. However, Bill Goodwine encouraged Sue and me to go out on another loop. Bill was still feeling good, exhibiting some real toughness for a Barkley Virgin, and his encouragement was very helpful. It helped me get motivated. We went back to our campsites and set about preparing for a second loop. I cooked a can of chicken noodle soup on a small camp-stove, and offered some to Bill. While the soup was heating, I rinsed my muddy feet, lanced and bandaged a toe blister, and changed into clean socks and shoes. Bill Losey, another friend from past Barkleys but who was not running it this year, kindly offered his help and assisted me in getting resupplied for loop two. By the time Bill Goodwine and I were ready, Sue was also ready to head back *out there*. It was just beginning to get dark. We put our headlamps on, and went back to the gate. Gary gave us our new numbers for pages on loop two, and we headed out at 12:05:05 race time. We had spent about 47 minutes at camp. This was several minutes shorter than my time in camp last year between loops one and two. One of my goals this year was to shorten this turn-around time, so this was a small but notable improvement for me. At Barkley, I now must take what pleasure I can from these minor successes, because my major result in recent years is failure. As Andrew Thompson had noted in the article he wrote in last year's *UltraRunning* after the Barkley, the reality of Barkley is failure. I believe that this insight of Andrew's is true, almost always. However, as we will soon see, one of the major exceptions to this failure rule was about to unfold in front of us.

During the second loop, we had more light rain. I was grateful to have a hooded Gore-Tex jacket that had been given to me recently by my friends back home, Reid and Lisa Kelly. Even when it wasn't raining it was foggy.

In the dark and fog, our visibility was limited to just a few feet in front of us. For a while I thought my vision was getting blurry, but it was just the light from my headlight reflecting off the fog back into my eyes. After a few miles of this, Sue and I both admitted that we were afraid that we would not be able to find Fyke's Peak in the dark and fog. We rationalized that since we had had trouble finding it in daylight, we would be unable to find it in this poor visibility. After some discussion, we decided to head back to camp before we got farther away. Bill believed that he would be unlikely to navigate the loop by himself, so he also decided to drop out at this point. The three of us left the course at the familiar Bald Knob cut-off. There is now a new trail there connecting the NBT near the top of Bald Knob to the jeep road. We took this trail and within a couple of minutes were on the Quitter's Road and made our way back to camp. Gary logged us in at 1:41 AM, exactly 17 hours after the start. We were each tapped out by Davey Henn playing his bugle.

Later I spoke with Buttslide Martin, who had gone on to Fyke's Peak in the dark on loop two. He told me that he had spent about six hours going from the Garden Spot to Fyke's Peak and then to Coffin Springs, where he too headed down the Quitter's Road back to camp. This seemed to vindicate my decision to quit before trying to find Fyke's Peak on loop two. If Leonard had had that much difficulty finding it, I probably would have had more trouble. Leonard lives relatively close to Frozen Head, and had told me that he had been there probably 50 times over the years to train and learn the course.

My DNF on loop two was a sad ending for me. I had thought that I would really finish two loops this year, for the first time since 1992. In retrospect (as I write this 16 days later), I realize that the cause of my failure was mental weakness. I was afraid of being lost in the dark. In the past Gary has used the phrase "skeert of the dark" as an explanation for why most runners do not complete even two loops at the Barkley. I now know what he means. I can find no better explanation for my failure this year. I now really regret my decision to quit. I should have just gone on even if it meant spending the night on Stallion Mountain. But I was skeert of the dark.

The meager good news for me this year was that I was slightly stronger and faster on my partial second loop than the previous year. This year I was slightly better trained physically. I had done about 6% more mileage and 20% more elevation climb in an eleven-week training period before Barkley, compared to the previous year. I did the first four Barkley miles of loop two this year in about 3:20, whereas last year that section of loop two had taken me about 3:39. So my increased training apparently helped a little. Last year I had dropped out at the same point on loop two, because of knee pain and stiffness. This year I did not have that problem. This gives me hope that next year, I can train even more and be even stronger. This in turn gives me a renewed feeling of determination to do better next year. But mainly, I need to find a way to increase my mental strength and courage in facing the mountains *out there* in the darkness.

Meanwhile, other runners were having varying degrees of success but mostly failure. Back at camp, I had the pleasure of becoming an observer of one of the most interesting events in the sport of ultrarunning. I learned that

Flyin' Brian had already finished two loops and was sleeping at his campsite! He soon arose and headed out on loop three, going in the reverse (counter-clockwise) direction relative to the first two loops. After Brian left, runners trickled in after DNFing or finishing loop two. Nine runners finished loop two within the time limit. Seven of them started loop three: Brian Robinson, Jim Nelson, Byron Backer, Greg Eason, Carl Laniak, Andrew Thompson, and Blake Wood, in that order. Eason, Laniak, and Thompson were running together; the others were each running alone.

Those of us in camp on Sunday afternoon had a special treat. Jim Nelson's wife, Rebecca, and Rebecca's sister, Annelise LeCheminant, were at the campground while Jim and the others were *out there* on their third loop. Rebecca and Annelise had both been to Barkley with Jim last year, and Rebecca had run one loop of Barkley this year. Annelise is a professional musician and songwriter. She had composed a song about the Barkley, and she sang the song for us while accompanying herself on guitar. There were probably a dozen or more of us around Gary's campfire for this performance. The song was so beautiful it nearly brought me to tears. In the refrain she sang: "I am not done with this race that eats its young." In order for her to sing about it as she did, Annelise, with the poetic insight of a songwriter, must have somehow been able to see something deep in the soul of the Barkley runners, about our driven obsession with this race. It was very touching to me, as I realized that I was one of the small number of people in the world about whom she was singing. The reader can listen to part of this song, "The Race That Eats its Young," from Annelise's web site, at <http://www.annelise.us/Music.html>. Fittingly, this song is on a CD titled "Driven." Note that the phrase that became this song title was first used by Gary in describing the Barkley Marathons as far back as 1988.

Eventually, all seven runners who had started loop three completed it within the 40-hour time limit. The finishers of the three-loop Fun Run, in order, were: Flyin' Brian, Jim, Byron, Blake, Greg, Carl, and Andrew. The latter three runners finished together. Gary seemed especially impressed with Byron and Carl, both first-timers at Barkley. Gary pointed out to Byron that if he came back next year and was just a little faster on the first three loops, he could make a run at the 100-mile. Byron dismissed this idea by stating: "I have no unfinished business at the Barkley." But as well as Byron had done, it is easy to imagine him coming back. We will see later if he could resist future attempts.

Notable among the names *not* on this list of Fun Run finishers was Joe Decker, the world's fittest man. Joe was making good progress until he had a problem with a new, untested flashlight that left him in the dark on loop two. He then fell and twisted a knee coming down the Zip Line. He did finish two loops, in 23:37:30. However, he then withdrew. He later described this on his website blog, and summarized his Barkley experience as follows: "What an absolutely incredible, wonderful, powerful, painful, discouraging, enlightening experience. Am I depressed or upset that I didn't finish Barkley? I don't think so. I actually feel a little giddy maybe even happy. Why you might ask? Even though I didn't complete the 5 loops that I so desired, I did learn a considerable amount about myself out there on the trail. They say adversity creates character. If that's true, my character just doubled." The Barkley had asserted itself as tougher than Joe, but I admire his reaction to his defeat. In April 2009, he wrote further that: "The Barkley 100 Mile trail run ... is the toughest race I've ever run in my life. Having completed the Badwater 135 (twice), the Marathon des Sables, the Grandslam of Ultrarunning and countless other endurance events, I thought I'd have no problem at Barkley, was I seriously mistaken! Last year I completed 2 loops of the 5 loop race before pulling myself at the end of loop 2 due to injury." Joe also stated in this 2009 blog that he will be back: "I broke the Guinness World Record when I turned 30 and plan on taking Barkley out next year when I turn 40!" It will be interesting to see if this prophecy will be fulfilled.

Flyin' Brian was the only runner to proceed onto the fourth loop. He was really doing very well and looking strong. After finishing four loops in the middle of Sunday night/Monday morning, in 43:19:20, he again lay down and got about an hour or more of sleep. Then he was up and headed out on loop five before daylight on Monday. Gary signaled this rare moment by ringing a Swiss cowbell that Milan Milanovich had given him in one of the past years that Milan had been here. This bell-ringing was the Barkley version of the traditional "bell lap" of a track race, when a bell is rung to indicate the final lap. This was only the tenth time in the history of Barkley that a runner had started a fifth loop (six previous 100-mile finishers + Blake in 2000 + Andrew Thompson in 2005 + Brian in 2007). At the time that Gary rang the bell, I was trying to sleep in my tent, but the bell woke me enough to realize that Brian was starting his fifth loop. I was really happy and impressed to realize that a remarkable feat of human endurance was happening right then and there.

During the day on Monday, those of us remaining in camp speculated as to when Brian would finish, and whether or not he would break Cave Dog Keizer's 2003 course record of 56:57:52. Gary said that Brian's sleeping for an hour or more in each of the nights, after loops two and four, was a "high risk" strategy. The risks involved are the possibility that the time spent sleeping would not leave him enough time to complete the course in the 60-hour time limit, and that by stopping to sleep, he may not be able to get up and continue at all. However, Brian's strategy made sense and was familiar to me. As the reader may recall, in both my three-loop finishes (1988 and 1991), I had slept during the night after the second loop. The one time I had attempted loop three without sleep was 1992, when I soon met my demise by becoming fatigued, falling into Phillips Creek, and becoming disoriented and unable to follow the trail. So for me, the strategy of sleeping at night between loops seems like a good one.

Brian settled the speculation soon enough. At about 4:23 PM, Flyin' Brian came running up the road into camp. He touched the gate at 55:42:27 race time, setting a new course record by well over an hour! We were all amazed and congratulated him. Brian hardly seemed tired or sore, although I was stunned to read later that he had fallen down a cliff in the dark on his third loop, and dislocated a clavicle. We gathered around and took pictures. Amazingly, Brian then held the equivalent of an impromptu seminar, in which he read excerpts from his training log to the assembled crowd of admirers. It was inspiring to learn that he had been running 60-90 miles per week in most weeks prior to the race. Even more impressive was the approximately 50,000 feet of elevation change per week that he had included in those training runs. He tapered for only the last few days before Barkley, not wanting to lose his "edge." Brian also later told me that he had been eating about 4,000 calories a day and was barely able to keep his weight up during that training period. He said that he ate a lot of nuts, and put olive oil on many of the foods he ate, as a way of trying to take in enough calories.

Below is a picture I took of Flyin' Brian as he was triumphantly approaching the finish gate to win the 2008 Barkley 100-mile in a course-record time.

As I have stated throughout this book, I believe that the Barkley Marathons is the toughest foot-race in the world. And we had just witnessed the fastest finishing time ever on one of the most difficult Barkley courses ever. Combining these observations, I conclude that those of us who had the privilege to be there and see Flyin' Brian's run in 2008 had just witnessed perhaps the greatest trail race performance in modern history, and one of the most incredible feats of human endurance running ever accomplished. To witness this was at once both a humbling and uplifting experience. I am grateful to Brian for providing us with that experience.

Below is the list of starters, their numbers of Barkley starts, and their loop-finishing times for 2008.

1. Flyin' Brian Robinson (3)	7:07:43	16:47:30	29:56:49	43:19:20	55:42:27
2. Jim Nelson (6)	8:22:20	20:00:57	33:42:34		
3. Byron Backer (1)	8:03:15	21:53:37	36:28:29		
4. Blake Wood (6)	9:11:52	23:17:20	36:52:27		
5. Greg Eason (3)	8:52:23	22:14:45	38:15:57		

6. Carl Laniak (1)   8:52:25   22:14:44   38:15:58
7. Andrew Thompson (9) 8:56:35   22:14:55   38:15:59
8. Jason Poole (5)   9:03:09   23:19:46
9. Joe Decker (1)   9:17:24   23:37:30
10. Will Harlan (1)   8:08:36
11. Todd Holmes (5)   9:03:10
12. DeWayne Satterfield (9) 9:03:15
13. Michael Graz (1)   9:05:15
14. Heather Graz (1)   9:05:16
15. Andras Low (3)   9:11:53
16. Jon Barker (1)   9:17:25
17. Wendell Doman (4)   9:33:00
18. Hiram Rogers (5)   10:33:24
19. John Tyszkiewicz (1)11:09:58
20. Fatboy Trahern (2)   11:09:59
21. Frozen Ed Furtaw (12) 11:18:19
22. Bill Goodwine (1)   11:18:22
23. Andrew Hackett (2)   11:19:45
24. Buttslide Martin (15)11:19:55
25. Sue Thompson (9)   11:27:11
26. John DeWalt (20)   12:04:33
27. David Hughes (9)   12:17:06
28. Matt Mahoney (12)   12:17:06
29. Merrianne Brittain (3)~18:58* Finished loop one over the time limit.
30. Steve Durbin (2) ~19:07* Finished loop one over the time limit; missed two books.
31. Stu Gleman (11)   Quit during loop one.
32. John Price (2)   Quit during loop one.
33. Rich Limacher (7)   Quit during loop one.
34. Rebecca Nelson (1)   Quit during loop one.
35. Joe Trujillo (1)   Quit during loop one.
35 Starters

+++++++++++

Below is the essay I wrote as an entry requirement for the 2008 Barkley Marathons.

Why I Should Be Allowed To Run The Barkley:
Quantum Theory and the Barkley Marathons
Essay #12 in a series
By Frozen Ed Furtaw
February 6, 2008

I should be allowed to run the 2008 Barkley Marathons because this will be the 20th Anniversary of my historic first-ever official completion of a Barkley Marathons in 1988.   In subsequent runnings of the Barkley Marathons, numerous other ultrarunners have accomplished 55-, 60-, and 100-mile completions far superior to my initial 55-mile finish in 1988. However, I will forever be proud of my accomplishment because it was the first, and in fact, the only official completion in the first four years of the Barkley Marathons. In that sense, my completion was a psychological break-through event because it showed that with enough determination, the Barkley was doable. Furthermore because I am not and never was an elite or national-class runner, my finish demonstrated that even a non-elite runner could complete the Barkley. These facts confirm that I have a rightful place in the Barkley Marathons, and thus should be allowed to run it again in 2008.

Beyond this, I have something very interesting to write about in this essay. In recent months, I have seen the movie "What the Bleep Do We Know," and read several books that further elaborate on the theme of this movie. (If you, the reader, have not seen this movie, I recommend that you do so.) In the remainder of this essay, I will give my brief summary of the important message I derived from this movie, and how it further constitutes a reason why I should be allowed to run the Barkley Marathons.

Quantum theory in physics can be interpreted to suggest that human consciousness interacts with the behavior of sub-atomic particles. This in turn affects the behavior of molecules and larger objects in our every-day world. Hence our consciousness or minds affect reality. A further implication of this line of thinking is that we humans have a significant amount of freedom and power to create and alter the world around us. We have vast power over reality that we can exercise by using our imagination and will to envision what we want, and then acting to make that vision become reality.

As an interesting example of this application of vision and will, I recently thought that I needed a good rain-proof jacket for running in the rain. I had never owned a Gore-Tex jacket, but I began to mention my desire for one to some friends and relatives, and began to do some pre-shopping catalog comparisons and visualizations of various brands. Before I knew it, and without having to buy one, I had four Gore-Tex jackets given to me by friends and a sister!

This philosophy and example have renewed and strengthened my belief that we humans can accomplish much by using our mental power to decide what we want and then using our willpower to achieve what we envision. I recently asked myself what I would like to use this power to acquire or achieve, and one answer that occurred to me was that I very much want to finish two loops at Barkley this year. This is something that I have not been able to accomplish since the loop was lengthened in 1995. Thus my run at Barkley this year will be an experiment in the role of consciousness affecting reality, and hence an experiment in quantum theory.

Chapter 28
2009: An Epic Harrowing Tale of Success

The 23rd running of the Barkley Marathons started on Saturday, April 4, 2009. In many respects, it was much like many past Barkleys. Fortunately for those of us who witnessed it, it was also like the 2008 Barkley in that it provided an awe-inspiring performance that again showed that the limit of human endurance is way *out there*, far beyond what most of us can approach or comprehend.

The largest-ever starting field of 40 runners was filled with the usual combination of returning former Barkley "sickos" and Barkley Virgins. Notable among returners was Mark Williams, the Englishman who was the first-ever finisher of the Barkley 100, back in 1995. Mark now lives in California, with an American wife and a child. We were all interested in seeing how he could do at the Barkley after 13 years since his last appearance here in 1996. He was apparently still a strong ultramarathoner, as he had by now completed the 153-mile Spartathlon 13 times in 15 starts, including 2008, when he finished it in 35:43. The Barkley course had changed significantly since Mark had last run it, so his attempt this year would not be a simple repeat of his 1995 accomplishment. It is worth noting that no runner had ever yet completed the Barkley 100 more than once, although five of the seven finishers (including Mark, in 1996) had attempted to repeat.

Although Mark Williams was the only returning 100-mile finisher this year, there were several other noteworthy previous Barkley runners back this year, including three who had finished the three-loop Fun Run last year: Andrew Thompson, Byron Backer, and Carl Laniak. Byron especially seemed like a prospective 100-mile finisher, since he had done so well here the previous year, as well as in numerous other ultras in recent years. Andrew Thompson, still holder of the Appalachian Trail speed record of approximately 47 miles per day for 47 consecutive days, was at the Barkley for his tenth appearance. The reader may recall that Andrew had had a dramatic hallucinatory ending to his attempted fifth loop in 2005. He had been back to the Barkley subsequently, both in 2007 when he had completed two loops, and in 2008 when he finished three loops for his fifth Fun Run finish. This left Andrew as the only person to have completed a fourth loop but who had not subsequently completed a fifth loop.

Other returning Fun Run finishers were Mike Dobies, John DeWalt, and myself. Returning non-finishers were Pat Costigan, John Price, Stu Gleman, Leonard Buttslide Martin, Bill Andrews, Chip Tuthill, Bill Losey, Steve Durbin, Allan Holtz, Mike Bur, David Hughes, DeWayne Satterfield, Hiram Rogers, Wendell Doman, Davey Henn, Paul Melzer, Robert Andrulis, Jon Barker, and Kerry Trammel. Kerry did not know until the day before the race began that he would be starting; he came to Frozen Head while still on the waiting list, and gained entry when Elise Harrington withdrew the day before the race due to travel problems resulting from a snowstorm in Colorado.

In addition to these returners, Barkley Virgins this year were Claudio Bacchi from Italy, Bob Haugh, Kevin Dorsey, Alan Geraldi, Jim Harris, Abi

Meadows, Rita Barnes, Marcia Rasmussen, Mike O'Melia, Jason Barringer, Joel Storrow, Carl Asker, Bob Jones, and Lora Mantelman. At fourteen, this was one of the largest fields of Barkley Virgins since the first Barkley, when all thirteen starters were Virgins.

In the months prior to this year's Barkley, the Barkley e-mail list had been highly active and entertaining. Hundreds of e-mails had been exchanged among list members on many Barkley-related topics such as sawbriers, clothes, women runners, and potential course changes. The latter topic is frequently a pre-race subject of interest and conjecture. This year, Gary had fanned the fires of speculation about course changes, especially with mention of a new part of the course that he called the Yellow Indian Trail, and by referring in a couple of e-mails to Wagon Rock, which is on the side of Big Fodderstack Mountain. In 2008, Gary had also hinted at the possibility that Big Fodderstack might be included on the course, but that turned out to be a devious trick intended to fuel needless speculation and worry by the runners. This year, there was also pre-race speculation about the possibility of a counterclockwise-direction start, as there had been e-mails about "reverse directions" that Gary said he was preparing.

I arrived at the Frozen Head campground on Wednesday evening, three days before the race was to start. I had intended to spend some time Thursday hiking on Stallion Mountain to better familiarize myself with the area that had caused me navigational problems in 2006 and 2008. However, on Thursday morning, I decided to stay in the campground and rest, rather than expending the considerable amount of time and energy that would be required to get to and explore Stallion Mountain. Instead, I spent some time in camp talking to other runners about Stallion Mountain and other parts of the course that presented navigational challenges. This strategy paid off for me, as will be described later.

The pre-race camp-out included the usual socializing among running friends old and new. I had the distinction of sharing a campsite with Mark Williams after he arrived on Thursday. There was a lot of speculation in the campground about putative course changes. There was also the all-too-familiar wind-driven rain, which fell for much of Thursday night. I had a new, larger tent with a large rain-fly this year, so I had not bothered to put a tarp over the tent as I had done last year. The result was water puddles on the floor of the tent Friday morning. Fortunately, the tent was large enough that my sleeping bag did not get wet, as I had placed it in a slightly elevated spot near the center of the tent. The rain water that had seeped into the tent during the night formed a small moat partially surrounding me and my luggage. The rain stopped on Friday morning, so I mopped up the water, and then put the tarp up over the tent, feeling annoyed at the seemingly ever-present rain at Frozen Head.

Gary arrived at the campground on Thursday afternoon, but he did not reveal the course instructions or map, and he did not set up his campsite. After visiting for a while, he left to spend the night at the Henns' house, thus wisely avoiding the night-long rain.

On Friday, Gary returned and set up his race-headquarters campsite as usual. Someone hung some small Buddhist prayer flags near where Gary hung the license plates around his site, thus adding to the colorful appearance of the race area. After the site was set up, the anticipated moment arrived when Gary began handing out course directions to the runners. We were all anxiously awaiting these directions to answer the questions about course changes, including possibly starting in the reverse direction. However, this issue had a hilarious resolution. In addition to the regular course instructions, Gary had included a copy of the directions in which the font characters were both reversed and inverted! We were all very amused by this stunt. However, as had been the case last year, the anticipated course changes again turned out to have been mostly red herrings. Course changes this year were minor. Several book placements were changed, but the route to be followed, and the loop distance and elevation change, remained the same as in the previous year.

The new book placements are worth noting. A book was placed on Bald Knob, along the NBT, for the first time. This book was located in the heart of the so-called clear-cut area, which has been causing navigational problems for runners since the area was logged prior to the 2003 race. Apparently, numerous runners in recent years had found a relatively easy way to skirt above the clear cut and re-join the NBT northeast of Bald Knob. I myself had inadvertently taken a similar route around part of the clear cut back in 2006. This bypass had the advantage of avoiding an area that was now heavily overgrown with the familiar sawbriers that seem to proliferate in disturbed places such as in the cleared areas under power lines. There were also many cut-down trees scattered in the clear-cut area. With the thick briers and felled trees on a steep slope, this area is very slow to traverse, as can be seen in the picture below, taken by Alan Geraldi during loop one of the 2009 Barkley.

Gary and Raw Dog had realized that many runners were taking the uphill bypass intentionally, so the placement of a book in the heart of the clear cut was intended to prevent this short-cutting. Although it turned out to be a nuisance to get to that book in the briers, I was glad that Gary had put a book there on Bald Knob, because this required all runners to go there instead of taking the easier bypass. I believe that this this is the best way to avoid problems such as the controversies that arose in 1988 and 2001 with runners missing parts of the intended course. Those controversies could have been avoided by more judicious book placement such as was done on Bald Knob this year.

The other significant book re-location was on Stallion Mountain. Instead of two books, on North Stallion Mountain and Fyke's Peak (South Stallion Mountain), as had been the case in recent years, this year there was only one book in that area. It was at a new location near North Stallion peak, but a few hundred meters southeast of the very peak, near the top of a cliff with spectacular views toward the east and south. I was happy with this new checkpoint placement, as it required us runners to go to the cliff top and be able to enjoy the view, which heretofore we had not visited. This new location was what Gary referred to as the Yellow Indian Trail, because the cliff that the book was on, when viewed in profile from the side, had a yellowish color and a shape reminiscent of an Indian's face.

Another minor book-location change was that the Rat Jaw book was placed about 3/4 of the way up Rat Jaw, in a cubby-hole in the wall of a rock cliff. The book had been placed near there at least once in previous years, but this location differed from the description in this year's instructions. This discrepancy happened because the book was placed by someone other than Gary, after Gary had written the description. This error in the course instructions was made known to all of us runners prior to the start of this year's race.

This year a film crew was at Frozen Head as part of a University of Tennessee videography class that was making a documentary video about the race. The presence of the film class was an interesting addition to the campground and activities at this year's race. I hope that the video they eventually produce becomes available to the public. I'm sure it will make an interesting story.

Another interesting aspect of this year's event was that Keith Dunn, a several-time Barkley DNFer, was there not as a runner but as an observer. Keith had a hand-held computer/telephone that he used to send "Twitter" messages to friends, including the ultra list of hundreds of ultrarunners, and a website throughout the weekend. Keith thinks that this may have been the first time that an ultra was "Tweeted" in real time. It was also helpful to the race participants in camp to be able to receive up-to-the-minute weather forecasts and weather-radar images throughout the event. As will be seen, the weather would be a significant factor during the event, as usual.

After Thursday night's rain, the weather took a turn for the better, and it did not rain during the day Friday. The forecast was for a warm and dry day Saturday. We were all happy that the rain had stopped, but concerned about the possibility of heat during the race. Saturday dawned as forecasted. It was a beautiful, clear, and sunny morning. We runners busily and somewhat anxiously prepared for the start of the race. As usual, Gary had not announced a specific starting time. He had stated only that the race would start one hour after he blew the conch shell, sometime Saturday morning. We knew only that he could start the race at any time between midnight and noon. This year, Gary dragged out this uncertainty to the extreme. Runners were nervously pacing around the campground as the morning passed slowly. Mark Williams was concerned that a start as late as noon would impose a tight schedule on him getting to the airport to fly home on Tuesday, if he were to finish the 100-mile near the 60-hour time limit. It was impressive to realize that Mark was thinking positively about completing the 100-mile again. As time passed on Saturday morning, I mentioned to some other runners that we were wasting hours of what would have been beautiful running weather. The morning had started cool, but with the clear and sunny skies, it was rapidly warming toward the forecasted temperatures in the 70s. I knew that Gary was using the late start as another tactic intended to make finishing the race just a little tougher. It is the kind of stratagem he must employ to ensure that Barkley remains the world's toughest trail race. It was certainly increasing the pre-race tension in the campground. At 9:48 AM, Keith Dunn Tweeted that: "Laz is being accused of just screwing with the runners."

Finally, Gary blew the conch at 9:53 AM. We had one more hour to get ready for the start, although by this time all the runners had already been ready for a few hours. I made use of some of the time to make a thermos bottle of hot instant coffee and give a brief interview to the video crew.

The 10:53 AM start was one of the latest in the Barkley's history. I tried to repeat last year's starting-gate scenario. As we runners gathered at the starting location, I positioned myself right in front of the gate, and even practiced ducking and scooting under the gate to make a fast start. Gary then made a formal-sounding announcement, stating that this was the time when it was customary for last-minute instructions for runners. He then said: "But this is the Barkley." He made no further announcement, but then lit his lighter and cigarette. Like last year, I quickly passed under the gate and took a few running strides, trying to be in first place. However, another runner had passed beside the gate, and was running ahead of me on my left. I quickened my pace, and briefly moved into the lead, like last year. I then relaxed my pace to a walk, and other runners moved ahead. Most notably, Byron Backer ran into the lead, and did not stop running all the way up the jeep road. He was actually running quite fast given the duration of the race that lay ahead. I commented to someone near me that it was not a good sign for Byron to run that fast at the start. I remembered the sad results of many past runners, including myself, who had run too fast early in the race, only to exhaust themselves well before the finish.

Soon a long single-file line of runners was hiking determinedly up the Bird Mountain Trail. There was plenty of chatter and banter among us. When we got to the top of Bird Mountain, where we were to turn and head down the other side, I commented that this was "one Barkley Mile." Carl Asker, a Barkley Virgin who is a Swedish native now living in Connecticut,

noted this comment. He later wrote a colorful story of his Barkley experience on a website blog at: <http://teamtfl.blogspot.com/2009/04/
barkley-marathons-2009.html>.   He wrote that when I pointed out that we
had done one Barkley Mile, he checked the reading on a Calorie-metering
instrument that he was wearing. This device apparently uses heartrate, body
weight, and time to calculate an estimate of the Calories burned by the user.
He reported that the instrument showed that he had expended 430 Calories in
this first "mile." As the reader may recall, I had wheel-measured this far last
year, so I knew that we had actually come about two miles. Still, it is reveal-
ing that his meter showed such a high energy expenditure. A common rule of
thumb is that a runner typically burns about 100 Calories per mile. This is an
interesting illustration of how far from "typical" running at the Barkley is.

Carl Asker has drawn several caricature pictures of humorous Barkley
scenes. One of his drawings is shown below. This picture represents the
Barkley loop, with "bird" mountain, the Garden Spot, some powerlines, Big
Hell, briers, and a bloody rat's jaw depicted.

My own run went very well on the first loop. I was here for the 13th time, determined as in the previous several years to complete two loops. My training this year had included both more mileage and more steep climb than in recent years. I felt very fit, at least relative to my normal for recent Barkley attempts. I got to Book 1, at Phillips Creek, in 1:01. This is the fastest such time that I have ever recorded in several years of using my "Pocket Guide." My six previously recorded times to Phillips Creek, for 1997, 2001, 2003, and 2006-2008, had all ranged from 1:08 to 1:23. Similarly, my time to the Garden Spot on this year's first loop was 3:18, compared to previously recorded times of 3:32 to 4:04. I attribute this fast early pace to three major factors: my improved training and condition; the good weather; and the fact that many sections of the NBT had been improved and maintained in recent years. After the Garden Spot, I had the good fortune to be running near Hiram Rogers in the Stallion Mountain area, where I had had problems with route-finding in prior years. Hiram, who lives near Frozen Head, said that he had been on Stallion Mountain eight times this year, training and learning the course. I followed him through the maze of faint old dirt roads and briers that cover the area. We made rapid time from the book at the Yellow Indian Trail near the top of Stallion Mountain, to Fyke's Peak, and down its south slope to the New River. My time between the Garden Spot and the New River was 1:10. By comparison, in the three prior years in which this section was part of the Barkley loop, my times for this section had been between 1:22 and 1:51. So I was continuing to make good time. My decision to conserve my energy Thursday and forego exploring Stallion Mountain turned out to have been a good one.

I spent little time at the New River looking for a place to cross. It seemed futile to try to find rocks or trees to cross the river without getting my feet wet, so I just looked for a relatively shallow place to wade across, and got my feet and legs soaked. On the other side, I scrambled up to Highway 116, there to find David Horton greeting runners and taking notes. I was happy to see him. I noticed that he was holding a copy of a draft of this book that I had brought and left for him at camp. After a brief conversation with David, I continued across the highway and onward toward the Testicle Spectacle. In addition to David, several members of the video crew were also at this road crossing, shooting video of us runners.

I paused for several seconds while ascending the Testicle Spectacle to entertain the video crew. Some of the crew members were standing in each of several places along this steep uphill. As I approached one group with a video camera pointing toward me, I asked if their audio microphone was on. They silently nodded that yes, I was being recorded. I then paused in front of their camera and quickly told the story of how this hill got its name... "Spectacles, testicles, vallet, and vatch!" The camera crew was quite amused. I continued uphill. In this area, I remember being with Carl Asker and Paul Melzer. We crested the Testicle Spectacle and went down the steep slope of Meth Lab Hill. When we got to the appropriate place, just past a steep downhill that Gary calls the Neo-Buttslide, we turned right into the woods and headed toward Raw Dog Falls. As we approached the book location near the waterfall, I was surprised and saddened to see Mark

Williams just leaving the checkpoint. I called out to him, that I was surprised to see him "way back here." I would have expected him to be much farther along on the course than we were. He said that he had gotten lost a few times, and hurried off. Carl and I got our pages and headed off after him, but that was the last time we saw Mark on this loop.

We continued onward and recrossed Highway 116 and headed up the next steep mountainside—Rat Jaw Junior. Gary had referred to the highway-crossing location as Pig Head Creek, because a pig's skull had been placed on a stick here to indicate the proper ravine where we started up the steep climb. Here I noticed that I was gradually pulling away from Carl. This was another indication that I was having a good day. Normally I would expect a younger runner like Carl to have no trouble keeping up with me. As Carl noted in his post-race report, he had trouble throughout the race maintaining his energy level, a problem that he attributed to not eating and drinking properly during the race.

I was alone going up Rat Jaw Senior, and this probably cost me some time. Recall that a book had been placed on the upper part of Rat Jaw, in a location that was not properly described in this year's course directions. I had trouble finding this book, even though I knew the vicinity of where it was. I walked back and forth a couple of times where I thought it should be near the cliff, but didn't see the book. Finally, I got to where I was sure I was beyond it, but still hadn't seen it. I tenuously continued up Rat Jaw, recalling that in previous years some books had been missing from where they should have been. I considered going on without a page from this book, under the assumption that it wasn't where it had been placed, and that when we all reported this, Gary would accept the loop without this page. However, I soon realized that this would put me at risk of being disqualified, so I turned around and went back into the cliff area where the book should be. After several more minutes, I did find the book, on a rock ledge about head high. I was relieved to finally have found it. This delay cost me about 10 minutes, during which Carl caught back up to me. I explained the problem I had had, and we continued trudging slowly to the top of Frozen Head Mountain. My time to the water-drop station near the base of the lookout tower was 6:46, my fastest time ever to that point on the Hell for the Highway course, and my best time to this checkpoint since 2001.

On the next two pages are a couple of photographs of me approaching the top of the Rat Jaw in the 2009 Barkley. These photos were taken by Rich Limacher, who was spending an amusing afternoon watching runners crawl up this incredibly steep hill.

I spent much of the rest of the first loop with Carl and Steve Durbin. We gradually pulled ahead of Paul Melzer going up Big Hell. It was already getting dark as we were going down from Chimney Top toward the campground. The three of us arrived at the start/finish gate together, in a time of 10:34 on my watch; however, Gary recorded my time as 10:29:37. I am not sure why we had this discrepancy. Regardless of the exact time, it was my fastest time to complete loop one since a 10:12 first-loop time in 1997, so I felt good about how things were going—except for the recurrent dreaded problem of a painful blister on the sole of my left foot. I had hoped that this

year I would avoid that problem, because I was wearing both toe socks and double-layer running socks. In a previous 10-hour ultra in January 2009, this combination of socks had successfully prevented sole blisters, so I was hoping it would spare me this perennial problem at Barkley this year. But I had no such luck. The wet feet and constant steep slopes that result in the feet sliding within one's shoes at the Barkley had taken the usual toll. I had started noticing the problem after about eight hours.

Steve, Carl, and I all planned to get something to eat, reload our packs, and head out on loop two. However, I knew that it would take me a while to

tape my foot blister and otherwise get ready to start loop two. So I told Steve and Carl to not wait for me if they were ready to go before I was. This is indeed what happened. I spent about 55 minutes in camp. I had trouble taping my foot because the blister was on the sole in a place that I could not see very well, and the skin was puckered from being wet for several hours. I was grateful to get some help from Chip Tuthill's wife, Bernadette, in taping the bottom of my foot. I also heated and ate a can of chicken noodle soup, and drank some of the coffee I had made that morning, before I started loop two.

When I got to the gate, Gary told me that Steve and Carl had already both started separately on loop two. I headed back *out there* alone.

It felt good and empowering to be hiking alone in the dark up the Bird Mountain Trail. But it also felt good to find Carl at the top when I arrived there. He too seemed to prefer company rather than the risk of trying to navigate the loop in the dark alone. We continued together, and got to the first book at Phillips Creek in 1:25 since I had started the loop. We continued past the Garden Spot without problems, but seemed to slow down going down from Fyke's Peak, and we had also had a little difficulty navigating to the river crossing. I was getting mentally fatigued and losing navigational sharpness. By the time we got to the river, I had painful blisters on the soles of both feet. I knew that getting them wet again in the river, and then climbing the steep uphills of the Testicle Spectacle, the Rat Jaws, and Big Hell would be very painful. I looked for a way to cross the New River without getting my feet wet. I tried to shimmy across on a thin log, but I ended up getting my feet and legs immersed anyway. By the time we got to the other side, we were about 7:58 into the second loop. It had taken me only 4:28 to get to this point on the first loop. I didn't think we could finish the loop on time, or even within a couple of hours of the time limit. Between this time concern and the sole blisters, I told Carl that I would drop out here and hike back to camp via the best way back. He was having problems too, including foot blisters. So we both quit at that point and hiked back. Unfortunately, this was about the farthest possible place on the loop from camp. It took us about 3 hours and 45 minutes to get back to camp, following Highway 116, the jeep road through the Frozen Head Natural Area to Tub Springs Junction, and the South Old Mac Trail. Gary recorded our time at the gate as 23:13. We were then both tapped out. For me this was another failure, but it was the farthest I had gone since 1992. I will have more to say about this later.

The photo on the next page, taken by Alan Geraldi, shows Gary tapping me out on Davy Henn's bugle.

Back in camp, we learned of some of this year's tales of failure from *out there*. Of this year's four Barkley Virgin female runners, all failed to complete one loop within the time limit. Abi Meadows had a pre-existing heel injury that had flared up starting early in the first loop, on the NBT. She gamely continued around the loop, but the heel injury continued to get worse. Abi was carrying a cell phone, and called an orthopedic doctor-friend from the top of Frozen Head, to get his recommendation on whether or not she should continue with the injured foot. The doctor advised against it, so Abi then phoned her husband who was down at the campground, and asked for a ride back from the nearest point where she could be picked up. She hiked tearfully down the jeep road to Highway 116, where her husband met her and drove her back to camp to be tapped out. Marcia Rasmussen sprained an ankle before reaching the first book, and eventually quit at the top of Rat Jaw and took the shortcut back to camp. Rita Barnes finished loop one, but was about an hour and ten minutes over the 13:20 time limit. The most dramatic story among the female runners this year was from Lora Mantelman. Lora got lost on the NBT on loop one, in the same area near Bald Knob where Dan Baglione had wandered off-course in 2006 and spent the night *out there* lost.

Lora apparently lost the trail and spent most of the day and part of the night unable to re-find it. She finally was able to get help when she saw other runners' headlights in the dark that night. One of those runners was Mark Williams, who then decided to quit and accompany Lora back to camp. They went down the Quitter's Road, arriving back at camp to be tapped out at 18:55. This spared Lora the humiliation of breaking Dan Baglione's futility record, but showed Gary to be somewhat prophetic, as he had identified her before the race as this year's "Human Sacrifice." She referred to Mark as her Garden Spot Hero, and claimed credit for "a really long 10K." The failures of the four women runners at Barkley this year are sure to add fuel to Gary's frequent taunting that women are too weak to run the Barkley.

In all, 27 of the 40 starters finished loop one within the 13:20 time limit. One of the other unfortunate runners who failed to complete the loop within the time limit was David Hughes. His time of 13:22:38 was agonizingly close, but two minutes and 38 seconds over the limit. I admire David's toughness to keep returning to the Barkley although he struggles to run at a pace needed to complete even one loop within the time limit. A couple of years ago, David had completed eleven different 100-mile trail races within their respective time limits, in the same year. This is a testimony to the difficulty imposed by the time limits at Barkley, even though they seem lenient compared to other races.

After coming back into camp with Carl on Sunday morning, I learned that four runners had already completed their second loop: Andrew Thompson, Byron Backer, Jim Harris, and DeWayne Satterfield, in that order. All four of them had begun their third loop. Interestingly, Andrew had slept for a little under an hour between loops two and three. Others who subsequently finished loop two were Mike Dobies, Pat Costigan, Wendell Doman, Chip Tuthill, Hiram Rogers, Steve Durbin, and Leonard Buttslide Martin. Buttslide finished his second loop in 26:37:44, just two minutes and 16 seconds before the 26:40 cut-off time. This was a good lesson for Carl Asker and me. When we decided to quit during loop two at the New River, Leonard was still behind us. We could see the light from his headlight as he was coming down from Fyke's Peak in the dark, although at the time we did not know who it was. Buttslide's great effort to continue and successfully finish two loops so close to the cutoff time was an excellent example of the determination that is required to do well at the Barkley. His toughness and persistence inspired both Carl and me to believe that we can do better next year.

Another gritty performance was shown by Allan Holtz. Allan had been to many past Barkleys, but with limited success. Last year he had completed the Grand Slam of Ultrarunning, completing four major 100-mile trail races. Here, he hung on to finish two loops, but he was over the time limit, in 29:50.

Yet another inspirational effort was given by the old man of the Barkley, John DeWalt, who was now 72 years old. Even though John was several hours over the time limit, he finished two loops in 31:33, showing incredible toughness and determination. John has slowed down over the years, but he is still one of the toughest ultrarunners in the country in his age group. He had completed the Hardrock 100 in July, 2008, in a time of 47:54:58, his 13th Hardrock completion.

Mike Dobies and Wendell Doman began the third loop together. However, they decided that they had had enough by the first climb, Rough Ridge. They returned to camp, with Mike reporting stomach problems, and Wendell claiming he was "not strong enough." Jim Harris, a Barkley Virgin, made it about half-way around the counterclockwise-direction third loop, but quit at the New River crossing. When he finally returned to camp, he stated that he had quit because he had "no tour guide" to help him navigate Fyke's Peak and Stallion Mountain. This left just Andrew Thompson, DeWayne Satterfield, and Bryan Backer on loop three.

Andrew was the first runner to complete three loops, in 30:51:33. His time to run the counterclockwise third loop was an impressive 9:48. He was already starting to reap dividends of having gotten some sleep after loop two. Upon finishing loop three, he ate, resupplied his pack, and again slept for about 45 minutes. He then began his fourth loop at 32:00 into the race.

The second runner to complete three loops was DeWayne Satterfield, in 35:35:50. This was DeWayne's first Barkley Fun Run completion, in his tenth start. This perennial winner of many ultras in the southeastern U.S. had finally completed the Barkley Fun Run! When he got to the finishing gate, he immediately sat down on the ground while Gary counted DeWayne's pages to verify his third loop. After a couple of minutes, DeWayne laid down right on the road by the gate, with a huge smile on his face, talking to the assembled small crowd of other runners and some of the video crew. He clearly had no interest in starting a fourth loop, even though he was under the 36-hour time limit to be allowed to continue, so he was summarily tapped out despite his great achievement.

Byron Backer was the only other Fun Run finisher, in a time of 37:40:39, an hour and 12 minutes slower than his three-loop finishing time the previous year. Byron reported having had repeated nausea on the third loop that prevented him from keeping food down. His fast start may have come back to haunt him. Still, he had done well, with two Fun Run completions in his first two years at the Barkley, a noteworthy accomplishment. Nevertheless, he too received his personal rendition of *Taps*.

Andrew finished his fourth loop in 44:58:12. He got something to eat and worked on his feet. I noticed that he had an open blister on the back of one of his heels. He said that he would use waterproof tape on it. Davy Henn and Carl Laniak were now acting as his handlers. Andrew asked Davy to wake him up in 45 minutes, and then he went to his tent for another nap. Andrew got up as scheduled, and started his final loop at 46:11:30. He was venturing back *out there* into that "hallowed territory" as he had called it in 2005, of the fifth loop that had defeated him then. Gary rang the Swiss cowbell with gusto as Andrew started his "bell lap," jogging downhill away from the gate. He had decided to run the fifth loop in the counterclockwise direction. He said that he would find it less confusing to do this fifth loop in the same direction as the previous two loops. The counterclockwise direction would also allow him to do some of the steepest sections, such as Big Hell and Rat Jaw, downhill rather than uphill.

Andrew would have an additional obstacle to overcome if he were to finish the Barkley 100 this year: weather. After two days and two nights of relatively good weather, that element of the Barkley was about to change. The forecast had been for Monday to turn colder with precipitation. The forecast proved correct. For those of us in camp, the weather was miserable Monday. It rained intermittently, sometimes very hard. It was cold and windy. These conditions made it difficult to break camp and pack things into our vehicles, as most of us remaining in camp were preparing to leave after seeing how Andrew would finish (or be finished off again). We knew that this nasty weather would make Andrew's attempt even more difficult. However, we also knew that Andrew was from New Hampshire, one of the coldest parts of the U.S. So if anyone could handle this sudden winter-like turn of the weather, it should be Andrew. He had seemed well prepared for the weather, wearing a rain jacket and rain pants as he had begun loop five.

We later heard an interesting story in camp of Andrew's fifth loop. Some of the video crew members had driven around to the highway and New River crossing about half-way through the loop. They saw and briefly talked to Andrew as he crossed the highway and then the river. They reported that as he approached the river, he picked up a long stick that he used to brace himself as he walked on a fallen log across the river, without getting his feet wet. Hearing this bolstered our belief in camp that Andrew was doing well on his fifth loop. We sat around the campfire between rain showers and took turns predicting Andrew's finishing time.

The reader may recall that after Andrew's demise on his attempted fifth loop in 2005, he had written about coming back into camp then and adding his story to Barkley's "epic harrowing tales of failure." I recalled those exact words, having written them into this book just a few weeks prior to the 2009 Barkley. While Andrew was preparing to again start his fifth loop, I had paraphrased his 2005 statement, saying to him: "When you get back here, we want to hear an epic harrowing tale of success."

That is exactly what we got. This time, unlike 2005, Andrew maintained control of his mental faculties to complete the loop. But not without an epic, harrowing struggle. He had to battle extreme fatigue. He took several 10-minute naps on the trail during the fifth loop. He experienced nausea and had difficulty holding down food and drink. He tried to take an ibuprofen and threw it up. Then there was the weather. The windy and rainy weather that we were experiencing in camp was delivering snow to Andrew on the mountaintops. He reported that near the end, there was a couple of inches of snow on the ground, and that it was snowing sideways with strong winds. He said that he was very cold. But he continued through these hardships and successfully completed loop five in 57:37:19. On the next page is a picture of Andrew being congratulated at the finish. This photo was taken by Rich Limacher.

When he finished, Andrew rested by the gate and answered questions from us runners and the video crew. He described how he had been well-organized for this attempt. He had a plan for food, a plan for sleep, a plan for clothes, a plan for his feet. However, he had had a dislocated clavicle in the winter, which had caused him to run what he called "minimal training." This is an ironic coincidence, given that Flyin' Brian had dislocated his clavicle during last year's Barkley. During his Barkley run, Andrew had taken one ibuprofen and one caffeine pill. The most amazing thing I remember him saying was that he had run this Barkley with "no pain." This seems incredible, given the difficulty of what he had done. I assume that when he reported "no pain," he meant that he had somehow managed to tolerate and overcome some obvious problems to prevent them from being significant factors in his mind. I had seen a raw blister on his heel, and know that he must have been aware of discomforts like this, not to mention the vomiting and cold. How-

ever, he had maintained mental control and transcended these problems. He had mentally committed himself to finishing, and carried out his plans perfectly. Recall that he had gone without sleep in his 2005 failed fifth loop. Like Flyin' Brian, who had failed without sleep in 2007 but succeeded with sleep in 2008, Andrew was able to complete the Barkley 100 in 2009 with short intervals of sleep between loops and during the fifth loop.

Andrew had written on more than one previous occasion about the failure aspect of the Barkley. Now, at last, he had finally achieved success. In 2007, he had written: "The universal currency at Barkley, however, is pain." Now he had completed it with "no pain." He had also written that: "The real Barkley doesn't end in victory. Its rare finishers are what statisticians call 'outliers.' The real Barkley chases down its strongest talent, its brightest stars, and annihilates them. It never ends the way it should. *That* is the real thing." However, now Andrew himself had demonstrated the opposite. As one of its strongest talents and brightest stars, he had made this one end the way it should: in victory. His five-loop completion, making him the eighth Barkley 100-mile finisher in its 23-year history, also showed us that the most amazing and beautiful tales from *out there* at the Barkley Marathons are those rare and wonderful instances of success, when runners transcend previous limitations and achieve what to most of us is still impossible. I think *that* is the real Barkley at its best!

Below is the list of runners, their numbers of Barkley starts, and their loop-finishing times for 2009.

1. Andrew Thompson (10) 8:28:49   19:51:44   30:51:33 44:58:12 57:37:19
2. DeWayne Satterfield (10) 8:36:30   22:12:37   35:55:50
3. Byron Backer (2)   8:23:39   20:13:01   37:40:39

4. Jim Harris (1)   8:36:28   22:08:48   Quit during loop three.
5. Mike Dobies (10)   8:41:37   23:34:95   Quit during loop three.
6. Pat Costigan (3)   8:42:40   24:29:33
7. Wendell Doman (5)   9:15:08   24:45:35   Quit during loop three.
8. Chip Tuthill (5)   10:09:54   25:01:53
9. Hiram Rogers (6)   10:23:53   25:12:00
10. Steve Durbin (3)   10:29:30   25:19:10
11. Buttslide Martin (16)   11:32:42   26:37:44
12. Allan Holtz (3)   11:32:39   ~29:50*Finished loop two over time limit.
13. John DeWalt (21)   11:27:37   ~31:33*Finished loop two over time limit.
14. Carl Laniak (2)   8:28:51   Quit during loop two.
15. Bob Jones   (1)   8:43:30
16. Jon Barker (2)   9:29:35
17. Bill Losey (4)   9:31:52   Quit during loop two.
18. Mike Bur (6)   9:55:13
19. Mark Williams (3)   9:58:39   Quit during loop two.
20. Carl Asker (1)   10:29:35   Quit during loop two.
21. Frozen Ed Furtaw (13)   10:29:37   Quit during loop two.
22. Paul Melzer (2)   11:06:55   Quit during loop two.
23. Davey Henn (3)   11:33:07
24. Jason Barringer (1)   11:33:15
25. Robert Andrulis (2)   11:34:05
26. Joel Storrow (1)   11:36:01
27. Kevin Dorsey (1)   11:50:40
28. David Hughes (10)   ~13:23* Finished loop one over the time limit.
29. <u>Rita Barnes</u> (1)   ~14:30* Finished loop one over the time limit.
30. Stu Gleman (12)   ~16:02* Finished loop one over the time limit.
31. <u>Marcia Rasmussen</u> (1)Quit during loop one.
32. Mike O'Melia (1)   Quit during loop one.
33. <u>Abi Meadows</u> (1)   Quit during loop one.
34. Kerry Trammell (8)   Quit during loop one.
35. Bill Andrews (3)   Quit during loop one.
36. Bob Haugh (1)   Quit during loop one.
37. Alan Geraldi (1)   Lost on loop one.
38. John Price (3)   Lost on loop one.
39. Claudio Bacci (1)   Lost on loop one.
40. <u>Lora Mantelman</u> (1) Lost on loop one.
40 Starters

The story of Andrew's victory in the 2009 Barkley is a perfect note on which to end the historical part of this book. However, the tales from *out there* at the Barkley Marathons are not over. The race will again be held in 2010 and, hopefully, for many more years to come. As I am completing this book in January 2010, I and 30-some other runners are again preparing for another adventure at Frozen Head.

For me personally, my failure in 2009 contained an element of success. I went farther in distance and longer in time than in any of my previous Barkley runs since 1992. I have been further inspired by stories from 2009, like those of Buttslide Martin, John DeWalt, and Andrew Thompson. I have learned more about my own limitations and how to overcome them. I had a significant personal success several weeks after the 2009 Barkley, when I ran a 24-hour ROGAINE, a form of long-distance orienteering. I taped my feet before the ROGAINE with a new technique that I learned from ultrarunning friends Nancy Shura Dervin and Morgan Murri, using benzoin tincture, KINESIO TEX® tape, and paper tape. I was on my feet for nearly the entire 24 hours of the ROGAINE without sole blisters. This was the first time in my memory that I have been in a race for that duration without sole blisters. So I will prepare for the 2010 Barkley believing that I can overcome this major problem that has nearly always plagued me at Barkley. My lifetime goal of again finishing three loops at the Barkley remains alive. As Annelise sang about the Barkley: "I am not done with this race that eats its young." I know that I am not the only one who feels this way. There are many of us who are still driven to continue to test ourselves against what Andrew Thompson has called "the greatest race among men and mountains."

The Barkley is not done with us runners either. The future holds more challenges for those of us who are willing to risk failure to find our limits. There was talk around the campground at Frozen Head in 2009 about the closure of Brushy Mountain State Penitentiary. In June 2009, Kerry Trammell informed the Barkley e-mail list subscribers that all prisoners have now been transferred out of Brushy Mountain. There is already speculation that the area around the closed prison may in the future be used for a new part of the Barkley course. This opens up some intriguing possibilities, for example, of the course including an "escape route" from the old prison into the mountains.

In any case, I expect that Gary will continue to find ways to keep the Barkley Marathons the most difficult trail race in the world to finish, *out there* at the limit of possibility. I expect that the Barkley will continue to draw runners from across the country and around the world, who will continue to attempt the impossible. And I expect that some of them will succeed at it.

+++++++++++

Below is the essay I wrote as an entry requirement for the 2009 Barkley.

Why I Should Be Allowed To Run The Barkley:
What If I Couldn't?
Essay #13 In A Series
By Frozen Ed Furtaw
January 14, 2009

I experienced a moment of sheer terror recently. It was the hour of unbearable uncertainty when I thought that maybe I wouldn't be able to run The Barkley this year.

At about 9 AM one recent morning, I opened an e-mail from Gary Cantrell that had been dispatched the previous evening. He was informing us waiting applicants about his status in choosing the 2009 Barkley Marathons starting field. Like about a hundred others, I had submitted my request for entry at the designated time. In the past my request for entry had always been honored. I read that, as of 13 hours previously, Gary was "sending confirmations as fast as i can." But I hadn't received a confirmation. Oh no! Could this really mean that, for the first time, I would not be allowed in? I feared the worst, and began the grief process.

First came denial. Surely he would still let me in. He couldn't leave me out. I was, after all, the first official finisher in the history of The Barkley Marathons. Then came anger. How could he exclude me? The nerve! I thought we were friends. And after all I have contributed to Barkley. What the #&@% was that Idiot thinking to leave me out? I was indignant! However, this soon dissolved into depression and sadness over the loss of one of the favorite parts of my life—my annual adventure at The Barkley.

The next step in my emotional roller-coaster was acceptance. I quickly realized that many other deserving runners should have the opportunity to run Barkley. It wasn't fair that I should always get in, only to be able to complete a paltry one-and-a-fraction loops. Gary was finally, justifiably, telling me that I had hoarded a coveted entry slot long enough. It was time to let another runner have the fun of which my repeated entry was depriving him or her.

Soon after accepting this inevitable and fair decision, I moved toward resolution. I saw this as an opportunity to try something new and different. There are other ultras that I would like to run in the springtime, but my constant obsession with running The Barkley had deprived me of that variety for many years. So being excluded from Barkley would free me at last from its grip, and allow me to try to live a normal winter and spring for a change. I hungrily snapped up the latest issue of *UltraRunning* magazine and began looking over the alternative options in the race calendar. Wow! It was great! There were lots of other interesting and challenging events that I could run instead of Barkley.

After making a tentative top choice of my new-found Barkley alternative, I began to get ready to go out with Gail and some friends. I decided to check my e-mail before putting the computer into sleep mode. And there it was! An e-mail received at 9:51 AM from my dear friend Gary, saying: "i regret to inform you that you did not make the waiting list... that means that you will have to run. see you the fools weekend, laz." I was in again!!! My hour of emotional turmoil ended happily.

When I reflect on what it felt like to think that I could not run Barkley, it makes me realize both that I am truly addicted, and that I love this addiction. The Barkley is one of the major motivating and defining aspects of my life. I am very grateful to have it in my life now, and to have had it in my life for the past 20-plus years. But I also realize that eventually, for whatever now-unknown reason, a year will come when I truly will not be able to run The Barkley. Fortunately, my one-hour tour of emotions that morning has helped me realize that ***whatever happens, I will cope***. That's one of the most powerful lessons that running The Barkley all these years has taught me.

Chapter 29
Barkley Data: Summary and Comparison to Other Races

Summary of The Barkley Marathons. The table on the next page summarizes the history of the Barkley Marathons in race distances and elevation change, numbers of starters and finishers, and winning times. Data in this table reflect the descriptions given in this book about the escalating difficulty of the event over the years. "Fun Run" refers to the three-loop race. Distances for the Fun Run are given in miles as both nominal distances stated by Gary Cantrell, and distances estimated by me using the method described in Chapters 2 and 27. Distances shown for the nominal 100-mile race are also my best estimates. Elevation gain for each year is estimated from topographic map contour lines, and reported in thousands of feet (K ft.) each of gain and descent. These distances and elevation change estimates are also given in the various chapters for the years of each course change.

The finishing results over the 23 runnings of the Barkley Marathons are further summarized in the following lists. Because the course changed significantly over the years, results are presented in three groups of years. The courses in each group had roughly the same configurations. Overall results for all years are also shown.

Course	Years	#Starters	% Fun Run Finishers	Fastest	% 5-loop Finishers	Fastest
Early Years	'86-'94	214	14.0 %	23:49:40	0.0 % *	*
Two Hells	'95-'05	330	14.6 %	28:52:57	1.8 %	56:57:52
Hell for the Highway	'06-'09	143	9.8 %	29:56:49	1.4 %	55:42:27
All Courses	'86-'09	687	13.4 %	23:49:40	1.3 %	55:42:27

* In the Early Years of the 55-mile three-loop course, there was no five-loop race. In those years, there was a six-loop 100-mile race with a 50-hour time limit.

In general, these statistics support the notion that the most recent course, the Hell for the Highway course, has the most difficult three-loop and five-loop courses to finish, compared to the earlier courses. However, as noted just above, the Early Years six-loop 100-miler with its 50-hour time limit was apparently the most difficult of all to finish. No one even tried.

Historical Summary of the Barkley Marathons.

Year	Bark- ley No.	No. Start- ers	Fun Run Miles Nom./ Best Est.	Fun Run Elev. Gain K ft.	No. Fin- ish- ers	Best Time	100- Mile Dist. Best Est.	100- mile Elev. Gain K ft.	No. Fin- ish- ers	Best Time	Highlights. Issues of *UltraRunning* magazine with Barkley Articles
1986	1	13	50/66.4	21.2	0	-	None	-	-	-	May 86 pp.14-15
1987	2	16	50/66.0	23.5	0	-	None	-	-	-	Hell added. Jun 87 pp.14-15
1988	3	19	55/71.1	24.2	1*	32:14:50	None	-	-	-	Garden Spot added. Jun 88 pp.20-21
1989	4	14	55/71.1	24.9	0	-	133.2	47.3	0	-	100-mile & Rat Jaw added. Jun 89 pp.19-20
1990	5	29	55/71.1	24.9	5	26:22:39	133.2	47.3	0	-	Jun 90 pp.9-11
1991	6	37	55/71.1	24.9	10	25:53:13	133.2	47.3	0	-	May 91 pp.8-11
1992	7	20	55/71.1	24.9	2	28:01:36	133.2	47.3	0	-	Jun 92 pp.8-9
1993	8	32	55/71.1	24.9	11	26:55:26	133.2	47.3	0	-	Jun 93 pp.8-11
1994	9	34	55/71.1	24.9	1	23:49:40	133.2	47.3	0	-	Jun 94 pp.14-15
1995	10	39	60/78.0	29.4	6	28:52:57	130.0	49.0	1	59:28:48	Big Hell added. Jun 95 pp.6-9
1996	11	24	60/78.0	29.4	2	34:58:06	130.0	49.0	0		Direction reversal added. Jun 96 pp.10-11
1997	12	31	60/78.0	29.4	3*	38:38:52	130.0	49.0	0		Jun 97 pp.15-17
1998	13	35	60/78.0	29.4	5	30:23:00	130.0	49.0	0		Jun 98 pp.17-18
1999	14	33	60/78.0	29.4	3	33:19:46	130.0	49.0	0		May 99 pp.38-39
2000	15	35	60/78.0	29.4	7	31:00:29	130.0	49.0	0		Jun 00 pp.16-19
2001	16	35	60/78.3	30.1	10	31:18:12	130.5	50.2	2*	58:21:00	The Hump added. Jun 01 pp.48-51 Sep 01 pp.4-5
2002		Race	Not	Held;		Frozen Head Park			Closed		Temporarily.
2003	17	33	60/78.0	31.3	3	32:15:51	130.0	52.1	1	56:57:52	Stallion Mtn. added. Jun 03 pp.48-50
2004	18	32	60/78.0	31.3	7	30:57:09	130.0	52.1	2	57:25:18	Final loop in opposite directions added. Jun 90 pp.23-25
2005	19	33	60/78.0	31.3	2	32:48:53	130.0	52.1	0		Jul/Aug 05 pp.62-63
2006	20	33	60/77.7	31.5	0	-	129.5	52.5	0		Race nearly cancelled. Highway 116 and Testicle Spectacle added. Jun 06 pp.54-55
2007	21	35	60/77.7	31.5	4	31:21:31	129.5	52.5	0		Jun 07 pp.54-58
2008	22	35	60/78.0	32.2	7	29:59:49	130.0	53.7	1	55:42:27	Aug 08 pp.38-39
2009	23	40	60/78.0	32.2	3	30:51:33	130.0	53.7	1	57:37:19	Jul 09 pp.86-88
Total	23	687			92	23:49:40			8	55:42:27	

* Controversial finishes. See details in respective chapters.

Lists of all finishers of the Barkley Marathons. Below is a chronological listing of all official three-loop finishers of the Early Years courses,
their numbers of Fun Run finishes through that year (in parentheses), and
their finishing times.

1986	No finishers	
1987	No finishers	
1988	Frozen Ed Furtaw (1)	32:14:50
1989	No finishers	
1990	David Horton (1)	26:22:39
	Dave Drach (1)	26:22:39
	Eric Clifton (1)	26:22:39
	Milan Milanovich (1)	33:39:01
	Fred Pilon (1)	34:09:28
1991	Dennis Herr (1)	25:53:13
	Fred Pilon (2)	28:21:38
	Peter Gagarin (1)	28:21:38
	Frozen Ed Furtaw (2)	30:42:50
	David Horton (2)	30:49:04
	Suzi Thibeault (1)	34:32:34
	Nancy Hamilton (1)	34:32:36
	Valeri Hristenok (1)	35:01:00
	Viktor Dobryansky (1)	35:01:00
	Dick West (1)	35:33:39
1992	Wendell Robison (1)	28:01:36
	Nick Williams (1)	34:44:31
1993	Fred Pilon (3)	26:55:26
	Wendell Robison (2)	27:17:50
	Dennis Herr (2)	30:34:11
	Nick Williams (2)	34:59:01
	Kawika Spalding (1)	35:17:06
	Rick Hamilton (1)	35:18:24
	Nancy Hamilton (2)	35:18:24
	Dick West (2)	35:21:28
	Steve Bozeman (1)	35:21:47
	Gerry Agin (1)	35:30:40
	John DeWalt (1)	35:30:53
1994	David Horton (3)	23:49:40

Below is a chronological listing of all finishers of three or more loops
within time limits on the Two Hells courses, their numbers of Fun Run finishes through that year, and their three-, four-, and five-loop finishing times.

1995	Mark Williams (1)	31:02:53	45:06:15	59:28:48
	Tom Possert (1)	28:52:57		
	Craig Wilson (1)	32:27:12		
	Milan Milanovich (2)	36:29:37		
	Gene Trahern (1)	39:22:13		
	Greg Shoener (1)	39:22:13		
1996	Craig Wilson (2)	34:58:48		

	Mark Williams (2)	34:58:49		
1997	Mike Dobies (1)	38:38:52		
	Blake Wood (1)	39:57:35		
	Craig Wilson (3)	38:38:55*Lost page; unofficial but included in counts.		
1998	David Horton (4)	30:23:00		
	Blake Wood (2)	35:32:46		
	Mike Dobies (2)	35:32:46		
	Fred Vance (1)	39:23:45		
	John DeWalt (2)	39:23:46		
1999	Blake Wood (3)	33:19:46		
	Randy Isler (1)	34:40:04		
	Mike Dobies (3)	34:40:05		
2000	Blake Wood (4)	31:00:29	46:46:31	
	Michael Tilden (1)	32:57:27		
	Sue Johnston (1)	32:57:56		
	Craig Wilson (4)	34:48:38		
	Mike Dobies (4)	34:48:39		
	Eliza MacLean (1)	37:19:08		
	Andrew Thompson (1)	37:19:09		
2001	David Horton (5)	31:18:12	45:40:49	58:21:00
	Blake Wood (5)	31:18:13	45:40:48	58:21:01
	Hans Put (1)	33:44:00		
	Sue Johnston (2)	33:44:01		
	Michael Tilden (2)	33:50:20		
	Mike Dobies (5)	37:03:42		
	Craig Wilson (5)	37:03:45		
	Andrew Thompson (2)	38:50:01		
	Randy Isler (2)	38:50:03		
	Steve Pero (1)	39:52:56		
2002	No Barkley race held			
2003	Cave Dog Keizer (1)	32:15:13	46:31:51	56:57:52
	Mike Tilden (3)	35:04:47		
	Jim Nelson (1)	35:05:16		
2004	Mike Tilden (4)	31:37:38	45:29:44	57:25:18
	Jim Nelson (2)	31:37:57	45:25:04	57:28:25
	David Horton (6)	30:57:09		
	Andrew Thompson (3)	36:19:21		
	Jason Poole (1)	36:19:22		
	Todd Holmes (1)	36:19:23		
	Craig Wilson (6)	36:19:24		
2005	Andrew Thompson (4)	32:48:57	47:26:59	
	Jim Nelson (3)	32:48:53		

Below is a chronological listing of all finishers of three or more loops within time limits on the Hell for the Highway courses, their numbers of Fun Run finishes through that year, and their three-, four-, and five-loop finishing times.

2006   No finishers

2007	Flyin' Brian Robinson (1)	31:21:31	47:49:43	
	Mike Dobics (6)	34:16:19		
	Andras Low (1)	34:16:20		
	Greg Eason (1)	34:16:21		
2008	Flyin' Brian Robinson (2)	29:56:49	43:19:20	55:42:27
	Jim Nelson (4)	33:42:34		
	Byron Backer (1)	36:28:29		
	Blake Wood (6)	36:52:27		
	Greg Eason (2)	38:15:57		
	Carl Laniak (1)	38:15:58		
	Andrew Thompson (5)	38:15:59		
2009	Andrew Thompson (6)	30:51:33	44:58:12	57:37:19
	DeWayne Satterfield (1)	35:35:50		
	Byron Backer (2)	37:40:39		

Here are some noteworthy observations from the above table and lists:
- There has been a total of 92 Fun Run finishes within the time limits.
- These 92 finishes were attained by 45 different runners.
- The number of five-loop 100-mile finishes was eight.
- All of the 100-mile finishes were by different individuals.
- There are currently five runners tied for the most Fun Run finishes, with six each: David Horton, Craig Wilson, Mike Dobies, Blake Wood, and Andrew Thompson.
- There have been six Fun Run finishes by four different women: Suzi Thibeault (1), Nancy Hamilton (2), Sue Johnston (2), and Eliza MacLean (1).
- No woman has finished a Fun Run or more on the Hell for the Highway course, nor on any course since 2001.

Barkley Sickos. In his *UltraRunning* article about the 1999 Barkley, Gary referred to those runners who keep returning to the Barkley as *sickos*. He credited "their amazing ability to forget last year's dismal failure before the next race" for keeping the Barkley entry roster filled over the years. In recognition of these diehards, I have compiled the following list of all runners with ten or more starts of the Barkley Marathons. These sickos are listed in order of most starts, followed by their numbers of starts, Fun Run finishes, and 100-mile finishes.

1. John DeWalt	21	2	0
2. Buttslide Martin	16	0	0
3. Fred Purloin	13	3	0
4. Frozen Ed Furtaw	13	2	0
5. Stu Gleman	12	0	0
6. Matt Mahoney	12	0	0
7. David Horton	11	6	1
8. Andrew Thompson	10	6	1
9. Mike Dobies	10	6	0
10. Craig Wilson	10	6	0
11. Dick West	10	2	0
12. DeWayne Satterfield	10	1	0

13. Jim Dill   10   0   0
14. David Hughes   10   0   0

++++++++++

Comparisons to Other Ultramarathons. I believe that the low per-centages of finishers (calculated as [the number of finishers divided by the number of starters] multiplied by 100), and the times of the finishes, support the claim that the Barkley Marathons is the world's toughest trail race. Only 1.3% of the starters have finished the Barkley 100-mile race, and only 13.4% have finished the three-loop Fun Run. Both of these completion percentages stand out as some of the lowest among the world's most difficult foot-races.

As a method of comparison of the Barkley races to other ultramarathons, I have examined finishing percentages and times of several other races that are considered among the toughest, or most difficult to finish, in the world. Some of the data used in this effort were obtained from Stan Jensen's website <http://www.run100s.com/>. Other data were obtained from the respective races' websites. The interested reader can find more information and stories about these and other ultramarathons, including the Barkley Marathons, by conducting an Internet search with the name of the race of interest.

The chart on the next page shows the completion percentages of these races, listed in order of lowest completion rates. Brief descriptions and dis-cussions of each of these races are given below. Several of these races are also rated by National Geographic as the world's most difficult. The Barkley Marathons is listed on the National Geographic list, ranked as the fifth toughest.   Their race rankings can be found at the following website: <http://adventure.nationalgeographic.com/2009/03/top-ten-toughest-races-text>. Not all of the races in the National Geographic rankings are human running races. For example, the bicycle Race Across America is included in the Na-tional Geographic rankings.

Wickham Park races. As shown in the chart, only five ultramarathon races about which I could find information have completion percentages be-low 20%: the two Barkley races (100-mile and Fun Run), and the three Wickham Park races (50-, 100-, and 200-mile).   Since only the Wickham races are comparable to Barkley in low percentage of completions, a detailed comparison among these races is given.   Information about the Wickham Park races can be found on Matt Mahoney's website at <http://mattmahoney.net/wickham/>.

The Wickham Park races are held annually on Memorial Day weekend at Wickham Park in Melbourne, Florida. These races were created in 1995 by Matt Mahoney.   This was the first year that Matt had run in the Barkley Marathons, and the Barkley was an influencing factor in his development of the Wickham Park races. Initially only a marathon distance was offered, and one runner finished out of four starters. The following year, a 50-mile race was added; a 12½-hour time limit was imposed because the park is open only 13 hours per day, during daylight hours. In the years that the 50-mile race has been held, it has had a 12.4% finisher rate. The 100-mile race was added in 2000, and has had a 2.2% overall finishing rate, although the rate has in-creased to 4.8% in the past couple of years. The 200-mile race was added in

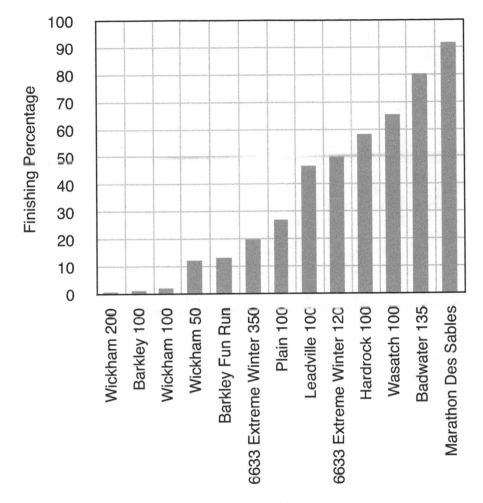

2001. It has had a 0.6% finisher rate. The 100- and 200-mile races are two-
and four-day repeats of the daily 12½-hour 50-mile course.

The Wickham Park course consists of multiple repeats of three-and-a-
fraction-mile loops on relatively flat trails in a swamp-like area. Thus it does
not have many of the factors that contribute to making the Barkley so tough:
extreme elevation climb, backcountry navigation, long times between aid,
running in the dark, and sleep deprivation. Some of the factors that undoubtedly contribute to the low completion rates at Wickham are: hot and humid
weather; poisonous snakes and alligators; and frequent repeats of a relatively
short loop—a feature that many adventure-seeking ultrarunners eschew.
However, probably the major factor contributing to the high DNF rates of the
Wickham Park ultras is that apparently most entrants are there on only the
first day to run the marathon. However, Matt considers them all to also be
entrants in the longer multi-day stage races. Hence, anyone wanting to run
only the marathon automatically becomes a DNF statistic of the longer races.

Besides completion percentage (and its inverse, % DNF), several other
measures of race difficulty include the following: longest course-record time;

longest time for the same runners to finish different courses; and highest ratio of course-record time to race time limit. Barkley and the Wickham 100 and 200 have had few if any finishers in common. However, comparing course records, the Barkley 100's is 55:42:27, the Barkley 60-mile Fun Run's is 28:52:57, the Wickham 200's is 42:43:13, the Wickham 100's is 20:16:05, and the Wickham 50's is 7:32. Using these course records as a metric of comparison, the ranking of these five toughest races is as follows: (1) Barkley 100, (2) Wickham 200, (3) Barkley Fun Run, (4) Wickham 100, and (5) Wickham 50. I think that the first four in this list, in the order listed, constitute a realistic ranking of the toughest trail ultras. However, I do not consider the Wickham 50 to be anywhere near as tough as virtually any of the dozens of 100-mile trail races held every year. Some of the other races that deserve to be considered among the world's toughest are described below.

6633 Extreme Winter Ultra Marathon. This race is listed as the #4 toughest race in the world in the National Geographic list. It has been held for the past three years (2007-2009), and offers races of approximately 120 and 350 miles over surfaces of snow and ice in the Yukon and Northwest Territories of Canada. The course crosses the Arctic Circle which has a north latitude of 66 degrees 33 minutes; hence the numbers which appear in the event name. Runners must carry or pull their provisions, clothing, etc. on a sled. In addition to runners, the race has also had cycling competitors. Extreme cold—down to about minus 40F—and high winds are major difficulty factors. Several runners have DNFed due to frostbite. Numerical results are difficult to extract from the narrative reports on its website <http://www.6633ultra.com/>, but it appears that there have been four finishers of 20 starters in the 350-miler, for a 20% finishing rate, and a course record of 5days:23hours:25minutes. In the 120-mile race, it appears that there have been three finishers of six starters, for a 50% finishing rate, with a course record of 39:08. Although its 20% finishing rate would not rank it among the first five races represented in the chart, the 350-mile race must certainly be considered among the toughest in the world. It is astonishing to me to realize that even the Barkley Fun Run is more difficult to finish, as measured by its lower completion percentage, than something as extreme as this 350-mile run in the Arctic!

The Plain 100. Like the Wickham Park races, the Plain 100-mile race can be considered as a descendant of the Barkley. The Plain 100 was created by Chris Ralph and Tom Ripley in 1997, the same year that Chris ran in the Barkley and finished one loop. These race directors have told me that the Barkley was an influence in their creation and design of the Plain 100. Information about the Plain 100 can be found on its website <http://www.cascaderunningclub.com/plain100.html>. This race has been held annually (except 2003 when it was cancelled due to forest fires) in the Cascade mountains of Washington State. It has about 21,000 feet each of elevation climb and descent, on trails and dirt roads, with only one aid station at about the 55-mile point; the course record is 23:53:52. Its overall historical finishing rate is 27.1%. However, it is interesting to note that its finishing rates have increased markedly over the course of its history. In the first five years of the Plain 100, its finishing rate was 3.9%. Over the next four races, the finishing rate went up to 21.8%, and in the most recent three runnings of the Plain 100, its finishing rate has been 46.9%. The course of the Plain 100 has remained the same in all twelve years that it has been held. This demonstrates that over the years, the ultrarunners who have attempted the Plain have become much better at completing it. A major factor that separates the difficulty of the Barkley from that of the Plain is that the Barkley has been a dynamic challenge: it has changed over the years to intentionally keep it at the outer limit of possibility. The Plain 100, on the other hand, has constituted a static challenge: its course has stayed the same over the years, allowing runners to learn what it takes to finish it, and adapt and improve their skills to do so. To me, this is a testimony to the remarkable ability of those in the endurance-running community to evolve to meet a tough challenge. However, the Barkley runners have not had the luxury of a static course, so the Barkley's finishing rate has not increased over its history as the Plain's has.

Leadville 100. This race has 15,600 feet each of climb and descent, with a peak elevation of 12,620 feet in Colorado's Rocky Mountains. Its website is <http://www.leadvilletrail100.com/home.aspx>. With a 15:42:59 course record, the Leadville 100 is not usually ranked as one of the most difficult ultras. However, it is included in my comparisons because it has one of the lowest finishing percentages of the 100-mile trail races. Over the past 17 years, the Leadville 100 has had a 47.1% finishing rate, one of the few major 100-milers with a historical finishing rate below 50%. This relatively low rate is largely attributable to the fact that the race's time limit is 30 hours, whereas most 100's with large amounts of elevation change have cutoff times of 32 to 48 hours.

Hardrock 100. The Hardrock 100-mile race is widely considered to be one of the toughest races. Its website is <http://www.hardrock100.com/>. It has 33,992 feet each of climb and descent with a maximum elevation of 14,048 feet, on a large loop in the San Juan mountains of southwestern Colorado. It has the highest average elevation of the 100-milers in the U.S. Its average finishing rate since 1992 has been 58.6%, in a time limit of 48 hours. Like the Plain 100, this race shows a historical trend of increasing finishing percentage in recent years. Over the past three years, its finishing rate has averaged a remarkable 72.3%. Its course record is an equally impressive 23:23:30. Ultrarunner Bob Boeder, a Hardrock finisher, has written a book about the Hardrock 100, entitled *Hardrock Fever: Running 100 Miles in Colorado's San Juan Mountains* (copyright 2000). In this book, Bob refers to Hardrock as "this wildest and toughest of all the 100 mile trail races." However, in all of its significant points of comparison—finishing percentages, course-record times, and amounts of elevation change—the Barkley 100 is clearly more difficult. This fact was pointedly underscored in an interesting statement made by Mark Williams, the first-ever finisher of the Barkley 100, in 59:28:48, in 1995. Mark also finished the Hardrock 100 in 1997, in 39:29:50. When asked which he thought was harder, Barkley or Hardrock, Mark replied: "The Barkley of course; it was 20 hours longer."

Wasatch 100. I have included the Wasatch 100 in my comparison list because this race was once considered the toughest 100-mile trail race, back in the 1980s when there was only a handful of 100-mile trail races in the world. I have finished Wasatch twice and have award plaques that are inscribed with, among other information, the statement: "World's Toughest 100 Miler."   This claim also appears on a race logo on the race's website <http://www.wasatch100.com/>. However, this assertion is no longer valid, as the Wasatch finishing rate over the past 17 years has averaged 65.6%, with a course record of 18:30:55.

Badwater 135. This is the race that is ranked on the above-mentioned National Geographic website as the toughest in the world. On the race's website <http://www.badwater.com/>, it calls itself "the world's toughest foot race." It is not a trail race, but rather a 135-mile road race on paved highways in and near the Death Valley desert in southern California. It has about 13,000 feet of climb and 4,700 feet of descent. It is held at the hottest time of year, when temperatures are sometimes around 120F. This race has a 60-hour time limit, in common with the Barkley 100. However, the Badwater finishing rate over the past ten years has been 80.2%. The course record is 22:51:29. Based on these data compared to those of the other races described above, its claim to be the toughest cannot be justified.

Marathon Des Sables. This is a multi-day stage race across part of the Sahara Desert in northern Africa. Its distance is usually about 150 miles, covered in four to six stages over several days. Runners must carry all of their own equipment and mandatory gear and food, with the exception of water which is supplied by the race organization. Not all years' results are available on the race's website <http://www.darbaroud.com/index_uk.php>, but over the past five years the Marathon Des Sables race has averaged 775 starters per year, with an overall finishing rate of 91.8%. The race record finishing time is 16:27:26. Comparison of these data to those of the Barkley shows that this race is simply not nearly as difficult to finish as either the Barkley 100 or the Barkley Fun Run, or virtually any of the other races in this comparison. Nevertheless, on its website, it calls itself "the most difficult race in the world."   I guess they have never heard of the Barkley Marathons.

+++++++++++

The above comparisons, in my judgement, definitively establish the statement that I have made throughout this book: the Barkley Marathons is the world's toughest trail race. This claim is most likely to be refuted by those who have completed one of the other difficult races. The challenge to those runners is to run the Barkley, and then judge for themselves which is the toughest.

Chapter 30
Barkley Philosophy

Hopefully the reader has perceived by now that the Barkley Marathons is a special event. It is *out there* on the edge of possibility. The great majority of attempts to run the Barkley end in failure in the sense of the runner not completing the full five-loop distance. However, those few attempts that end in success, epitomized by Flyin' Brian's course record run in 2008, are tremendous accomplishments of human endurance. Only the most fit and dedicated endurance athletes have attained this accomplishment.

Gary's policy of selecting entrants into each year's field of runners would allow virtually any top endurance runners in the world to test themselves at the Barkley. However, many of the top ultrarunners in other long trail races have disdained the Barkley. Many of these elite runners know that the Barkley is not for fast runners. It requires much more than mere speed. It takes a combination of running/hiking endurance, speed, navigation ability, planning, self-management, confidence, humility, and a sense of humor. The eight men who have finished the Barkley have all exhibited these characteristics. All have achieved a world-class accomplishment.

However, most of the rest of us who "fail" at the Barkley still achieve something important. We Barkley runners are willing to attempt something which we recognize as virtually impossible. I believe that this in itself is a form of victory. It is a victory over our own fears and limitations. It is also a victory over ego, because of the overwhelming probability of failure. To even attempt the Barkley, we runners must accept being humbled by our limitation of that which we take pride in—our running ability. We each prepare ourselves to perform at our best, even while realizing that it will probably not be good enough. I believe that there is value and virtue in even making such an attempt. As Peggy Cole, the mother of Barkley runner Abi Meadows, commented at the 2009 event: "There are no losers at the Barkley."

Gary writes a frequent column entitled *View from the Open Road* in *UltraRunning* magazine. In the May/June 2008 issue of *UltraRunning*, his *View* column was sub-titled: "Because we can fail." In this insightful essay, Gary notes that true success requires the possibility of failure. He thinks that this possibility of failure (or in the case of the Barkley, the high probability of failure) is an attracting feature that induces many runners to attempt the Barkley. I agree that the likelihood of failure is an intriguing factor that makes the Barkley nearly irresistible to me. In fact, I now go to Barkley with no hope or expectation of finishing the 100-miler. I go to test myself against something that to me is impossible. But in so testing myself, I see how far I can go, and then must learn to live with that self-limitation. Therefore the Barkley is an exercise in self-knowledge and humility.

In the weeks following the 2008 Barkley, I was interviewed for an article by a feature-story writer, Anna Lauer, from *The Pagosa Springs Sun* newspaper in Pagosa Springs, Colorado, where I live. I had previously met Anna as a social friend, and she was intrigued by my ultrarunning and especially by my stories about Barkley. In the article, I was quoted as saying: "Since most runners finish most ultramarathons they start, they are using a measuring stick that is smaller than they are. But the Barkley is the biggest measuring stick known to running. To me that's intriguing, knowing I can't possibly finish those particularly hard 100 miles in 60 hours. But, I do know I can go there and run until I can't run anymore. Run myself out before I run out of race. To know I can attempt a challenge I can't conquer. Not everybody likes confronting their own limits and failing. Some people hate the Barkley because of that. But some people, like me, go back again and again." Like Gary, I was trying to say that the possibility or probability of failure is one of the things that attracts me to the Barkley.

In an e-mail that I sent to the Barkley e-mail list in February 2009, I further elaborated on this measuring stick theme, while commenting on comparisons of Fun Run finishing times in different years. I wrote: "The underlying truth in all these comments is that the Barkley is an elastic measuring stick designed to measure an elastic parameter—the limit of human endurance. It has expanded (and possibly sometimes shrunk? any comments?) over the years. laz has changed the course as needed to keep it at the limit of do-ability. Some course changes have been intentional because it kept getting easier to do the same course, and some changes were the result of park directives to stay out of certain areas. Given that Barkley's historical finishing rate is about 1%, and there is no other race in the world (that I know of) that even comes within an order of magnitude of this low rate, I think laz has succeeded remarkably well at putting the Barkley at the edge of possibility. Isn't that a major reason why we love it so much?"

In *The Pagosa Springs Sun* interview, I referred to the Greek myth of Sisyphus. This mortal had enraged the gods by his defiance. For his impudence, he was condemned to eternally push a rock to the top of a mountain in hell. Once at the top, the rock would roll back to the bottom, and Sisyphus again had to push it to the top, only to see it roll again to the bottom. Sisyphus had to face repeating this cycle forever. He had no hope of escaping from this eternal task. The French existentialist philosopher and writer, Albert Camus, has written about Sisyphus. Camus portrays Sisyphus as the absurd hero. Camus writes: "Where would his torture be, indeed, if at every step the hope of succeeding upheld him?" Like Gary and I, Camus finds meaning in hopeless struggling. At the end of an essay on Sisyphus, Camus concludes: "The struggle itself toward the heights is enough to fill a man's heart. One must imagine Sisyphus happy."

Thus Barkley brings meaning into the apparently futile attempt against the impossible. In so doing, it teaches us the important lesson, applicable to all of life, that meaning and happiness are to be found in the *effort* to achieve something, not only in the accomplishment of the final goal of that effort.

The Barkley provides a playground in which we ultrarunners can push against the limits of the impossible. Furthermore, the lessons of the Barkley even show us a way toward achieving the impossible: stop believing that it is impossible. Our beliefs in our own limitations help to create those limitations. If we can let go of those self-limiting beliefs, we may discover that we can do far more than we originally thought possible. With the amazing performances of all the 100-mile Barkley finishers, we have seen these breakthroughs that allow some of us to transcend previously-conceived limitations. I think this is one of the profound philosophical lessons that the Barkley has given us.

Over the years I have frequently used the term "Barkley Training" to refer to the preparations that I put myself through in training for the Barkley. Barkley Training is somewhat different than training for more normal races. In Barkley Training, we accept and seek out conditions that we would normally eschew, such as running through brush and briers, and training off-trail in the dark. I have come home from many training runs that included off-trail running, with torn and tattered clothes and scratches from bushwhacking. When Gail asks what happened to me, I say it was Barkley Training. Below is a picture of me doing some Barkley Training. In this case, I was pre-soaking my shoes and feet in water before a training run, to test my foot-taping for its ability to stay in place when wet.

Barkley Training is when we push ourselves to extreme limits to try to get tougher and stronger. Barkley Training is when we accept seemingly meaningless harsh conditions and find meaning in it, because it helps us accept the difficulty and hardships that we know we will face during the Barkley. This again is a way in which the Barkley teaches us important philosophical lessons. It pushes us to extend ourselves toward unreachable goals. In this way, the Barkley helps us to be happy with what we can do, even though we cannot do everything toward which we struggle.

Camus was right. This struggle itself is enough to make one happy. To me, this is the ultimate philosophical meaning of the Barkley Marathons. It is an exercise in finding meaning and happiness.